Praise for *Fixing Fashion*

Fixing Fashion offers brilliant insight into all that is broken in the apparel industry. Michael Lavergne's brave and honest telling of what really goes on behind the scenes is an eye-opener that fuels the impetus for change. His thorough political and historical depiction that spans centuries makes for a powerfully evocative narrative that is crucial to solving the many problems facing the fashion industry. In order to fix what is broken, we must first learn how it came to be broken.

—Kelly Drennan, Founding Executive Director, Fashion Takes Action

A must-read for for every designer and apparel executive who does not yet have full transparency in their supply chain. *Fixing Fashion* outlines how exploitation has been entrenched in the apparel industry for over a century. Lavergne then uses this historical context to map opportunities for longterm change, including a long list of change makers who are redefining fashion.

—Kate Black, author, *Magnifeco: Your Head-to-Toe Guide to Ethical Fashion and Non-toxic Beauty*

Fixing Fashion is a fascinating personal and historical journey through the complex web of clothing supply chains. Author Michael Lavergne urges us to reflect on how we are linked, through that web, to people around the world (including millions of children) who are embedded in the clothes that we wear. The book is a compelling call to government, business and all of us towards increased transparency and greater action to ensure more just and sustainable supply chains.

—Harry Kits, Senior Advisor Corporate Engagement, World Vision Canada

A rare insider's globetrotting tour of the ethically challenged, complex, contradictory, and maddening global fashion industry. If you've ever wondered how an industry with so much potential to do so much good could permit thousands of vulnerable workers to needlessly die at Rona Plaza in Bangladesh, read Michael Lavergne's highly personal wakeup call.

—Dr. David Doorey, Professor of Labour Law and Supply Chain Governance, York University, Toronto

Through his seasoned and humble eyes, Michael Lavergne offers a rare glimpse into the complexities of the apparel industry in his book *Fixing Fashion*. Taking us through compelling stories from his personal experiences, and layering on news accounts of landmark human rights and environmental events in recent history, Michael invites us to question our assumptions about where our clothing comes from and how we, as consumers, can make better choices going forward. This is a must-read book for anyone who cares about the human and environmental toll of our clothing and the companies behind the labels.

—Amy Hall, Director, Social Consciousness, EILEEN FISHER

Who makes our clothes? How are they designed and marketed? After the shocking Rana Plaza factory collapse in 2013, people started asking these pertinent questions. Michael Lavergne's book *Fixing Fashion* soberly dissects the 'fast fashion' industry and looks at how to fix it. This should be compulsory reading for decision makers, designers and consumers.

—Paul Dewar, Member of Parliament Ottawa Centre, Foreign Affairs Critic for the NDP

His unique perspective as an industry insider who has travelled the world sourcing goods for global clothing brands gives us both a first-hand view of the social and environmental problems in apparel manufacturing as well as a deep understanding of why they persist. Lavergne's account will inform and inspire students of business and international development as well as present and future business leaders who will be called upon to tackle the serious and complex problems he uncovers. Thankfully Lavergne's detailed account also points towards paths for change.

—Kevin Thomas, LLM | Director of Shareholder Engagement, SHARE - Shareholder Association for Research & Education

In *Fixing Fashion*, Michael Lavergne offers a rare insider view of how the globalized garment industry works and why worker rights abuses are so endemic to that industry. He also offers hope that fundamental change is possible.

—Bob Jeffcott, Policy Analyst, Maquila Solidarity Network

FIXING FASHION

Rethinking the Way We Make, Market and Buy Our Clothes

Michael Lavergne

new society
PUBLISHERS

Cover design by Diane McIntosh.
All images © iStock — Jeans: shenor; Label: zoom-zoom; Background: chaoss
Printed in Canada. First printing September 2015.

New Society Publishers acknowledges the financial support of the Government of Canada through the Canada Book Fund (CBF) for our publishing activities.

Paperback ISBN: 978-0-86571-800-5
eISBN: 978-1-55092-595-1

Inquiries regarding requests to reprint all or part of *Fixing Fashion* should be addressed to New Society Publishers at the address below. To order directly from the publishers, please call toll-free (North America) 1-800-567-6772, or order online at www.newsociety.com

Any other inquiries can be directed by mail to:

New Society Publishers
P.O. Box 189, Gabriola Island, BC V0R 1X0, Canada
(250) 247-9737

New Society Publishers' mission is to publish books that contribute in fundamental ways to building an ecologically sustainable and just society, and to do so with the least possible impact on the environment, in a manner that models this vision. We are committed to doing this not just through education, but through action. The interior pages of our bound books are printed on Forest Stewardship Council®-registered acid-free paper that is **100% post-consumer recycled** (100% old growth forest-free), processed chlorine-free, and printed with vegetable-based, low-VOC inks, with covers produced using FSC®-registered stock. New Society also works to reduce its carbon footprint, and purchases carbon offsets based on an annual audit to ensure a carbon neutral footprint. For further information, or to browse our full list of books and purchase securely, visit our website at: **www.newsociety.com**

Library and Archives Canada Cataloguing in Publication

Lavergne, Michael, author
     Fixing fashion : rethinking the way we make, market and
buy our clothes / Michael Lavergne.
Includes bibliographical references and index.
Issued in print and electronic formats.

ISBN 978-0-86571-800-5 (paperback).--ISBN 978-1-55092-595-1 (ebook)
     1. Clothing trade--Social aspects. 2. Clothing trade--Environmental aspects. 3. Fashion--Social aspects. 4. Fashion--Environmental aspects. 5. Shopping--Social aspects. 6. Consumption (Economics)--Social aspects. 7. Social responsibility of business. I. Title.

HD9940.A2L39 2015   338.4'774692   C2015-903746-8
                                                                      C2015-903747-6

MIX
Paper from
responsible sources
FSC® C016245

For Wendy Diaz, a child laborer from Honduras
whose voice helped to stir industry actions against child labor
in the offshore apparel trade — and for all like her
who have yet to be freed.

Contents

Foreword

Carry Somers

THE VALLEYS OF THE PEAK DISTRICT where I live are dotted with buildings that bear witness to the legacy of the textile industry in the Midlands.

At Arkwright's spinning mill in Cromford, built in 1771, two thirds of the 2,000 workers who once toiled there were children. Some textile factory owners employed children as young as five, but Arkwright had a more enlightened approach — and did not employ children until they reached the age of six, providing them with clothes, accommodation and a basic education. He was seen as a model employer of his time.

The British government had made it illegal for textile workers to immigrate to the United States because they wanted to keep their monopoly on this new spinning technology. However, another Derbyshire man, Samuel Slater, made the trip disguised as a farm laborer, and in 1790 he reconstructed Arkwright's spinning machine from memory. Known in the United States as the Father of the Industrial Revolution, and in the U.K. by the less-flattering Slater the Traitor, Samuel Slater founded the U.S.'s first cotton mill. He continued to grow his business to 13 mills, all of which employed children.

Three centuries later, the fashion and textiles industry still employs millions of children throughout the supply chain. The Uzbek government forces about two million children as young as nine to miss school for two months a year in order to help with the cotton harvest. Young girls migrate to work in the spinning mills of Tamil Nadu, lured by the promise of earning enough money for a dowry.

Meanwhile, the owners of cotton fields, spinning mills and factories around the world continue to abuse national and international legislation and, like Samuel Slater, put personal gain ahead of ethics. From the cotton fields to the cutting floors, there has been progress globally, but the scale of the problem continues to grow as fast as the issues are being addressed. All over the world, people are still suffering, and our environment is at risk as a direct result of the fashion supply chain.

On April 24, 2013, 1,133 people were killed and many injured when the Rana Plaza factory complex collapsed in Dhaka, Bangladesh. A disaster on this scale made it hard to ignore the true cost of the current fashion business model.

Rana Plaza opened a policy window for significant change in the sector. Whilst this is a symptom of the problem, it has provided an opportunity to set a new agenda to overcome the causes. The Bangladesh Accord has seen an unprecedented level of collaboration and cooperation on a global level as all the actors involved worked together to strengthen due diligence along the entire length of the fashion supply chain. Brands and retailers are being challenged to take responsibility for the workers, communities and environment on which their businesses depend.

Fashion Revolution, founded in the days following the Rana Plaza disaster, is a global platform that asks questions, raises standards and sets an industry-wide example of what better looks like. Each year, on April 24, Fashion Revolution Day tackles some of the industry's most pressing issues.

Knowing who made our clothes is the first, small step toward transforming the fashion industry. The fashion supply chain is fractured, and the people who make our clothes have become faceless. A recent *Australian Fashion Report* found that 61 percent of brands didn't know where their garments were made, and 93 percent didn't know where the raw materials came from. This is costing lives. Greater transparency is the first step toward building a future in which an accident like the Rana Plaza collapse never happens again.

As consumers, we too must realize that we are not just purchasing a garment or accessory, but a whole chain of value and relationships. When we buy a new item of clothing, it holds within its threads the DNA of the workers who have touched it, sewn it, pressed it, and

wrapped it throughout its journey. Consumer demand can revolutionize the way fashion works as an industry. If we start to think more
about the stories behind the clothes that we wear every day and put
pressure on the brands to become more accountable, we could see a
radically different fashion paradigm.

Carry Somers, Co-founder, Fashion Revolution/Fashion Revolution
Day, www.fashionrevolution.org

Introduction

THE AMERICAN AIRLINES JET banked sharply before it dropped like a rock over the collection of ramshackle shanties on the outskirts of Tegucigalpa.

I gripped the armrest tightly, and a number of my fellow travelers quickly drew the sign of the cross in front of themselves as we barreled down into Honduras' Toncontín International Airport. The plane's wheels hit hard, then bounced a couple of meters off the ground before breaking to a turn at the end of the tarmac. We had narrowly avoided plunging off the sheer cliff that bordered the airport runway. As much as it might have felt like it, we hadn't just survived an emergency landing; this was routine procedure. For me, it was just one more day on the road, running around the world chasing down the lowest-priced pair of athletic pants for a major American brand. In a lengthy career that has taken me through war zones and earthquakes, factory fires and civil protests, that landing in Honduras was a walk in the park.

It was early 2003, and I had been on a sourcing trip to Central America for one the largest branded apparel groups in the world — with annual sales at the time of more than $US 4.5 billion. Few people would have recognized my employers, bakery giant Sara Lee Corporation of Chicago, Illinois, as the owner of the Hanes, Champion Athletics, Wonderbra and Playtex brands. Four years into my time with the company, I was an aggressive young manager with Sara Lee's Branded Apparel sourcing division responsible for coordinating logistics, production, pricing and quality at some two dozen contract manufacturing facilities scattered across Central America, Haiti and the Dominican Republic.

A few years earlier, brand procurement operations had gone global. And on more than one occasion during my six years with the firm's Canadian and U.S. business units between 1999 and 2005, I had had to convince suspicious immigration officers that no, Sara Lee did not source its cheesecakes from China and that, yes in fact, I really did need to plough through Honduras, Jordan, Egypt, Thailand and the Philippines in the space of a couple of weeks to ensure deliveries of critical garment shipments in support of our international expansion. The events of 9/11 didn't make the job any easier; tightened security for global logistics reached out to foreign ports of call, throwing many an overseas business traveler into a panic.

But why, exactly, would Hanes, one of America's largest and most respected home-grown manufacturers — with vertical operations and domestic partnerships that affected everything from garment sewing to the cotton fields — purposely seek to outsource its production needs from exotic locales so far away? Raw materials and cheap Southern labor had been plentiful for generations in the United States, even after the abolition of slavery on which the U.S. cotton trade had largely been built. Hadn't the 100-year-old textile giant been saving for the future or re-investing its profits in modern production methods, employee training and new machinery technologies at home? Weren't America's markets well protected by state politicians and robust legislation against the dumping of cheap foreign goods?

Hanes was founded in Winston-Salem, North Carolina, by John Wesley Hanes in 1901. In many respects, the history of the company *is* the history of the global apparel industry. In the later 20th century, organized American labor movements struggled against the perceived evil-doings of home-grown textile barons, but the international apparel industry had already survived for centuries by virtue of its mobility and ingenuity. The industry had followed in the footsteps of the 16th-century spread of mercantilism across the globe and then expanded with European colonization, while driving ever-greater levels of commerce between East and West.

The history surrounding Hanes' global expansion and how it related to the state of the global apparel trade is both simple and complex. A good starting point would be to examine, as we will, the historical foundations of modern apparel and textile trades along with the political and economic events that led to their rapid, international growth — from the development of European wool markets to the outbreak of global war in the early 20th century.

Arguably, consumer demand for items associated with the wealthy and famous has helped drive the creation of global markets for fashion goods and their facsimiles; arguably, because the evolution of marketing sciences and the increasing importance of mass media throughout the 19th and 20th centuries have played an integral part in nurturing, some would say manipulating, consumer desire. Meanwhile entrepreneurs, investment capital and artisans have each taken their turns by pursuing their own means of satisfying market demand — often blind to or ignorant of the long-term, hidden costs of their supply chain impacts and manufacturing methods. Each party endeavors to compete on those points they are best able to leverage; aesthetics, convenience, quality and cost have always been the most important measures for the purchasing public, so each of these offer possible points of competitive advantage. The offshoring of manufactured goods production has been one of the solutions used to ensure a profitable enterprise. As we shall see, though, modern-day divisions of labor and the internationalization of production have not been a wholly recent phenomenon; it is, rather, a centuries-old cycle once again repeating itself.

I have yet to meet anyone in the industry who has purposefully set out to do harm to others or the environment, and I am sure that none of the well-known *maison de couture* across Europe's fashion capitals or trend gurus in New York has set out to perpetuate the toxic pollution of our planet by way of carcinogenic dyestuffs or agricultural dependence on petrochemical fertilizers, which are staple inputs of worldwide cotton farming. But they do, in fact, do so, however indirect many designers and creative directors may feel the connection to be. There is a long but direct line of sight from the catwalks of Paris, Milan and Manhattan to the local neighborhood shops of fast-fashion retailers, and it is growing shorter every season. High fashion labels certainly may charge more for access to their designs and cachet, but many of their garments are manufactured at the same facilities as fast-fashion brands, and thus the big labels face the same social, community and environmental impact challenges as do fast-fashion brands.

Across the vast majority of the planet, the past two decades have seen a transformation in technology and communications — well-known drivers of global trade and business. Only the most remote reaches of civilization remain ignorant of the tsunami of information that mass media and the Internet age have washed over us. It is a very simple act today, for example, to snap a smartphone pic of the latest window display at Coach's 9,400-square foot flagship boutique on Queen's Road in Hong Kong and then forward it to an unaudited, clandestine handbag factory in the Jiangsu province of China — where the bags can be copied, assembled and shipped to global markets. The technology is a good deal more complex, though, when you are trying to plan retail inventory in a virtual, web-based manufacturing environment across thousands of developing country factories while, at the same time, attempting to ensure all the facilities involved are free of negative social, community and environmental ills.

These two brief examples touch on the extremes of new technology applications that have transformed multinational retailers and brands into on-demand manufacturers, indirectly owning production commitments to thousands of third-party facilities scattered across the globe, all in a drive to maximize company profitability by gaining the most competitive *first cost* possible (the direct price that buyers or their agents negotiate from a factory's loading dock).

The speed with which original, creative ideas or designs can be copied or communicated is breathtaking. Multinational operators such as Spain's Inditex group (owners of the Zara retail organization and a half-dozen other brand holdings) have built their business and manufacturing models around the frenetic pace of media-driven trend adaption. But much of the fast-fashion model depends on expedited logistics and air shipping of finished goods and materials between manufacturing facilities and suppliers, adding significantly to already carbon- and water-intensive product footprints.

Moving from actual, owned production toward virtual or outsourced manufacturing is only one model — albeit the now-predominant one — being followed by global brands. Gaining a deeper understanding of the business models and supply chain paths for mass fashion will help us to measure the impacts of our buying choices or, at the very least, will raise our awareness past the point of an ability to claim ignorance.

At the macro level, most brands have two basic choices: they can either make their goods themselves or they can buy their goods from others. The "Make or Buy" question becomes a key strategic choice. Both scenarios have a subset of options that we will explore further in the chapter dealing with business models, but they essentially come down to either those companies that are primarily marketing driven, that is, a company selling the image or aspirations of its products without any previous tie to the history and pride of product found at self-owned manufacturing firms, and those that still own to some degree their manufacturing facilities. Companies that still make their own goods (or did at one time) have a strong leg up on competitors because their technical knowledge, manufacturing DNA and deep understanding of engineering practices allow them to better deconstruct the true costs of doing business. But some retailers find this a burden, preferring their buyers not to negotiate from a place of real knowledge or awareness; they prefer the ignorance that allows buyers to focus purely on achieving better pricing than competitors, thereby adding unsustainable costing practices to the menu of social and environmental ones.

I have been very fortunate to have gained experience with both types of organizations through hands-on practice in functional roles across the entire product lifecycle of a garment and have learned from deep-knowledge experts how each step in the process presents its own set of challenges. For example, during the initial creative concept and technical design phases, many early decisions dealing with materials selection and assembly processes can be made (or put off) that result in later-stage social and environmental fallout. The management of pre-production planning and shipments to multiple factories of components such as yarns, fabrics, price tags, buttons and packaging is a critical, cost-driven stage of the product lifecycle, and it warrants understanding as well. The total number of people and processes involved in making and delivering a simple garment from an initial designer's sketch to the rack at the mall is truly astounding (as many carbon footprinting consultants have found while trying to map the environmental impacts of the apparel industry). The great majority of brands unfortunately, have still gathered little information or dedicated few resources to understanding their own supply chains' repercussions.

Once through the actual stages of sewing and quality inspections, garments make their way to us by international air or ocean shipments that can often only gain entrance to export markets under special bilateral or multilateral trade agreements. The management of and planning for access under these types of deals have generally fallen to sourcing and supply chain teams, and this is where I have spent a good deal of my career. But owned outright or not, most leading brands these days do take a significant amount of ownership of the production process, and many retailers often find themselves narrowly removed from becoming the *de facto* owners of their key vendor-partner facilities.

I use this term "vendor-partner" carefully, especially when it comes to talking about the thorny topics of a factory's social, safety and environmental accountability — the manufacturing-specific offshoots of the greater corporate social responsibility movement that has evolved over the past 30 years. It is unfortunate to note that too few of the brands and retailers I have worked with seem to effectively approach meaningful, collaborative partnerships with their suppliers as part of their core business strategy. Behind the lip service paid to collaboration, confrontation, strong-arm pricing practices and a lack of trust are too often the norms of buyer-supplier relationships in the retail world. As a result, the general attitude of "I am the buyer and I hold the power" often spills over into efforts at enforcing responsible business practices, negating any real progress from being achieved.

Meanwhile, a multi-billion dollar industry of accountability consultants and service providers, legitimate and not so legitimate, has grown up around the controversial issues of labor and human rights, ethical trade and environmental management. An entire alphabet soup of acronyms has been created by industry bodies, nonprofit groups and organized labor movements aimed at tackling the issues of worker's rights, overtime hours and pay, child and forced labor, workplace discrimination, gender equity and other contentious topics head-on. As we shall see in Chapter 3, titled "Alphabet Soup," WRAP, ETI, BSCI, BSR, SEDEX, FLA, and SAI, among other groups, have all developed, adopted or supported to one degree or another a host of principles, codes of conduct and performance standards for measuring a factory's adherence to or ignorance of labor, health, safety, human rights and environmental laws. In many cases, brands and retailers are all too aware that they are sourcing from factories that break these or local laws; factories may feel that they have to, in order to meet the aggressive pricing pushed upon them. The game is to keep the process moving, pushing shipments and cost benefits along while incremental improvements in factory performance are pursued.

Generally speaking, the environmental regulations and labor laws on the books in developing countries hold up quite well to the scrutiny of international observers. Often, these robust regulatory frameworks have been a requirement for developing countries to gain access to Western markets through so-called Free Trade agreements or to take full advantage of multilateral trade rules. But the gaps that exist between paper laws and their practical implementation can range from minimal to extraordinary, depending on the country in question. One only has to look closely at the issues at the heart of the 2013 Rana Plaza tragedy in Bangladesh, in which more than 1,100 people lost their lives, to understand the stark costs in human suffering caused by such failures. The collapse of the multi-story building housing numerous apparel factories was due primarily to shoddy construction standards and exacerbated by an inefficient inspection bureau, a culture of corruption, and a lack of training in firefighting and emergency evacuation techniques. The response of some local industry leaders has been that if the regulatory standards actually had to be met, then how could Bangladesh continue to be cost competitive against rivals in Cambodia, Haiti, East Africa and the Middle East? As up-and-comers saddled with a host of developing country problems, the logic goes, rapidly rising economies should be given leeway to ease their industries into global markets. Perhaps, then, Myanmar or even Cuba will be the next low-cost destinations for the industry as trade agreements write in social and labor standards knowing they will be set aside in support of development goals. But this argument is a house built of cards, a fabrication of global trade policies driving the well-known race-to-the-bottom approach of neoliberal economics, and this remains true for dozens of countries far beyond Bangladesh.

To be sure, important achievements have been realized over the past 20 years; growing numbers of brands and retailers — under pressure from activist shareholders, organized labor, consumer pressure groups, NGOs and the media — have reached down through their supply chains to try and ensure the use of decently managed factories. For many, however, this has meant a cookie-cutter, checklist approach to one-off, annual factory audits and corporate codes of conduct that do little to change factory practices. Focused as they are on costs and stripped of engineering competencies, many buying groups have avoided deeper involvement in a supplier's social, safety and environmental practices, let alone taken on capacity building, employee training, supply chain transparency or collaborative re-invention of the demand production model.

Thankfully, there are industry outliers, companies driven by engaged, ethical professionals from the very top of the organizational chart. In later chapters, we will look at the practices of some of the most responsive brands and the people behind them to identify concrete examples of a better and still profitable way to do business both on and offshore. Profiles of industry efforts such as the Better Cotton Initiative and the Responsible Sourcing Network highlight robust, collaborative actions that engage critical members of the supply chain and promote sustainable change. These are but two examples of industry and stakeholder leaders willing to break new ground while contributing funding and expertise to meaningful alternatives in the way fashion apparel businesses operate.

When it comes to examining the CSR (corporate social responsibility) and public relations communications of some branded apparel groups, the same general market trends seen across all consumer products are evident. A considerable amount of green-washing is involved, as marketing hype often replaces real investments and hands-on efforts in production countries. Deciphering the sometimes confusing messages can be a challenge for consumers, especially because supposedly commonsense trends like the benefits of organic materials can be shown to be misleading or not quite as responsible as we might first believe. Like all things labeled "environmental," some understanding of the chemistry and biology behind both natural and synthetic textile products is needed to gain a grasp of the facts. Surprising to many consumers and NGOs alike, textile and apparel firms have often excelled at sustainably and safely managing the chemistry. We don't need to look any further than iconic sportswear brands Nike and Adidas to understand how significant such innovation can be both in building a leadership organization and in driving responsible manufacturing practices down to the factory level. Their work in the continuous reduction of hazardous chemicals and volatile organic compounds from their products, the recycling of production waste into after-use, extended-life products, and the enviro-engineering of new product lines from early concept and design stages fully supports the premise that doing good can also be good for business.

Leaving benchmarks such as these aside, the choices for most of us when we buy or use any given consumer product are still more often than not driven by its cost, the perceived quality or style that a given brand name may extend, and a purchasing convenience that matches our hectic, modern lifestyles. If forced to consider the question, I don't believe that anyone would knowingly seek out clothing made in sweatshop conditions, or in a factory that uses child labor, or that has been processed by a facility discharging its toxic waste into nearby water systems, or one failing to pay its employees for the full average 65-hour work week that is currently standard for offshore apparel manufacturing. But we are often left to make choices that both reinforce and perpetuate the worst excesses of our disposable culture. As I have often commented when asked for an opinion about public attitudes, it is not that people *don't care*; but people often do not care *to know*.

From early 1995, when I first hit the ground running in Mexico City, charged with opening the first Americas sourcing office on behalf of Wal-Mart stores at the outset of the North American Free Trade Agreement (NAFTA), until 2010, when I returned home to Canada from China some 15 years later, I clocked hundreds of thousands of miles traveling by planes, trains and automobiles (with the occasional *burro* and oxcart thrown in for good measure). I traveled across 32 countries, spanning every continent on the planet save Antarctica — all in the service of multinational brands and retailers keen to gain a competitive price advantage over their rivals by direct sourcing from factories in the developing world. To say that I have an understanding wife and resilient, adaptable children would be a gross understatement! By the time our eldest son had celebrated his eighth birthday in China, he had lived in five countries in North America, Latin America and Asia, picking up three languages along the way. A career in this industry certainly comes with its own advantages, both personal and professional, and for me the opportunity to gain a firsthand look into the globalization of manufacturing has proven both rewarding and challenging.

If this book has one goal above all others it is this: to firmly place the burden of knowledge foremost in our minds the next time we head off to the mall for a little retail therapy. Our decisions do matter; they affect the lives of real people and our planet in very real ways. And, as new social business models and trends toward localized, high-value apparel and the greater reuse of secondhand fashions begin to take hold, we should be aware of the ethical consequences of what, where and how we buy.

Vote your values with your wallet, and business *will* follow your lead. The power *is* in our hands, not as consumers, those faceless units of economic consumption, but as individuals seeking connections to the people, the communities and materials imbedded in our apparel. It will take the actions of us all in order to truly fix fashion.

1

Manchester to Mumbai

M Y EARLIEST MEMORIES FROM CHILDHOOD are vividly sensual: the spiced aroma of *nasi goring*, a Javanese dish my grandmother's family had adopted from their time in Indonesia; the velvety hand feel of the Persian tapestry my grandfather had brought back to Canada along with his war bride at the end of World War II; and the grainy black-and-white images of the fighting in South Vietnam that flickered across my grandparents' television set. These are all still with me. An early exposure to all things international, my upbringing as a military brat, and time spent living with my worldly grandparents all planted within me the roots of a lasting curiosity for the great, wide world beyond Canada.

My grandfather's influence was especially formative on me. As a career military man and later as a federal civil servant with Canada's Department of Justice, my grandfather's lifelong example was one of responsibility, service and a quiet sense of right and wrong. At 18 years of age, like so many young men and women of his generation, he had given up his own dreams (of becoming an English teacher) to enlist in the army at the outbreak of World War II. His early years of service with the Royal Canadian Corps of Signals took him across North Africa, up into the bloody battles for Sicily and the Italian mainland, and then on into Holland. There he met and fell in love with a stunning young blond while attached to units of the 5th Canadian Armoured Division that liberated her hometown of Hilversum. He would later travel to the Far East, spending time in Hong Kong, on his way to Indochina with the Canadian contingent supporting United Nations' efforts to implement the Geneva Accords that had ended the

First Indochina War in 1954. He returned from his mission deathly ill
and spent nearly a year recuperating before taking on a series of staff
roles at Canadian Forces bases across Canada before finally settling
in Ottawa. He retired at the rank of Major and went on to dedicate
another 20 years of service to Canada, working out of the West Block
on Parliament Hill. When I look back on his travels and youthful adventures across war-torn Europe and the remnants of former colonial
outposts, I have often wondered if wanderlust is a genetic trait as I
later followed in his footsteps to many of those same places.

As a descendant of United Empire Loyalists who had abandoned
the United States for Nova Scotia, Grandfather had been a staunch
Conservative and Royalist himself. He was very liberal with his library,
however, and as a boy I spent hours poring over books on Canadian
history, espionage, foreign wars and the British Age of Empire.
Everything from *The History of the Canadian Army* to Churchill's bi-
ography of the Duke of Marlborough to Vincent Massey's *On Being
Canadian* captivated me at an early age. My father's own military travels and the trinkets he sent home from U.N. duties in Cyprus and the
Sinai Peninsula only added fuel to the fire, and I dreamed of traveling
the world. I was proud of our country's role as a liberator and international peacekeeper, but, with a drill sergeant for a father, I turned away
from a career in the military. I had already lived the life without joining
up or getting paid for it! My mind was more on writing and history,
keen to learn of exotic cultures and languages, having grown up in an
era of increasingly liberal thought and social revolution.

By the mid-1980s these early influences, together with my growing
fascination for the Sandinista Revolution and ensuing Contra War in
Nicaragua, were responsible for my decision to study political science
and history. With a little luck and a solid performance through a tran-
sitional year program, I was admitted to the University of Toronto's
prestigious Trinity College without completing high school. There I
followed in the footsteps of such notable Canadian thinkers as historian
Margaret MacMillan, diplomat George Ignatieff and former Governor
General Adrienne Clarkson. It was during those years at school when I
first began to understand that my boyish dreams had been built upon
misconceptions and untruths. Behind carefully crafted textbook histories of honor and sacrifice lay a foundation of colonial oppression,

slavery and mercantilist expansion that had fed the voracious engine of empire, global trade and the ensuing Industrial Revolution.

Despite this academic awareness and a theoretical affection for revolutionary causes, I cannot honestly say I did much with that knowledge at the time — other than write a few letters to the American Embassy in Canada. I was by all accounts an immature and self-centered student, happier to jet off to Mexico and the Caribbean on March Break getaways than to put any real effort into university politics or social activism. But those holidays in Latin America helped me to build language skills that would lead, in a few short years, to an incredible accident of luck — one I still find hard to believe today — that landed me in the retail industry.

Have Passport, Will Travel: Wal-Mart, NAFTA and Mexico

Like many other university students fresh out of school, I had set off backpacking one summer with little but adventure and girls on my mind. In lieu of the typical European trek, which many of my peers headed off on, I struck out instead for Mexico, hitchhiking my way from the ancient Mayan ruins of Tulum across the Yucatan peninsula to Mexico City.

Those adventures are for another, very different book, so suffice it to say that two years later I returned home to Canada looking for a way to maintain my newly honed Spanish language skills. I ended up in Toronto, working part-time for the trade development office of Valencia, Spain, helping the general manager with market research and administrative duties. The pay was next to nothing, but it was interesting work, and I could use my Spanish every day. Enrique Cosi, the Valencian native I worked for, was a generous boss and as sharp as a tack. More importantly, he encouraged me to learn as much as I could about the merchandise export trade.

I took him at his word, and within a year I was looking for something more substantial to sink my teeth into. Quite by accident, I came across an advertisement in *The Globe and Mail* newspaper looking for ambitious young managers with experience in international trade and an interest in working in Southeast Asia setting up buying offices for an unnamed North American retailer. The ad provided a fax number in Hong Kong (as this was well before most people had even heard of the Internet or email) and, excited at the prospect of further travels,

I proceeded to whip together my first resume. It turned out to be a sparse, one-page effort, but nonetheless I faxed it off, naively expecting a phone call back in a day or two.

A week went by, then a month. By the start of the second month, I had forgotten all about the promising opportunity in far-off Asia — until early one evening a call came to my mother's home where I had been staying since my return from Mexico. An elderly lady with a thick Southern drawl addressed me: "Mr. Lavergne?" She started inquiringly. "Our man Mr. Wong would like to interview you next week in Toronto. Do y'all know who Wal-Mart is up there in Canada?" Did I ever!

It was mid-1994, and the American retailing giant had only recently entered the Canadian marketplace after acquiring the Woolco retail chain from Woolworth Canada. But aside from retail industry veterans, few Canadians seemed to know much about the Arkansas-based discount chain. What was less clear to me at the time (and what the Southern lady was quite vague about over the phone) was what exactly Wal-Mart had to do with the ad I had responded to. I would find out soon enough.

Over the coming weeks, I met first in Toronto with Charles Wong, a Hong Kong-based businessman and chief operating officer of Wal-Mart's secretive buying agent network, Pacific Resources Export Limited (PREL). From this brilliant merchandising executive I would gain a rapid education on exactly who PREL was and what they did as the exclusive global buying agent for the American retailer.

Next, I was flown down to Bentonville, Arkansas, to be looked over and quizzed in the back office of a local travel agency by a tall, lanky gentleman named George Billingsley. George was more than just the CEO of the PREL buying group (which had taken over Wal-Mart's own small network of Asian procurement offices in the early 1990s). He was also a close personal friend and longtime tennis buddy of Wal-Mart founder Sam Walton. Next, I was sent to see J.R. Campbell, then head of Wal-Mart's International Merchandising Division at the Wal-Mart home office across town. I learned over my two-day grilling that the good old boys at PREL had little interest in sending me to Asia, where I had zero experience or history at the time. What they were keen to talk about were my impressions of Mexico, my experiences there, and my abilities in Spanish.

With the North American Free Trade Agreement having gone into effect on January 1, 1994, and with Wal-Mart looking to maximize the vendor relationships it had bought into with its 1991 entrance into the Mexican retail marketplace, PREL was keen to grow its presence in the region. But as an Asian-staffed and -managed organization with its hands full in the Far East, and little cultural or business experience in Latin America, I was asked point-blank how I would feel about going back down to Mexico to start up the company's operations there from scratch. Not a single employee yet existed, no legal entity was in place, and no operating budget had yet been put together. I had to decide then and there, I was told, and if my answer was a positive one, I needed to be ready to start immediately. It took me all of five minutes to think about it, and, though I hadn't a clue how to go about starting up a *greenfield* buying office in a foreign country (a greenfield is a new business start-up generally in a new market, often an international one), I said yes without even asking about the salary. We shook hands all around, and I was in, going overnight from a part-time desk job in Toronto making a couple of hundred dollars a week to being a salaried country manager for the exclusive buying agent of the world's largest retailer. And, as I would learn very quickly, the most important product category PREL had targeted for export to Wal-Mart's U.S. stores was *apparel*.

It was an industry I knew little about at the time, but one which I would come to understand very rapidly and very successfully. My experiences in the industry took me across Latin America, the Caribbean and the Middle East, on to Asia and Africa, with stints back in U.S. and Canadian head offices for good measure. The apparel industry also introduced me to my wife and to a good many generous people who shared with me their knowledge and expertise not only of fabrics, materials and machines, but of people as well. I am not sure though, having learned everything that I have over the past 20 years, if I would have embraced it in quite the same way had much of the knowledge I've acquired been shared with me early on.

The Roots of Global Trade

Very few of the aspiring young designers, sourcing managers, or up-and-coming merchandisers I've had the pleasure to work with over the years had anything more than a cursory understanding of the historical context of the textile and apparel industries. Even today, with more recent efforts at leading design and business schools to broadly examine growing trends in environmental sustainability, cultural development and social responsibility, the knowledge gaps are significant for those without a background in global studies, history or political science. The American writer and social activist Pearl S. Buck has often been quoted as saying, "If you want to understand today, you have to search yesterday." And so a deeper look into the foundations of today's global industries, which evolved out of Western society's early industrial past, is well worth the effort. This is especially true if we are to make sense of how we have gotten to where we are today and what it will take for us to change these industries for the better — for both our planet and our race.

That era of incredible innovation in manufacturing technologies, transportation and scientific endeavor also witnessed the beginnings of the world's first multinational organizations: the infamous East and West India trading companies. From 1600 until the 1780s, the British, Dutch, Portuguese, Prussians, French and Swedes all created new stock-issuing enterprises the likes of which had never been seen. These companies were not simple commercial organizations aimed at wresting from each other the riches of newly opened trade routes to Asia or the burgeoning American colonies of the European powers. They were near-states unto themselves, and with them was born an era of truly global commerce. Along with their government-endorsed trading monopolies, the companies raised armies, waged wars, built up new colonies, negotiated treaties on behalf of home countries, imprisoned and executed whom they liked, and subjugated local peoples — all in pursuit of financial profit. Imperial Germany followed suit later, in the 18th and 19th centuries, with less grandiose designs, though by no means less violent ones.

By far the largest of these enterprises in terms of financial scope and raw tonnage of goods was the *Verenigde Oostindische Compagnie* (VOC), the United East India Company of the Netherlands, better known in English as the *Dutch East India Company*. Granted its charter and a 21-year monopoly on Asian trade with Holland in 1602, the VOC became a massive organization of commerce and exploitation far surpassing European rivals in scope, violence and early profitability. This was due in large part to its stranglehold on the so-called Spice Islands of Indonesia and the Malayan Peninsula. Between 1602 and 1796, the Dutch sent nearly one million of their countrymen to the Far East on more than 4,700 ships. They brought back to Europe more than 2.5 million tons of pepper, cinnamon, silks and porcelains through the ports of Rotterdam and Amsterdam, paying out an annual dividend to shareholders of 18 percent annually for nearly 200 years.

To grasp the enormity of the Dutch trade, we might compare it to that of its better-known competitor (at least here in North America), the British East India Company (EIC), which put to sea half as many ships as the VOC while managing to extract only one fifth of the volume of cargo. But in similarity to many modern-day counterparts, it was dissolved amid scandal and corruption in 1800; by that time, the full extent of territories under its control covered much of the Indonesian archipelago. As an outcome of the Congress of Vienna in 1815, what was to become modern-day Indonesia was officially granted as a colony — The Dutch East Indies — to the newly created Kingdom of the Netherlands, which retained its colonial grip on the island nation until it finally gained U.N. recognition of its independence in 1949.

As successful as the Dutch were, even given their massive size and financial muscle, the VOC was not, it would appear in historic hindsight, either as well managed or as ambitious as the British East India Company which, in 1600, received the first of its various charters from Queen Elizabeth I. Nor, for our purposes, did Dutch colonial trade have as profound or as lasting an influence on the social, political and economic development of global textile and apparel industries as did that of Great Britain.

This was hardly the intent at the start of the British East India Company's commercial endeavors. They had rather hoped to muscle in on the Asian spice trade (which would prove such a lucrative enterprise for the Netherlands), offering significant rates of return for bulk shipments of highly prized pepper, cardamom, ginger and turmeric. But the Dutch were already well entrenched in the region, and competition between the two companies was fierce. So much so that otherwise cordial relations between the newly crowned King James I of England and the Dutch government became strained. Under pressure from their national leaders, both companies were forced into a treaty in 1619 that aimed to build cooperation between the two ventures while sharing home markets between them.

Peaceful coexistence was short-lived; in 1623, the Dutch discovered a plot by Japanese and English merchants at the trading post of Amboyna Island in present day Maluku, Indonesia, to seize the fort and kill the Dutch governor. After torture and interrogations (which included the Dutch practice of "waterboarding"), some 20 men were executed on charges of treason. Although the facts were later found to be largely true, England was enraged when the details of the case were brought home by a few of the men whom the Dutch had pardoned. The episode provided significant propaganda material during the series of Dutch-Anglo wars that raged between 1652 and 1674.

More significantly for future generations across the developing world and for England's wool-based textile industries of the day, the immediate result of the Amboyna Massacre, as it came to be known, was that the British East India Company turned its attentions increasingly toward India. From their earlier outpost established at Surat on India's west coast in 1612, the company expanded, adding trading forts at Madras in 1639, Bombay in 1668 and Calcutta in 1690. From these bases they built a brisk exchange in English-manufactured goods, metal-wares and tools for local spices, silk, indigo dye, tea and most fortuitous of all, cotton.

The histories of cotton and the human race have long been intertwined, so to speak. In fact, cotton had been processed by ancient Mexican and Indus valley cultures from around 3,000 BCE. Alexander the Great was among the first Europeans to enjoy its benefits; his troops left off their hot, woolen garments in exchange for cotton ones after briefly invading India in 326 BCE. By the eighth century, the Muslim conquest of Spain had helped to expand trade into Europe where Venice, Antwer and Haarlem all became key centers for the transportation and sale of the material. An early technological innovation that helped to further speed its adoption occurred when the spinning wheel was introduced to Europe around 1300; by the time of the Renaissance, cotton fabrics had become highly sought-after goods.

When the Portuguese explorer Vasco da Gama became the first European to reach India by sea in 1498, a new age of trade between East and West was begun. The great cargo ships of the Iberian Peninsula would over time mean the death of overland caravans of the old Silk Road from Asia. Soon, brightly colored Indian textiles were being cheaply shipped by the ton to European markets, earning healthy profits for Portuguese merchants. Their exotic patterns, washability and low cost made the fabrics accessible to many on the Continent, and demand for Indian calicos and chintz exploded. Little did the weavers and traders of the subcontinent understand that their initial good fortune would mark the beginning of a long period of de-industrialization for Indian textile industries. Just as monumental a transformation tied to the bulk introduction of finished cotton fabrics would soon impact tens of thousands of people who depended on the woolen apparel and textile industries of Europe and the British Isles.

Since Roman times, the people of Europe had depended largely on leathers, linen and wool to clothe themselves, and sheep's wool provided the staple yarns for most of the population's apparel. By the Medieval era, as traveling fairs began to stimulate the growth of regional trade, wool production centers in North-Central France, fed by raw materials from England and Spain, were sending their wares out to markets in Naples and Sicily and as far afield as Constantinople. Limited supplies of silk from China were also available thanks to the Silk Road, but were a class of luxury goods far beyond the reach of the average farmer or craftsman.

Throughout the 13th century, commercial trade in wool increased dramatically — so much so that it was providing a surplus of capital that became central to the economies of various Italian states, Belgium and the Netherlands. Wool exports also earned the English Crown a sizable income, having been made a dutiable item of export under the infamous Edward Longshanks' (King Edward I) Great Custom law of 1275.

British North Sea ports, supplied by large landowners and Catholic religious organizations like the Cistercian Order, whose emphasis on manual labor and self-sufficiency supported such trade, shipped massive quantities of material to the textile centers of Ypres and Ghent. There, the wool was processed and dyed for cloth making. In an effort to develop England's own manufacturing, in 1331 King Edward III extended his support to Flemish master weavers escaping war on the Continent to settle in his kingdom. But by midway through the bubonic plague, which raged throughout Europe from 1340 to 1400 decimating a third of the population, only ten percent of England's wool output was being absorbed by local production.

By the late 14th century, as the Medici and other Florentine family banking houses grew their wealth through the management and financing of the trade, Italy became the dominant player in European wool markets, which depended heavily on English raw material exports. Efforts to support local production back in Britain intensified, but taxes levied by the Crown had the effect of *reducing* exports, which only further fueled merchant efforts to convert raw materials to cloth. The 15th-century wealth, not only of England but increasingly of Wales and Scotland, was tied to sheep; both landowners and commercial interests benefited from these developments. From 1651 onwards, for a period of some 200 years, a series of laws known as the Navigation Acts sought to regulate the exchange of both merchandise and hard currency among Britain and her colonies and to exclude the ships and merchants of other European powers and their respective overseas territories. The result was to drive up prices for British textiles while guaranteeing captive markets.

Labor, Guilds and the Scourge of Slavery

On the social front, the 14th century had seen the rise of urban-based craft guilds aimed at protecting the shared interests of artisan communities; these can be considered early forms of the unions that would one day take such a prominent place in English politics and society. Much of the added value and profits from wool came from the successive division of processing and labor. Thus, a collection of tradecrafts developed around the sorting, scouring, dyeing, spinning and finishing of wool. Rural areas, however, were beyond the reach and rules of these guilds. Enterprising entrepreneurs who had ready capital or credit could purchase raw materials, and, together with small advances to cottage-based artisans, would "put out" work for each consecutive step of production. Written contracts stipulated the arrangements each artisan would work under, and full payment was made once goods had been returned as completed. Thus the *cottage industry system* allowed merchants and small entrepreneurs to clear tidy profits which, in urban settings, would have found their way into the accounts of guild cooperatives. As exploitive as this might have been to those rural workshops unable to band together with their rudimentary supply chain peers, in an era of near-unregulated commerce, their lot was infinitely better than millions of unfortunates who fell under the yoke of a far more abusive and inhumane system of labor tied directly to the global trade in materials and textiles: slavery.

For most of us today, it is incomprehensible that a completely legal trade in human lives from the early 1500s through the mid-1800s allowed for the uprooting, kidnap and sale of between 10 and 15 million men, women and children to the so-called New World. At times with the collusion of African rulers and often through direct capture by European slavers, the West African slave ports of Dakar, Freetown, Christiansborg and Gorée Island, as well as those on the East Coast at Zanzibar and Mozambique, shipped their human cargo to European colonies in America, the West Indies and South America. Estimates put the number of African slaves brought forcibly to the United States at somewhere between 450,000 and 650,000 souls, while Brazil accounted by far for the largest number of lives stolen, at over three million.

It was around the same time that the British were establishing their toehold in India in the late 1600s that their activities in Africa were turning them into the largest and most efficient slave traders to the Americas. English ship builders, banking houses and shipping lines amassed vast wealth through their involvement in the slave trade for over 200 years. It is no exaggeration to say that the economic foundations of the British Empire and those of the nascent capitalist expansion born out of mercantilist and colonial policies held by all the major European powers, and to a great extent those of the American South, were built on the backs of slavery and subjugation. Even when the Abolition of Slavery Act of 1833 ended official state violence against Africans in the U.K. and the Americas, vested commercial interests continued their exploitation of enslaved peoples elsewhere. The law explicitly exempted U.K. territories in India, Ceylon (modern-day Sri Lanka) and China, and granted reparations to the British owners of slaves for the loss of their "property" long after they had extracted what value they could from them. The government of the day paid out the unbelievable sum of £20 million (nearly $US 25 billion in today's

currency equivalent) of government income — equal to half of its annual budget — to some 47,000 slave owners.

The work of Professor Catherine Hall and a team of researchers
from University College London has investigated, traced and identified
the families and business interests who benefited from this government
largesse. These payments added greatly to the financial foundations
of some of England's wealthiest banks, insurance companies, railways,
trading companies and families. Among the most noteworthy were
P&O lines (the Peninsular and Oriental Steam Navigation Company),
Baring Brothers Bank, Lloyd's of London, Cambridge/Oxford Railways,
the Bank of England, dozens of West Indian merchant traders, and the
ancestors of George Orwell, David Cameron, Graham Greene and
Sir Peter Bazelgette, current chair of the Arts Council of England. As
for the "freed" slaves themselves, many were forcibly converted under
a system of apprenticeship to unpaid, bonded laborers for a period of
four to six years. For the average former slave, Britain's newfound abo-
litionist bent left much to be desired.

The British center of slave trade activity was the Caribbean island
of Jamaica, the wealthiest of their colonies by then, which served as
the labor supply base for sugar plantations scattered across the West
Indies. From Jamaica and directly from Africa, slaves sent to the
American colonies labored first on tobacco and rice plantations all
along the eastern seaboard of the United States. By the early 1700s,
Sea Island cotton (as it came to be known for its coastal origins) was
being successfully grown in Georgia's and South Carolina's sandy soils,
but it would not be until 1793 and Eli Whitney's invention of the cotton gin that the technical issue of sorting the valuable fibers from seed
waste was overcome. This would help to fuel the spread of the crop
across America's South and Southwest, where it soon became an important and vital component of the new nation's economy.

Short of manpower to facilitate cotton's expansion, Southerners
turned increasingly to the use of slavery as a means of production;
without slaves, these agricultural pursuits simply would not have been
feasible. Both slavery and land use expanded as the nature of tobacco
and cotton farming quickly depleted the soil of nutrients, thus pushing
an ever-growing encroachment Westward. The early age of globalized
fiber and textile trades was not shaping up to be a pleasant one for

much of the world's population; people were enslaved, lands stolen from indigenous races, wars of conquest were fought, and colonization expanded as these industries grew.

The India Trade and Cotton's Rise

Meanwhile, in the Far East, the monumental changes had been steaming ahead that would wreak havoc on traditional Indian cotton and textile industries; these were the same changes that would both revolutionize business and decimate British guilds and cottage industries alike. From its network of trading ports along the Indian coast, The East India Company had integrated its commercial activities directly into an already existing and highly developed local economy. Indigo dye, opium bound for Chinese markets, spices, sugar and artisan cloth were all commodities of interest to them, with opium and cotton fabrics becoming the most significant for a variety of social, economic and, by extension, political reasons.

Not unlike many multinational companies today, the EIC had not originally sought more than a trading relationship with the Mogul rulers of the day, content to align itself with existing power structures that could guarantee it a secure commercial operating environment. This proved a prudent policy to follow until the mid-1750s, when the English began to turn to more heavy-handed and violent means to exert both political and economic power, particularly in the wealthy Indian province of Bengal.

As mercantile competition from the French increased in the region and internal political struggles within the Mogul empire took their toll, the company was all too ready to take full advantage of events at hand. By the late 18th century, EIC dominance over the southern peninsula was firmly in place. The English then turned north toward Delhi and for the next half-century battled, negotiated, placated and connived to impose themselves on the remaining Indian states.

As mentioned earlier, the demand for Indian calico had become a particularly lucrative trade. Traditionally produced by caliyan weavers in and around Calicut in the Southwest, it was an economical, plain woven cotton fabric much less coarse than the canvases or *serge de Nîmes* (the origins of today's denim) wovens of the day. Calicos' brightly colored prints appealed greatly to English home markets. Along with chintz, calico fabrics of particularly large, floral prints that had been glaze-finished began to flood into European and British markets at volumes that soon worried established wool merchants and factory owners. Two sets of highly political economic forces were set to collide.

Wool had become by the late 15th century "the great staple trade of the kingdom,"[24] and the commercial interests tied to its profitability would not step aside so easily for the new India trade. These commercial interests could wield considerable political might, and from 1690 to 1721 a series of trade policies known as the Calico Acts were passed by the British Parliament. Ostensibly aimed at protecting employment among the poor, the real beneficiaries of these protectionist actions were the entrenched interests of the kingdom's wool trading and manufacturing industries. Both entrepreneurs and the landed aristocracy stood to lose financially from The East India Company's import competition, and they lobbied hard to have restrictions imposed. But these were not the only arguments against the newly emerging cotton trade and open-market access to British home and colonial markets. Policy makers within government were also keen to prop up the mercantilist ideology of the state, which viewed a strong balance of trade and the maintenance of inward cash flows as paramount to the economic dominance of the British Empire.

The first of such laws, passed in 1700, specifically banned the import of dyed and printed calico fabrics. Merchants were quick to exploit the obvious loopholes in legislation and for the next 20 years continued importing unfinished Asian cloth. This served to facilitate the growth of local dyeing and finishing industries in cotton, dominated by descendants of the earlier wave of French Huguenot immigrants. Anti-calico forces were just as quick to manipulate anti-foreigner feelings among the populace in their fight against imports. In 1719, riots broke out in the calico quarter of London that fueled further Parliamentary actions in an effort to ensure peace and order while curtailing the import of cotton goods in support of local industry and mercantilist policies. The 1720 update to the earlier act explicitly outlawed not only the import of nearly all cotton fabrics and goods but also their sale and use.

Two quite surreptitious exceptions to the law were allowed for, which served the interests of the upper classes in reinforcing the existing social order of the day: muslins and blue calico. Muslin was a

sheer and delicate fabrication most associated with wealth and priv-
ilege, while blue calico cottons were primarily used for working class
uniforms and work-wear. There had been much upper-class conster-
nation at the growing trend of those classes deemed beneath them
copying more expensive fashions with cheap calico fabrics. Thus the
law was created in an attempt to enforce a code of class dress and to
keep working people in their "proper place." The impending revolu-
tions in commerce, investment, scientific innovation and the means of
mass production just around the historical bend would only serve to
lower the station of under classes in both Europe and the Americas to
new depths of despair.

Cotton, Industry and the Birth of Class Struggle

In the introduction to this book, Carry Somers wrote authoritatively of
Sir Richard Arkwright's cotton mill at Cromford in the East Midlands
of England. The Derbyshire town is today a quaint village of fewer
than 2,000 inhabitants, 100 kilometers southeast of the industrial
city of Manchester. Here, and in a handful of similar factory towns, is
where the Industrial Revolution was truly born. Aside from the social
challenges that the growing working classes brought to manufacturing
towns, the importance of the Cromford facilities was not only that they
housed the first water-powered cotton mill. Sir Richard also brought
together a series of technological advances that led in great part to the
textile sector's role as a critical engine of Industrial Revolution growth.

In the space of a little more than 40 years, from 1733 through 1775,
innovations such as the flying shuttle, spinning jenny, Arkwright's own
water-powered spinning frame and cotton carding machines, and
James Watt's steam engine would set the textile world on fire as the
age of mechanized production was launched. With it, the role of cotton manufactures escalated; raw material imports ballooned from less
than two million pounds of the stuff in 1720 to more than 30 million
pounds by the 1790s. Competitors launched their own mills as the
demand for spun cotton surged (still allowed under the Calico Acts
for the manufacture of re-exported goods to English colonies across
the globe). New investments in innovations and the continued growth
of the trade in England led to the repeal of the Calico Acts by 1774.
Arkwright licensed his technologies to new operations in Lancashire,

Scotland and Germany, while the apprentice Samuel Slater made good his escape to America with plans to copy Arkwright's designs, setting up the first of his 13 U.S. mills in Pawtucket, Rhode Island, in 1793. By this time the export of cotton goods accounted for some 16 percent of the U.K.'s exports and would grow to an astonishing 40 percent by 1806.

The Atlantic trade that England had nurtured through restrictive practices aimed at its American colonies still continued after the colonies had gained their independence — but in reverse. By the early 1800s the United States was supplying the majority of the world's demand for cotton. This cash crop industry built on the backs of African slaves exceeded the value of all other U.S. exports — combined — at the time. Ever-growing demand for cotton lint would see the numbers of enslaved women, men and children in key plantation states like Georgia, Alabama, Mississippi and Louisiana burgeon to 50 percent of the population. With the impending American Civil War and Southern attempts at leveraging "cotton diplomacy" to secure European support for the Confederate cause, England turned its efforts toward colonies in West Africa and the Caribbean. When these failed (largely due to inhospitable soil and weather conditions combined with a lack of manageable local labor supplies), empire mercantilists fell back on their original source of cheap cotton: India.

The British East India Company's subjugation of that industrious country continued, and the subcontinent was reduced under English rule to the role of raw materials supplier and captured market for home country exports. Finished cloth production was outlawed in an effort to artificially eliminate competition; EIC authorities resorted to draconian measures including the amputation of weaver's thumbs if they dared to disobey British directives. Operating largely as an empire of extraction, Great Britain's policies purposefully converted and then maintained its Indian colonies into a state of de-industrialized under-development and forced an economic wedge between global North and South.

Once India's resources were tied to England's demand for raw cotton, the U.K.'s industrialization would pick up steam, and, along with it, growing pressures on the lowest levels of society and working classes at mills like Cromford.

Along the same route from Manchester to Cromford, the equally famous Quarry Bank Mill was constructed by the Greg family some 13 years after Arkwright's endeavors had begun. Quarry Bank, however, often suffered from seasonal water shortages as well as facing a greater degree of competition from neighboring facilities in and around Manchester proper, just 12 miles to the north. As technology advanced to free them from dependence on water, they adapted. The Greg's conversion to steam power allowed them to run their facilities for 24 hours a day, seven days per week. This had, of course, the same devastating effect on their employees as it would in other mills introducing the same technology; many soon found themselves out of work. Those who were left, overwhelmingly women and children, faced the same drudgery of 12-hour days as did Arkwright's laborers.

More often than not, technological advancements served to push ever-greater numbers of rural workers into teeming urban centers like Manchester. Rapid population shifts into the cities driven by industrial efficiencies quickly outstripped municipal infrastructure. By the early 1820s, the population of Manchester had soared to 140,000 from about 90,000 people just 20 years earlier. Pay in the cities was miserable, and food costs were soaring due to the effects of British import tariffs on foreign grain. Living conditions for the working classes were squalid, dirty and unhealthy. It wouldn't be long before people began to organize themselves and call on authorities to make improvements.

On August 16, 1819 a crowd of some 60,000 men and women dressed in their Sunday best gathered for a non-violent demonstration at St. Peter's Field, Manchester, calling on the government for labor and political reforms centered on Parliamentary representation. Rather than listen, local authorities called on military units in the vicinity to arrest event organizers and break up the crowds. Inexperienced cavalry units attempted to execute the arrest warrants and, becoming stuck fast in the multitude of people around them, they panicked. Swords drawn, they began hacking their way toward their objective, and, seizing upon the men in question, were met with a pelting of rocks. At this point, additional mounted and foot units pressed in on the field with sabers and bayonets drawn before charging the crowd. By the time a senior officer could regain control of the troops, a dozen civilians had been killed and more than 400 injured. Men, women and children were all counted among the dead.

The field cleared quickly, but it wouldn't be until the following morning that order was fully restored. Rioting continued throughout the day with further episodes of troops firing on civilians. Reports ensued of children whose fathers had attended the St. Peter's Field rally losing their factory jobs, and other protestors who had been gravely wounded by the military were refused medical treatment. British historians would later refer to the Peterloo Massacre as one of the most significant political moments of the age. But Parliamentary reformers and labor activists against the factory systems of the day were far from finished with their work.

The St. Peter's rally, the first large-scale political event of its kind in modern England, proved a catalyst for reforms, but they would take more than a decade to bear fruit. By 1832, the Great Reform Act of Parliament became the first step toward achieving universal suffrage in Great Britain. It extended the right to vote to middle-class merchants and property owners, but fell far short of the general population's expectations. Rather than relieve the pressure on government, the Act caused growing divisiveness between the commercial class and the working poor — who felt more isolated than ever.

Still, some significant advances were achieved with the help of trade union activists when the Factory Act of 1833 attempted to relieve some of the harshest conditions faced by child laborers. Under this law, children below the age of nine were no longer allowed to be employed in manufacturing, while those between nine and 13 years of age were limited to a 48-hour work week. They were also to be provided with at least two hours per day of education, could no longer be made to work at night, and were to be given no fewer than eight half-days off per year, in addition to Good Friday and Christmas. Work day limits were further extended to women in an addition to the Act in 1844, and in 1847 a maximum ten-hour work day was legislated for all factory workers in yet another amendment to the Act. Workplace health and safety standards were also addressed, covering issues related to sanitation, proper ventilation and machinery safeguards. Initially aimed at laborers in the textile industries, by 1910 numerous other trades were brought under the Factory Acts, extending protections to workers in nearly every other manufacturing industry in Great Britain. Unfortunately, such practices did not immediately extend to British colonies. With the passing in 1899 of the Masters and Servants Act, child labor practices were encouraged in overseas territories, particularly in Africa; in Canada, the Breaches of Contract Act allowed for the imprisonment of uncooperative working children.

Factory owners like the Greg family were outraged and railed against what they termed governmental interference in commerce and private industry. This was a time, remember, when business operated with nearly unlimited freedom. Industry had brought the empire new roads, railways, commerce, canals and technologies, driving wealth and advancements. Factory owners declared that it would all be imperiled by political meddling. They could see no logical need for an end to the unregulated use of their employees as they best saw fit. In the face of increased labor costs and lower productivity, they pursued what did seem logical; they turned to ever-greater automation and the efficiency of machinery.

The Promised Land: America's Industrial Revolution

In the United States, age minimums, wages and hours of work for children were not federally regulated until 1938 with passage of the Fair Labor Standards Act. In pushing this law forward, President Franklin D. Roosevelt lectured the American people through one of his famous "fireside chat" addresses to "not let any calamity-howling executive with an income of $1,000 a day … tell you … that a wage of $11 a week is going to have a disastrous effect on all American industry." [39] Yet that was exactly the type of argument businessmen had been making since the earliest arrival of the Industrial Revolution to American shores.

The rapid industrial growth and population shifts from rural to urban employment that had affected Great Britain were echoed in the newly expanding American economy of the day, further fueled by the millions of immigrants escaping European poverty for the "New World." Significant numbers of children were put to work on American farms, in coal mines, and in textile and glass factories for 12 or more hours a day. And, as had been the case in Europe, it would be trade union activists, beginning this time in Massachusetts, who first called for limits to the use of child labor.

By 1836, the state enacted the first local statute requiring workers under 15 to attend school at least three months of the year. Six years later, work day limits at textile factories of 10 hours per day were also legislated in Massachusetts and Connecticut. Other states followed suit, though practical enforcement was irregular at best. According to the census of 1870 (the first to officially include working children), there were some 750,000 children under the age of 15 working for a living (and this did not account for those laboring on family farms or in family businesses). By 1911, the number had climbed to two million. Although numerous union and religious organizations took up the plight of working children, progress was slow and uneven. State representatives in Congress and the business interests tied to them could be counted on to fight whatever legislative attempts the forces of social justice pursued. For millions of working children in America, the 1938 Fair Labor law came far too late to be of much good.

Why History Matters

The point of looking back at the historical rise of early multinational trade practices, the emergence of global business and the roles specifically played by the raw material, textile and apparel trades in that ascendancy is not simply to leave us amazed at the extent to which entire swaths of the economic structure of modern society have been constructed on oppression, violence and the enslavement of our fellow human beings. Nor is it to argue on the side of those who would relegate the historical context of such practices to another era of ignorance or see them as the sad but necessary byproducts of human cultural development that we have happily left behind. Rather, this examination has a two-fold objective, which may already prove obvious to many readers.

Firstly, it is to underscore that, at its root, capitalism as a belief system and set of practices has intrinsically, since its earliest forms under mercantilist and expansionist colonialism, been constructed on a foundation of one, inalienable practice of its faith: exploitation. What "exploitation" means may certainly prove subtle; it may simply refer to the conversion of one material into another. But as has more often been the case, capitalist exploitation is ruthless in its single-minded determination to achieve a profit and create monetary growth at the expense of all else. Ecosystems have been laid to waste, cultures ravaged, genera-tions of humanity sacrificed to the greater good of "economic progress." Little has changed since the earliest days of the Industrial Revolution; when change does come, it is rarely brought about without external pressure being exerted on those benefitting most directly from such exploitation.

But much more interestingly for the arguments put forward in this book, by scratching just below the surface of the commercial and economic pursuits of our recent ancestors, we can clearly identify persistent patterns of behavior that foreshadow those of the leading economic and political interests of today:

+ the use of multinational trade policy to manipulate underdeveloped markets and raw materials pricing to the benefit of more developed ones;

+ alignment with existing power structures in foreign countries to guarantee order and security while safeguarding the investments and operations of multinationals overseas

+ both Neoliberal and Conservative calls for reducing the role of government interference in private industry;

+ holding companies to stricter local standards of ethical practice at home while requiring no such responsibility outside of national borders

+ and the reallocation of labor-intensive industries to low-cost and often dependent territories that lack the motivations or capabilities to enforce their own environmental, community, safety and labor safeguards all the while, as Europeans once did from the Jacobean Era through the Victorian age, espousing a determination to educate, enlighten and improve the lot of the poor in faraway lands.

These issues are more relevant today than ever before; they exist in today's headlines just as easily as they might have in those of the past. The history of global textile and apparel industries, as well as the practices of most modern retail and fashion sectors that depend on them, are mired in vicious cycles built on a foundation of exploitation for profit. To break free from the systems of production, distribution, employment and trade policies that have grown out of this shared history will take not only visionary leadership. It will take a re-engineering of our social values and economic constructs nothing short of revolutionary. It is to our great fortune that a handful of outliers has already begun to both identify and implement the social and structural "ecosystems" needed to facilitate just such a revolution in both thinking and action.

2

To Make and Market

MEXICO PROVED TO BE AN IMPORTANT EARLY MILESTONE in both my personal and professional life.

I returned home to Canada in late 1999 with a young family in tow after three years in-country servicing Wal-Mart stores and another year working under contract to regional retail group *Corporacion Supermercados Unidos* (CSU) in Costa Rica.

It might have been something of a cliché for me to have married my best friend's sister. And as she was the only daughter in a traditional rural family with three brothers and firmly Catholic parents, I don't recall that our friendship made the ordeal any easier on me! Still, with my friend's recommendations and my own mother's trip down to Mexico to help facilitate the official *pedida de mano* when I formally asked permission to marry Angélica, things came together quite nicely. The first of two baby boys came along a year later, just two months before we were due to relocate to Central America.

CSU, the Costa Rica-based retailer that had offered me a one-year contract to help start up their direct import procurement team, operated multiple stores in multiple formats across most Central America countries and the Dominican Republic. In 1998, they brought in North American and European management talent to help facilitate the launch of the region's first *hypermarket* store (based on French retailing giant Carrefour's mixed merchandise format). The new *Hipermas* chain was launched in 1999 in an effort to improve the group's stature and its value — ahead of the expected entry of Wal-Mart into Central America's retail market.

(Note: In a series of investment transactions over a ten-year period involving Costa Rica's wealthy Uribe family, the World Bank's

International Finance Corporation, Dutch retailer Royal Ahold, and Wal-Mart itself, the CSU group would be fully acquired by the Arkansas-based giant's Mexican operating arm in 2009.)

Including a couple of months spent at Wal-Mart's home office, my four years in the region being indoctrinated into the global company's worldview provided a wealth of early learning opportunities in the world of merchandising and offshore procurement. I had been bitten by the "merchant bug," fascinated with the series of processes that I would later come to know as the *product lifecycle*. PREL and Wal-Mart opened doors to me that had been beyond my reach as an ambitious but naïve young student of the world including my first trip to China and South Asia in 1995. While attending PREL's annual meeting, I was sent to visit manufacturing units of state enterprises and cross-border, Hong Kong-based entrepreneurs as part of that education. Later, on behalf of CSU, I had traveled to Taiwan, Korea, Panama and South America to scout out new suppliers and make the first of what would become numerous working contacts over the years with the global trading outfit Li & Fung. But it was not until my return home to Canada in 1999 as a manager with the local arm of Sara Lee Branded Apparel that my sourcing career really took off. The opportunity would mark the beginning of a six-year, in-depth and hands-on education in apparel manufacturing, technical product development and supply chain operations on a truly global scale.

From Cheesecake to Champions; Sara Lee Corp., Hanes & the Global Apparel Trade

It still comes as a surprise to many outside of the textile trade that Chicago-based Sara Lee Corporation, best known for its baked goods, was one of the world's largest global clothing and fashion companies prior to the 2005 spinoff of its branded apparel holdings. At one time, it held ownership in a diverse collection of international brands and manufacturing companies including Coach leather goods, Champion athletic wear, Hanes t-shirts and underwear, Israel's Delta Galil, French hosiery brand DIM, and the venerable British textile firm Courtaulds.

At the time that I joined up with the firm, there were some 60-odd people in the Hanes Canada offices, which were just outside of Toronto in the fast-growing suburb of Mississauga, Ontario. Sara Lee had also previously acquired Canadian intimates company Canadelle in 1968 (its designers were the original visionaries behind the world-famous Wonderbra). The Quebec operations and the Ontario Hanes organization were run separately, and a sharp, young management team under Canadian General Manager Kirk Erlich was put in charge of the margin-challenged Toronto business, with plans to execute a turn around.

One of the Toronto group's challenges stemmed from the fact that it was required to buy merchandise for Canadian retail clients out of U.S. inventories under a "cost-plus" model. The plus in this equation averaged 15 percent over and above the true cost of goods that Hanes' U.S. arm had paid to manufacture its apparel lines in self-owned facilities in Mexico, the Caribbean and Central America, which were then imported into stateside distribution centers. This was where my newly created role came into play; Hanes Canada was struggling to find its own home-grown solution to the same "make or buy" conundrum many consumer goods companies were facing at the time.

As the sourcing manager heading up a department of one, I was charged with helping the Canadian operation to procure its finished garments directly from manufacturers at more competitive costs than simply purchasing them from its U.S. parent. The idea, logically for Kirk and his team, was to eliminate the cost-plus markup, so as to improve their own margins. For a short time beforehand, a small team out of Canadelle's Montreal office had attempted to deal with their American counterparts to procure materials from the same U.S. fabric being shipped down to Latin America for assembly by the U.S. parent. They had planned to use a different set of factories to assemble these textiles for Canada's needs — factories that were primarily in Mexico versus Central America and the Caribbean in order to take advantage the tax-free benefits extended under the NAFTA trade deal.

In early 1998, Sara Lee's executive team in Chicago took the first step in their publicly disclosed plans to begin divesting from the vertical manufacturing structure Hanes had spent decades building by selling off nine yarn and fabric facilities in Virginia, Tennessee, the Carolinas and Georgia. The organization's responsibilities to thousands of employees were terminated. The associated overhead expenses that went with them freed up an estimated $US 600 million of cash flow to the benefit of shareholders. Those working out of the executive offices insulated from such cost-cutting back in Chicago (who also held large blocks of shares) made it clear that self-owned sewing facilities across the Americas would be next on the chopping block.

The food-dominated conglomerate had taken a page from peers at marketing-driven brands like Coke and Adidas. The labor-intensive apparel divisions were earmarked to be the first to fall under management's new goal of shedding engineering and manufacturing know-how as they focused their efforts on becoming a marketing-driven mega-brand powerhouse. The axed textile facilities were gathered together under the umbrella of a newly structured limited liability company called National Textiles along with service agreements and preferential pricing contracts selling back to Sara Lee's apparel businesses.

It was National Textiles that Canadelle had called on to begin shifting supplies to external factories in Mexico. But with no Spanish-speakers in-house at the time and one lone quality inspector — who was given limited time and no travel budget to speak of — to cover a half-dozen facilities across Mexico, the well-intentioned project soon fell off the rails.

It would take me three to four months of hard work crisscrossing Mexico to consolidate contract sewing facilities to put things in order. Between container-trucks of unaccounted-for fabric, late delivery shipments affecting sales to Canadian retailers and fluctuating exchange rates, it soon became doubtful that an independent supply chain strategy could provide the total cost savings expected of the Hanes Canada management team. Instead, through back-and-forth discussions with the apparel group's American headquarters, there appeared to be sufficient interest in keeping factory manufacturing outputs or rates of production required for Canadian market demand in-house to allow a compromise deal to be struck. A lot of time, effort and money could have been saved had the right folks simply sat down to talk through the issues collaboratively.

But the realities faced by Sara Lee's Canadian and U.S. operations in forcing a choice between in-house manufacturing versus the shedding of technical skills to outsource labor-intensive steps of the supply chain weren't going away anytime soon. Brand competition was fierce for a share of the American consumer's dollar. As my experience with

PREL had shown, national retailers like Wal-Mart, Kmart and Target had begun to put significant resources behind the overseas sourcing of their own private label goods. By the time I had left PREL, their network had grown to 20 offices around the world; they were managing combined global factory-cost purchases of nearly $US 2.2 billion. U.S.-based apparel companies still manufacturing at home found themselves under increasing pressure both to meet buyer's pricing demands and to retain their space on store shelves.

Century-old Hanes exemplified the challenges faced by thousands of North American apparel manufacturers. They certainly weren't alone in looking to downsize their vertical operations — which covered every manufacturing step from cotton to garments — in a bid to remain competitive. In the 24 years between 1990 and 2014, U.S. apparel and textile firms shed over 1.3 million American manufacturing jobs, according to the Department of Labor's Bureau of Labor Statistics. During the same period, some 3,200 textile operations and more than 8,000 sewing facilities across the United States closed their doors.

Canadian industries have fared little better, despite a temporary uptick in the opening years of the North American Free Trade Agreement. Garment factory jobs fell from a high of 94,000 in 2002 to a dismal 21,000 by 2013. With Canadian apparel imports ballooning by $CND 2 billion from 2009 to $CND 10 billion in 2013 (mostly from Cambodia, Bangladesh and Vietnam), the trend shows little sign of letting up. It is no exaggeration to say that when North American clothing brands turned to developing countries to help improve their margins, they decimated the ranks of American and Canadian workers dependent on factory jobs in both the textile and apparel sectors. Businesses were careful, it would seem, in sharing some of the cost savings achieved with their customers by bringing down average prices on clothing for more than a decade.

Founded in Winston-Salem, North Carolina (also home to R.J. Reynolds and Wake Forest University), the Hanes brand and companies were born out of the state's tobacco legacy at the turn of the 20th century. The town of Salem itself had grown up on tobacco and textiles. In fact, its founders, who were followers of the Protestant Moravian Church that first settled the area in the mid-1700s, opened the way with their Salem Cotton Mill in 1837. These facilities expanded over the next 50 years to include spinning operations and hand looms that produced dyed woolens and heavy jean fabrications, providing — among other things — the fabric for the Confederate army's uniforms during America's Civil War.

Around this time, local brothers John Wesley and Pleasant Henderson Hanes sold out their thriving tobacco business to the R.J. Reynolds Company, and in 1901 and 1902 respectively, invested in the start-up of separate textile enterprises. Wesley, as he was more popularly known, built his Shamrock Hosiery Mills to make infant and men's socks; later, he changed the company name to Hanes Hosiery Mills as it expanded into ladies stockings and pantyhose. It would soon become the largest provider of knit hosiery in the world. Pleasant's effort, the P.H. Hanes Knitting Company, became the first large-scale Southern manufacturer of knitted underwear; by 1910, it had expanded its operations to ensure an ongoing and stable supply of yarns as well.

With the outbreak of World War I, the textile and tobacco businesses in the region grew rapidly as the market to supply U.S. servicemen with cigarettes and undershirts surged. To keep up with demand, Hanes Knitting expanded its facilities twice, building a new plant and cotton mill. Thousands of new workers streamed into the nearby towns of Winston and Salem (which amalgamated in 1913, the same year P.H. began selling goods under Hanes' own label instead of continuing to provide contract production to others). Between 1910 and 1920 the new city's population doubled, to nearly 50,000 residents. Many of those working for the Hanes brothers took up residence in the growing company enclave of Hanes Village, which P.H. had built on the model of earlier English industrial towns complete with homes, stores, a church, a school and its own railway stop.

With the onset of the Great Depression following the stock market crash of late 1929, American industries were thrown into a decade and a half of severe economic contraction. Millions joined the ranks of the jobless as U.S. unemployment rocketed past 20 percent, making the recession of 2008–10 seem like a tea party by comparison. International trade dropped by half. But even during such dire economic times, people still needed underwear, and the better-run Southern textile businesses like Hanes were able to hang on. Still, life was hard for those on the factory floor, where a five-and-a-half-day work week of 10-hour days might garner $6.75 in wages — at a time when room and board would eat up half that amount.

The companies continued to innovate and grow under family leadership. Hanes was among the first apparel brands to begin shifting its hosiery production away from traditional Asian silk after DuPont launched commercial production of the nylon polymer in 1939. Unlike rayon, which had been produced in the U.S. by Courtaulds & Co. since 1910 and was derived from plant cellulose, nylon was a petrochemical byproduct that could be synthesized en masse while reducing reliance on Asian imports. But with the outbreak of World War II, American women would have to wait for the less expensive, more comfortable legwear because the U.S. government took control of all available nylon production for the war effort.

With the advent of nylon, the era of oil-based synthetic fabrics began in earnest. Manmade fibers — acrylic, polyester and spandex — would all follow in the 1950s, while on the technological front Hanes again pushed new boundaries in manufacturing by using significantly improved circular knitting. Unlike "full-fashion" leggings produced on expensive, fine-gauge flatbed knitting machines, which required highly skilled operators and sewn-back leg seams, circular-knit seamless hosiery was more efficient to make, comfortable to wear, and much more economical to manufacture.

Under the guidance of James Gordon Hanes Jr., great-grandson of company founder P.H. Hanes, investments in engineering, research and technology kept the Hanes clan at the forefront of apparel innovation. During his time as CEO, seamless hosiery revolutionized the marketplace and positioned the newly formed Hanes Corporation, which had brought the two former textile enterprises together in 1965, as an undisputed global leader in apparel manufacturing and know-how. In a U.S. Securities and Exchange Commission filing of June 2, 1965, it was noted that the combined companies had expanded their original product lines to include a wide range of ladies hosiery, underwear, sportswear apparel and sleepwear. With nearly 10,000 employees, Hanes' revenues had climbed to over $US 110 million from zero in a little more than 60 years. Not a bad legacy at all for a couple of good ol' boys from North Carolina who had started out trading chewing tobacco.

Besides simply building a profitable business, these descendants of pious German immigrants had built a community, invested in child welfare and education, brought roads, municipal waterworks and infrastructure to their region. Along with this success and commitment to local development came thousands of jobs not only in sewing but in technical trades and management, engineering, research, marketing, product design and development. But by the late 1970s, the company that successive generations of the Hanes family had built up from nothing to become a world leader would be taken in directions that would undo much of its history.

From June through September of 1978, Consolidated Foods Corporation of Chicago quietly spent $US 41 million buying up more than 20 percent of Hanes, which had been listed on the New York Stock Exchange. Plaintiffs in a class action lawsuit alleged that the $US 5 billion food company had worked with brokerage firm Morgan Stanley to secretly purchase the apparel company's shares through blind accounts at a number of secondary traders in order to mask its identity. Hanes itself launched a separate legal action in the United States District Court of North Carolina. It alleged that the buy-up of stock was in fact an illegal market manipulation violating both the Securities Exchange Act of 1934 and the North Carolina Tender Offer Disclosure Act, as no disclosure of the intent to purchase had been made to authorities. An era of hostile corporate takeovers was underway, and Hanes Corporation was ripe for the picking.

Consolidated itself had grown out of humble beginnings. Canadian entrepreneur Nathan Cummings, born in Saint John, New Brunswick in 1896, started his commercial career in his father's shoe store and by 21 years of age had his own footwear factory up and running. He expanded into general merchandise imports, later buying, then selling, a profitable candy and biscuit business.

By 1939, the astute businessman made his first foray into the U.S., borrowing a large sum of money to purchase a Baltimore-based wholesaler of coffee, tea and sugar, the C.D. Kenny Company. The business grew successfully and allowed Cummings to expand by buying out Chicago-based Sprague, Warner & Company in 1942, a national distributor of canned and packaged foods. By the mid-1940s the businesses were taking in $US 120 million in sales, and Nathan took the company public on the New York exchange.

With increasing competition among smaller, regional brands, Consolidated Foods pursued an aggressive strategy of acquiring established, family-owned companies, saving significantly on product development and marketing costs throughout the 1950s and '60s. In 1953, the firm made a small investment to buy up Chicago-based Kitchens of Sara Lee (with sales of only $US nine million annually) in exchange for a block of existing shares in a deal that would significantly impact the future of the growing company. Cummings' growing conglomerate struggled with its new size yet continued to diversify in an effort to spread risk among its businesses; they acquired Shasta Beverages, Toronto-based Monarch Foods and a Venezuelan vinegar firm in the 1960s. Ahead of his pending retirement, the company's founder invested significantly in the Sara Lee brand, opening new production facilities that tripled its bakery products output in 1964, driving Consolidated's sales past $US 600 million that same year.

With Nathan's retirement in 1968, the company made its first foray into the apparel business when it acquired Gant shirts, based in New Haven, Connecticut, home also to prestigious Yale University where the brand had a strong following among students and faculty. The Canadelle purchase followed soon after. This would mark the beginning of a long period of non-food diversification for the packaged foods and bakery giant.

Over the next decade, everything from home furnishings and Electrolux vacuum cleaners to household chemicals and the Fuller brush brand were gathered under the company's growing umbrella of purchases. These decisions had been made in the light of government action that required the divestiture of some of the firm's assets while food price-controls under the Nixon administration limited Consolidated's profit margins. Sales had continued to climb with ongoing acquisitions, hitting $US 2 billion in 1973, but profitability at the firm lagged that of competitors. Diversifying into new businesses was seen as the best way to avoid further regulatory action while bringing new growth to Consolidated. Thus was born the strategy that led to the hostile raid against Hanes Corporation and a further ten-year drive into non-foods categories, which would soon account for over 50 percent of company income.

As an outcome of the earlier legal suit, trading in Hanes stock was suspended on September 5, 1978, and two days later North Carolina's attorney general weighed in with further action prompting a restraining order against Consolidated's continued purchases. Over the next ten days, the corporate officers of both companies met to hash out a deal, setting an offer price of $US 61.00 per share for outstanding stock, well above the average $US 40.00 it had commanded on the open market prior to knowledge of the takeover bid; Consolidated had saved themselves in excess of $US 15 million on their earlier transactions based on purchases made before market news of the takeover was released.

Financial markets welcomed the acquisition of Hanes, which Robert Metz at *The New York Times* called in his 1978 "Marketplace" column, a well-regarded company known for both its sophisticated management style and disciplined merchandising prowess. The decade also marked two important milestones for the organization, highlighting the opportunities and challenges faced by Hanes and its competitors, one in the emerging science of marketing and the other in manufacturing.

Hanes Heads South

On the manufacturing front, Hanes began its first steps toward the offshoring of its production model with the opening of facilities on the Caribbean island of Puerto Rico in 1973. Long before cross-border manufacturing in Mexico took place or NAFTA and globalization became household words, the U.S. government had set about to facilitate the relocation of American factories to lower-cost jurisdictions in its own backyard.

President Roosevelt's New Deal policies of the early 1930s that aimed at softening the blows of the Great Depression on America's poor had excluded the U.S. territory of Puerto Rico. Along with Cuba, the Philippines and Guam, the United States had gained effective control of these colonies in its successful war against Spain in 1898. In 1935, the U.S. Department of the Interior created the Puerto Rico Reconstruction Administration (PRRA). Under it, Teodoro Moscoso led the *Compañía de Fomento Industrial* (the Industrial Development Company, or PRIDCO), which was in charge of implementing *Operation Bootstrap*. This program had been developed with the help of consultants Arthur D. Little and Robert Nathan as a series of actions intended to transform the island's economy from one of agricultural dependence to that of an industrial powerhouse.

Together with public relations companies such as McCann Erickson and Young & Rubicam, the development policy was aggressively marketed to U.S. corporations through all major financial media of the day. A dollarized economy, lower wages than the U.S. mainland, duty-free shipments to markets back home, and exemptions from federal and local taxes were all identified as clear benefits to industrial investors. With a per capita income of only $US 113 at the time, or one sixth that of the U.S. mainland, low wages were central to the plan's efficacy. Officially launched under the Industrial Incentives Act, new American investment in Puerto Rico was extended a ten-year tax holiday, and by 1950 some 80 new facilities were operating and a further 20 were under construction. While the government itself invested directly in the start-up of manufacturing units that would later be sold off under some of the first privatization programs of the modern era, American companies like Textron and Beacon Textiles moved to set up their own dyeing, cutting, sewing and textile operations on the island.

Hanes' North Carolina competitor Julius Kayser & Company may have been among the first name brand American textile firms to set up in Latin America, choosing Mexico as their production springboard in 1950; but until the 1970s, the Winston-Salem-based family had worked to keep their manufacturing close to home. When the U.S. Internal Revenue Service enacted a series of rules (beginning with Section 931, later to be replaced by Section 936) allowing for the tax-free repatriation of profits from Puerto Rican subsidiaries, the opportunity proved too hard to resist. Ultimately, the combination of these artificial marketplace dynamics and the company's new masters at Consolidated Foods would put the vertically integrated company on a steady path toward greater overseas activity; by the 1980s, they had established factories in Costa Rica and the Dominican Republic, to be followed later with facilities in Jamaica, Honduras, Haiti, El Salvador and Mexico.

No decisions could have been made solely in a black-and-white comparison of home country versus offshore operational costs. Without explicitly manipulating the taxation and duty rules of the game in favor of large-scale manufacturing interests starting with *Operation Bootstrap* (including the cross-border Maquila programs first launched in the 1960s; the Caribbean Basin Initiative of the 1980s; NAFTA in 1994; and current efforts to push forward the Trans-Pacific Partnership trade and investment treaty), North American apparel and textile production and the jobs tied to it would not have logically flowed overseas. We'll come back to these issues shortly by looking at the challenges faced at Sara Lee during one of the largest new brand launches of the past two decades as the company joined forces with trend-right retailer Target stores to bring active sportswear styles to mass markets, but first let's turn to marketing.

Marketing: A Brand's Best Friend

The second major milestone of the 1970s for Hanes evolved out of the collaborative efforts of merchandisers, advertising execs and marketplace analytics. The divisional president of the company's hosiery business in 1968 was a methodical, Princeton-trained engineer by the name of Bob Elberson who had gone on to Harvard to earn his Master's degree in business. Elberson began looking at how his team's hosiery unit might break out of its dependence on department store sales, where product line growth had hit a brick wall. The marketing folks came back to Bob with a competitive analysis that laid bare the challenges of penetrating the highly fragmented supermarket and drug store formats of the day. While he was sure new opportunities lay in expanding sales to these clients, space was tight and shared by multiple competitors. Hanes needed a stand-out solution.

Having challenged the team at iconic design firm Herb Lubalin, Inc., Elberson was presented just the innovation he needed to make the merchandising breakthrough Hanes was after: a sleek, simple, yet original egg-shaped package for ladies hosiery. Rhyming "egg" with "leg," designer Roger Ferriter nonchalantly gave the product a French accent, and the L'eggs brand was born. The unique product required its own store fixture — which competitors had no way of filling; and the shrewd hosiery exec hit upon a consignment sales model in which

Hanes' own staff would be responsible for maintaining the displays. Both store owners and their customers loved it. Early product testing fared so incredibly well that the effort was cut short to enable a nation-wide launch of the product in late 1970.

While competitor sales struggled in a declining hosiery market, *L'eggs* helped Hanes to drive 140 percent growth in the category over the next six years as it firmly held onto first place among brands, not only in pantyhose but also in ladies bras and men's and boy's underwear markets. It was these kinds of results that made the company such a hot takeover target. But in the 1960s and '70s, as a growing number of consumer product companies competed for the attention of the public and retailers, the emerging pseudo-science of marketing — and its half-brother, advertising — were being called upon to help understand and ultimately to shape our buying habits.

The roots of early fashion advertising and promotions grew out of the rising 18th-century urban culture of Europe's largest cities, principally London and Paris. Newspaper and press advertisements were not yet widespread in an era of pamphleteering and handbills. Shopkeepers and tailors focused instead on presenting attractive windows and façades with comfortably appointed interiors more akin to private clubs. As limited advertising began to appear toward the later 1760s, a growing number of merchants began to display engraved pictorials in their shop-fronts depicting their wares. Early pictorials and publications aimed at middle- to upper-class ladies such as Heidelhoff and Ackermann's *Gallery of Fashion* and John Bell's literary fashion magazine *La Belle Assemblée* left their marks on 18th- and 19th-century readers, providing editorial commentary on period style and fashion trends.

The turn of the century and Europe's *Belle Époque* era leading up to the outbreak of World War I gave rise to a flourishing arts scene in Paris while growing ranks of working class citizens enjoyed a rare period of peace and prosperity in the French capital. On the other side of the Atlantic, America was emerging from its post-Civil War depression and entering the so-called Gilded Age of increased employment (including, as we have seen, significant numbers of children), immigration and opportunity. As leisure time grew along with disposable incomes, all sorts of new pastimes and products vied for the public's attention and wallets.

To promote the plays, cafes and consumer goods of the time, colorful, large-scale lithographs began to appear around Paris as a particular style of commercial art emerged. Toulouse-Lautrec (1864–1901), Jules Chéret (1836–1932) and Alphonse Marie Mucha (1860–1939) pioneered this pre-modern movement, bridging art and the growing consumerism it depicted. Mucha's focus on beauty and style gave birth to the Art Nouveau movement that he led, obsessively redefining architecture and new forms of transportation as well as jewelry, furniture and fashion design.

The outbreak of the war in Europe in July 1914, put a damper on consumption and fashion advertising, but some newly emerging industries would evolve greatly during the coming interwar period. Of particular importance was the growth of available ready-to-wear clothing as new mechanization and mass tailoring techniques, which had their earlier start in men's military wear, were converted to civilian use from the 1920s onward.

Unlike the rather simple and plain designs that have characterized menswear since the beginning of the modern era, women's clothing prior to the turn of the century was much more technical, depending on individual fit, complicated pattern work and ornate tailoring. Those who could afford it would order entirely new outfits in line with changing styles, but the vast majority of women depended on alterations to their existing apparel to keep up with trends.

Adopting industrial production methods, department store retailers and the more industrious designers turned to mass fashion to meet the demands of a population tired of the drab shades and coarse fabrics of the war. The growing professionalization of publicity and the use of statistical methodologies from the social sciences in investigating the buying habits of a burgeoning middle-class added to the transformation of the advertising trade. Influenced by a new generation of minimalist photographers such as Clarence White and Man Ray, commercial artists like Hans Schleger and Paul Outerbridge wielded the growing medium of photography as an evocative tool for building fashion brand awareness.

Vogue and *Harper's Bazaar* in the U.S. and *The Queen* magazine out of the U.K. all came into their own in the 1920s, providing their readerships with updates on continental fashions, popular style and sewing patterns to copy at home. *Vanity Fair* and *Ladies' Home Journal* also carried adverts by top fashion photographers and designers whose work steadily replaced illustrations through to the World War II and beyond.

Even with the impact of that horrific war, the U.S. population grew more than 14 percent from 1940 to reach over 150 million people by 1950. With an average age of only 30 and more than 50 million Americans between the ages of 12 and 30, U.S. apparel industries and their advertising consultants clearly identified the growing teen and young adult markets as critical to their continued success. Sexual iconography and masculine/feminine stereotypes began to be predominantly featured in advertisements of the day, building off Hollywood's portrayals of rebellious teen angst in movies like Brando's *The Wild One* or of film noir's "Bad Girls" of the '50s like Audrey Totter and Marie Windsor. By the 1960s, images of women in fashion media relegated them to the role of the provocative woman-child, wispily thin and pouting from ads dressed in men's shirts or hanging on adoringly to young men who themselves were portrayed as ornamental objects of desire.

Consumerism as a practice was taking hold as marketing began to hone the craft of identity-molding young North Americans for a lifetime of brand-influenced buying. At the same time that boys and men were being more greatly encouraged to follow what Harvard Medical School psychiatrist Dr. Susan Linn has termed "hyper-masculine behavior,"[60] girls were being influenced to look outside of themselves and their traditional family and friend relationships for new measurements of self-esteem and value. Marketeers turned increasingly to psychology not only to help model pleasurable physical environments that might induce shoppers to relax and spend more time — and by extension, money — in their stores, but also recruited them to collude with brands and advertising firms in helping to build "cradle-to-grave" loyalty.

Today's youth-driven fashion markets represent a significant slice of the $US 15 billion in advertising that seeks to capture teen and preteen spending, which is somewhere in the neighborhood of $US 600 billion annually. Marketing has not often been subtle in its messaging that material consumption is what matters, while selling us on the myth that popularity, beauty and a sense of belonging can be bought and sold. Popular fashion has long been associated with identity, but not until our modern age of advertising across so-called omni-channel retailing markets — selling to us from mobile phones, Internet, TV, radio and traditional stores — has the importance of branding so profoundly altered patterns of socialization, particularly among young people.

As Dr. Allen Kanner explained, while discussing his intriguing book *Psychology and Consumer Culture: The Struggle for a Good Life in a Materialistic World,* "It's the meta-message that you can solve all of life's problems by purchasing the right products that's having the most profound effect."[61] By focusing on teens during the most formative years of their social and psychological development, marketing efforts of recent decades have acted on the natural insecurity of adolescents in pushing material values to define identity. And by developing what Dr. Kanner calls "particularly insidious" practices, youth-targeted, identity-oriented branding attempts to drive a wedge of rejection between teens and their parents by reinforcing age and cultural differences as the acceptable norm. How children and young adults see themselves and those around them has adversely changed due to the overwhelming amount of advertising telling them how important a given brand is for their self-esteem and sense of worth. Manipulating the need for peer group acceptance takes advantage of adolescent vulnerabilities by warping the natural processes of identity development. In light of such industry efforts, it is hard to see Dr. Kanner's comments as an exaggeration of the facts.

Such surreptitious efforts are only a stone's throw away from the more nuanced practices of environmental psychology and anatomical mechanics researched by self-described urban geographer and retail anthropologist Paco Underhill. Having worked with the likes of Microsoft, Adidas and Estée Lauder while gathering research on more than 900 different measures of interactions shoppers make while actively browsing through retail outlets, Underhill has pioneered the use of behavioral analysis, a practice with roots in psychology, in helping to understand buyer decision-making in lieu of a dependence on financial analytics, which rely heavily on economic data.

Rather than a focus on traditional quality/value perceptions and a customer's willingness to spend on a given product, the work Underhill and his associates at New York-based consulting firm Envirosell have undertaken places greater emphasis on the mechanics of the shopping experience. Physical store layouts and the aesthetics of retail environments, together with an understanding of how consumers respond psychologically to fixture placement, product packaging, signage and the like, have helped retailers to make subtle adjustments that result in significant sales performance impacts. Strategically located seating and complementary coat check services, for example, influence shoppers to stay longer in stores while freeing their hands to pick up, touch, or try on goods, greatly increasing the likelihood of a purchase. Underhill's early work and his first bestselling book *Why We Buy: The Science of Shopping* identified important operational lessons to retailers tied to our phobias and biases. One to avoid at all costs turned out to be poor fixture placement, which results in the so-called butt brush, the accidental contact of one shopper with another's derrière. It turns out that few experiences put off store customers more, especially female ones, than someone brushing up against their backsides due to tight space between racks or those that force shoppers into the oncoming traffic of busy store aisles.

Dr. David Lewis, founding neuropsychologist and director of the consumer behavior research group Mindlab International in the U.K., has spent much of his career looking at how brain sciences have provided advertising firms and marketers with insights into why we buy. More than simply understanding consumers better, Dr. Lewis argues that what he calls *neuromarketing* is being used to stimulate our buying by influencing our emotions.

One might better call this sensory manipulation, which psychologists often refer to as *subliminal priming* — attempts to stimulate the unconscious mind to increase the probability of later cognitive actions, i.e., buying more of something or choosing a particular brand of jeans over another. Neuromarketing researchers believe that through the use of color, imagery or music, brands seek to trigger emotive responses and attachments to our subconscious minds.

In a recent blog posting for e-commerce platform Shopify, content designer Humayun Khan urged small retail store owners to emulate some of these practices by delving into examples of sensory stimulation as employed by teen apparel brand Abercrombie & Fitch. He referenced research by Nobel Prize recipients Richard Axel and Linda

Buck into how our olfactory sense has been identified as the most emotional and memory-linked of our senses. This knowledge was apparently not lost on the marketing team at A&F who, according to Khan, dosed their stores with the brand's own "Fierce" fragrance for men in a sensory attempt to make teens better identify with the chain's model-like staff and classic, cool image of youth. He also asserts that their penchant for playing loud, club-like music has a dual purpose: to drive purchase-controlling parents from their stores and to over-stimulate adolescent brains to trigger impulsive buying.

The blatant recommendations are a bit startling and hardly actions that could be called responsible business practices. Yet these manipulative efforts at driving ever-higher levels of consumption have become completely acceptable norms in an industry that shows no qualms at employing psychological trickery to get us to spend. From the afore described examples of "atmospherics" to the emotional engineering of advertising, to the creation of "want-needs," marketing strategies drive the perception of scarcity and exclusivity. Fashion brands have excelled at provoking feelings of both desire and inadequacy. As Dr. Lewis stated in a 2013 interview for the *London Evening Standard*, "From playground to playing field and schoolroom to boardroom, brands are increasingly perceived as the outward and visible signs of personal accomplishment and social inclusion."[67]

Supply Chain Strategy for Launching a New Brand

Astute market positioning and the challenges of managing offshore supply chains affected by global trade regimes came together for Sara Lee's apparel businesses in 2003 when I was promoted to director of global sourcing under then vice president of the team Claudia Runkel. The boost up the ladder came with new responsibilities. I was asked to lead the sourcing team effort supporting plans by the company's Champion athletic wear label to launch *C9 by Champion*, a new sub-brand to be sold exclusively at Target stores in the U.S.

Claudia had become one of the most important mentors in my supply chain career two years earlier when the Hanes Canada offices and warehouse in Toronto were abruptly shut down. The management team's financial goals hadn't been met, and, in one of a long string of Sara Lee's corporate restructuring efforts, some 60-odd employees in the Canadian apparel business were let go; operations were consolidated back to Canadelle's Montreal headquarters. Three or four staff members were kept on to manage Toronto-area retail accounts. Through the efforts of General Manager Kirk Ehrlich, and by calling on the relationships I had built with U.S. colleagues while sorting Hanes Canada's Mexican contracting debacle, I was offered a relocation to Winston-Salem. By early August of 2001, my wife Angélica, baby Mike, and I settled into a five-year-old bungalow just one mile from the Sara Lee Branded Apparel group's headquarters.

My first role with the U.S. team once again leveraged the skills I had developed in Latin America. For the better part of two years, I would be one of a small team of managers charged with overseeing supply chain relationships at two dozen contract sewing facilities in Central America and the Caribbean. These external manufacturers mimicked the work Hanes had previously done themselves in the U.S., sewing up cut parts sent to them from Southern textile mills into sweatshirts, tees and underwear for mass market retail customers and printable t-shirt wholesalers across North America. By this time, Sara Lee had made good progress toward the accomplishment of its internally-named "Project 2000" business plan, which called for the deverticalization of many of their businesses — from food to apparel — closing more than 100 facilities, including those that had affected my friends and co-workers in Canada.

Those of us who had built our networks and could help the company drive savings and maintain profit margins by shifting production to lower-cost countries while dealing with their inherent cultural, linguistic and bureaucratic challenges were given a greater profile in the organization. Sourcing as a supply chain function had begun to move away from a historic role reserved for offshore buying agents or the bastard-child of old-line manufacturers like Hanes toward an acceptable profession. Frankly, I was thankful to have hung onto my job at a time when my young family was just getting off the ground and globalization was pushing ever-greater numbers of jobs overseas.

With Sara Lee's help, we were able to buy our first home and move beyond the hand-to-mouth existence we had faced since our days in Mexico. Shortly after our arrival in Winston-Salem, my wife became pregnant with the second of our two children. Ensuring their care and well-being became paramount to dealing with the conflicts I felt about how my improving career depended on the job losses suffered by others. While I was able to push it out of my mind at the time, it was a theme that would come back to haunt me time and again.

Those first couple of years with Hanes' U.S. operations provided me my first real insights into the complexity of engineering and management smarts needed to effectively and profitably run all the operations of an apparel factory. With self-owned facilities still scattered across Mexico and Central America, the organization's knit goods and intimate divisions fought to maintain that know-how against growing industry trends of downsizing. It was by spending time on the production room floor visiting such facilities that I built my own understanding of the challenges they faced.

Of all the tiers in the apparel industry's global supply lines, running a sewing factory has to be one of the most thankless and difficult tasks imaginable. Infrastructure and machinery start-up costs are significant, and the business licensing processes — even in developing countries — can be onerous. Many of the factory owners I came to know over the years felt a real responsibility to the hundreds of employees and the families that depended on them for their livelihoods. That is not to say that a good number didn't. Like any industry, there are good and bad players — with all shades of grey in between — and to generalize would be a mistake.

Manufacturers also make the leanest margins of all the entities in a business model, where brands reap the largest reward, while arguably doing the least amount of work. For so-called full-package goods, factory owners take responsibility for all costs of providing their buyers with a complete garment — from patterns, thread, trims and fabric to the final packaged product in wholesale cartons. Margins average 10–20 percent . . . gross. Retail apparel margins range considerably, from the low 30s for discount retailers like Wal-Mart to mid-40 percent for leading sports brands like Nike, and into solid 50+ margins for European fast-fashion giants like H&M and Inditex. And with a growing number of developing countries in recent years having turned to labor-intensive, textile trade employment as a way out of poverty, buyers have a glut of options to choose from. It is anything but a level playing field.

In any event, I had apparently done a decent enough job of haggling for per-minute sewing costs in Haiti, troubleshooting quality issues with Korean manufacturers in Guatemala, and planning security contingencies on Mexican trucking routes northbound to have earned the director promotion to the C9 team. The opportunity tied to it was a significant one, both for me and for Sara Lee because it would help break new ground at the company by securing distribution for athletic apparel at some 1,400 Target stores across America while completely replacing Target's own private label brand. The exclusivity deal worked out between the two corporations was nothing short of a coup for the sales and marketing team at Champion. Less than $3 million worth of product would be shipped for the brand's 2004 launch, yet by 2012 Target would be opening its first stand-alone C9 by Champion store and realizing sales of $1 billion at retail.

Heading up the sourcing team that delivered the first couple of years' worth of product was one of the most challenging and rewarding highlights of my career. But there was no way that the half-dozen of us assigned to the project could ever have managed such a feat on our own. The product line across men's, ladies' and children's wear was simply too expansive, the volumes too large, and the manufacturing resources required too far outside the scope of Hanes' internal factory footprint or technical capabilities. To support the hometown team in managing the global factory network needed to deliver on commitments, Claudia and the executive group called in the big guns. In the world of offshore sourcing, none was bigger than the Hong Kong-based trading firm of Li & Fung.

Founded in 1906 as a small-scale export trading company in South China by the son of a local merchant family and a Chinese English teacher, Li & Fung is now a Hong Kong-based multi-billion-dollar global enterprise. Their businesses extend from supply chain services, product development and design support to retailing, product distribution and brand ownership. I first worked with their merchandising export teams while on contract to the United Supermarket Corporation in Costa Rica. After coming across a 1998 interview in the *Harvard Business Journal* with Victor Fung, the company's leader, I had sent the astute businessman an email asking for help in procuring Asian goods for the Latin American retailer. For the next decade, it would be an on-again off-again relationship.

When Sara Lee execs called on Li & Fung as a sourcing partner to support the C9 launch at Target, I was happy to learn I would be collaborating with a former PREL colleague. Mark Agius, a native of the Mediterranean island nation of Malta, had previously run a PREL subsidiary in Egypt servicing Wal-Mart's sourcing needs in the region and had only recently signed up with the Li & Fung organization.

Together, Mark and I would go on to build an international merchandising and quality control support team of more than 20 associates scattered across the globe. They were charged with supporting my own team of six in the U.S. and an additional four staff sitting in Sara Lee's Asia apparel office in Hong Kong. Every one of them would be needed to oversee the vast global network of factories signed up to manufacture the C9 brand — from Kenya and Lesotho in Africa to Indonesia, Cambodia and Vietnam in Southeast Asia. China, Jordan and Egypt in the Middle East and Honduran suppliers in my old Central American stomping grounds would round-out the core countries targeted in our supply chain and financial plans.

The other integral piece to solving the C9 puzzle would require a new and innovative design-and-development team to churn out exciting product capable of meeting Target's high-bar expectations without overshadowing the sub-brand's parent at Champion proper. To spearhead these efforts, the company turned to Ned Munroe, a passionate, driven and inspiring design professional who had learned his craft at New York's prestigious Pratt Institute. By the time he joined the Champion team in 2003, Ned had already proven his mettle as divisional VP of men's design at outdoor apparel retailer Eddie Bauer and as vice president of men's design with iconic American style brand J. Crew. His close working relationship with Target's vice president of design and development, Michael Alexin, another longtime Eddie Bauer creative lead, would be instrumental in helping to guide Sara Lee's design and sourcing teams through the challenge of understanding Target's timelines and development process.

Target's own efforts to re-engineer import apparel calendars — reducing the number of weeks needed from initial creative concepts through the delivery of goods to a customer in their stores — had been making waves in the retail industry. From my point of view, exposure to and understanding of their entire product development lifecycle would be just as valuable to Sara Lee's apparel teams as the new sales growth that C9 would deliver. Even today, many apparel brands struggle with a 52-week calendar; that's how long it takes from start to finish, covering every process from competitive market shopping through receipt of the next season's garments in retailer warehouses. In 2003, Target was pushing the new C9 team right from the get-go to shave ten weeks off this 52-week standard, and they had built in a number of ingenious yet simple and quite logical ways to achieve this.

For my team and the extended one at Li & Fung, our more immediate concerns at the outset of the project were two-fold. First, we needed to push a new and under-staffed design team operating out of Winston-Salem and New York to provide us the building blocks of a product lineup, so we would know what to make. Secondly, we needed to identify a manufacturing footprint that would allow us to produce a new range of goods that Sara Lee and Hanes teams were not yet familiar with — while hitting the wholesale price points (read: margins and profitability) and delivery dates needed to keep our internal and external masters happy.

Both the brand and the retailer had clear margin goals to achieve. Added to the mix was a global buying agent that required a commission on the factory purchase price of goods. Not to mention factory owners who needed to keep their machines humming and their employees active and paid. That is quite a number of profit margins to deliver while still providing the great pricing and design to retail shoppers that is a hallmark of Target's commitment to its customer.

Who Makes What: Profits, Margin and Mark Up

Let's just take a moment to add those margins up (to do this, I'm making some assumptions about the similarity of certain types of brand/ retailer agreements):

15 percent to the manufacturer of the factory selling price, most commonly negotiated as the FOB price of goods. (Freight On Board refers to the cost of fully finished and packaged goods delivered by the factory to the port of export in their country and placed on board an ocean-going vessel.)

28 percent to the brand of the wholesale price to their retail client. The FOB includes the cost of shipping garments from their export country of origin to the importer's country, clearing customs and paying associated costs and delivery (in most cases) to the brand's own warehouse or distribution center. A markup (not to be confused with the margin earned by the brand) is added to the total cost of goods to establish a wholesale price.

45 percent of the retail selling cost goes to the retailer. Major national retailers generally collect a host of fees from brands or wholesalers for advertising, warehouse, shelf space, etc. These miscellaneous fees range anywhere from three to ten percent, but to simplify the exercise, we won't bother with them here.

Here is how those numbers look in real dollar terms based on a retail selling price of, say, an average $US 40.00 sportswear apparel top.

Retail sales price $US 40.00. Having paid a wholesale price of $US 22, a discount or mass retailer will have earned $18 gross profit per top, which is a comfortable 45 percent margin.

Wholesale price $US 22.00. Having paid $US 13 FOB to the factory offshore and an additional $US 2.00 per unit in freight, handling, customs fees and import duties, for a total cost of $US 15 into their warehouse, the brand wholesaler will have earned $US 7 gross profit per top, and a reasonable 32 percent margin. After paying their offshore buying agent seven percent of the factory FOB price ($US 0.91), they are left with $ 6.08 per unit, which further deteriorates margin to 28 percent, a tight one on which to run a business.

Factory FOB price $US 13.00. In order to earn a minimum margin of 15 percent on a top costing $US 11 to produce, the factory owner must sell the tee for $US 13, earning just $US 2 per unit of sale.

In the above exercise, $26.99 in gross profits was earned by the major stakeholders, without considering fabric, trim, packaging and transportation suppliers nor the "services" of import taxation and customs bodies. 66 percent of those dollars were earned by the retailer, who essentially put the goods on sale in their home market. Just seven percent of those profits were earned by the manufacturer who made the goods. Three percent was paid to an agent who may or may not have provided a significant amount of value in the entire process. (Agents may also be earning fees from the factories as well, which is generally frowned upon by agent clients but is not an unheard-of practice. They may also earn fees — as has been the case for Li & Fung projects I have worked on in the past — from extending financing on fabric purchases or short-term working capital to the factories they manage, ostensibly on behalf of their retail and brand clients.)

Less than one percent of these earnings went to the sewing operators and laborers who actually made the garment. When looking at these black-and-white numbers, it becomes startlingly obvious why so many grassroots civil and labor organization stakeholders have taken exception to the economic models of consumer goods industries. (How exactly we might re-balance an equitable share of total product profitability back into manufacturing costs and stakeholders will be discussed in subsequent chapters.)

What also becomes obvious is the economic reason why so many brands have turned to designing and sourcing goods on their own. Using the above exercise, a retailer would stand to gain significant additional margin dollars or be better positioned to share that income between improved profits and more competitive pricing to customers.

In the case of the C9 brand, there is little doubt that Target would have loved to have negotiated a licensing agreement with Sara Lee's apparel group in order to source and manufacture the goods themselves. With an in-house design team of some 300 associates across all product categories and together with their formidable sourcing arm, Target Sourcing Services (TSS), which operates over 20 in-country procurement and quality hubs around the world, the retailer was more than qualified to do the job.

TSS was once an external buying agency group, similar in scope to that of PREL, where I had worked on behalf of Wal-Mart stores in Mexico. In fact, before taking up the more challenging job in Costa Rica with the United Supermarket group in 1998, I had been offered the general manager's role at the Guadalajara arm of Associated Merchandising Corporation (AMC), the previous incarnation of the TSS organization. AMC, as it was better known since its founding in 1916, had once operated as a client-owned buying cooperative for a number of retailers including TJ Maxx, Marshalls and Bloomingdale's in the U.S. and Canada's Hudson's Bay Company. In 1998 Target bought out AMC, which subsequently closed down its department store division to wholly focus on servicing its new parent company as a buying agency, thus becoming TSS.

Trade Agreements and Why They Matter

With its eye on the long-term growth of the fledgling brand C9, Sara Lee firmly and strategically held control of it. But to service the rapid start-up of the agreement while achieving its multi-tiered financial goals would require a carefully balanced mix of manufacturing sites. Pricing generally drives and limits brand and retailer options when it comes to choosing exactly where to make what, and very few cost demands from buyers these days allow for local U.S. or Canadian manufacturing to be considered.

But simply chasing large, multinational retailers offshore is no guarantee of success, as evidenced by the recent spate of retail chain closings in North America. Examples like Canada's Tabi Stores, Smart Set, and Jacob, and American retailers Delia's and Wet Seal abound as the global scale and pricing muscle of the H&Ms and Zaras of the world increases. Technology-driven supply chains, significant buying power and efficiently structured sources of supply are needed to win in today's retail apparel markets, not just trend-right fashion and good design skills.

The reality is that just as there has been for a long time now a glut of available apparel production capacity in the world, too many fashion retailers without well-developed supply chain plans have crowded the developed markets of Western Europe and North America.

In dealing with the manufacturing challenges of C9's launch, as with any apparel sourcing strategy, we had to take into consideration a variety of critical factors — from the fabric compositions and technical construction of the garments to global and regional trade regimes and geo-political risks. Entering the U.S. market is no easy feat; the U.S. has built up some of the most complex sets of customs and tariff rules in the world, while expanding a hodgepodge of regional, bilateral and multinational trade agreements.

We will look more carefully at global trade structures in the chapters ahead, but for the time being suffice it to say that "free trade" deals are more correctly described as *managed trade agreements*. As much as we may be told differently, the vast majority are not entered into with an eye to helping poor nations create employment and alleviate poverty. They are not, in fact, grandiose international development efforts. For the most part, they are put in place by and for the benefit of international business interests and the global financial markets to which they are beholden.

Thus, in the U.S., when formulating a strategy for apparel that makes significant use of synthetic fabrications like polyester, nylon and spandex, import duty considerations are high on the list of issues to deal with. This is primarily because the U.S. is still a major producer of cotton, cotton yarns, and fabrics; import duty rates on manmade textile goods are double those for cotton apparel. While a men's cotton tee might pay a rate of 15.9 percent of the FOB factory price, polyester track pants are hit with a 32 percent duty. It logically follows, then, that for an apparel line that includes synthetic fabrications in over 60 percent of its items, an importing brand would try as much as possible to purchase goods from countries that pay no import entry or duty tax to access its markets.

As luck would have it, those countries strongest in economically priced, volume synthetic fabric manufacture such as Thailand, Taiwan and China did not have such agreements with the U.S. If we wanted the biggest margin bang for the buck, we had to choose from the still-lengthy list of potential nations that had put in place trade pacts that would reduce or eliminate duties altogether. These agreements with other nations included:

AGOA: The African Growth and Opportunity Act signed by President Bill Clinton in 2000. Extended US market-access benefits to a number of countries that targeted building up their apparel exports to that country, including Lesotho, Swaziland, Kenya, Madagascar, Namibia and Mauritius.

ATPDEA: The Andean Trade Promotion and Drug Eradication Act of 2002, which had amended the previous ATPA or Andean Trade Preference Act of 1991. Relaxed duties on some apparel items, while allowing others to enter the U.S. duty free.

CAFTA-DR: The Dominican Republic-Central America-United States Free Trade Agreement. Signed with five Central American countries in late 2004 (Costa Rica, El Salvador, Guatemala, Honduras and Nicaragua) and the Dominican Republic.

CBPTA: The U.S.-Caribbean Basin Trade Partnership Act of 2000 was an expansion of the Caribbean Basin Initiative (CBI) originally launched in 1983; it affects 17 Caribbean and Central American countries, and Guyana and Trinidad on the South American continent.

NAFTA: The North American Free Trade Agreement was signed by the U.S., Canada and Mexico in late 1993 and came into effect January 1, 1994.

QIZ: The Qualifying Industrial Zones agreements beginning in 1996, which, under the U.S.-Israel Free Trade Agreement, allowed for the processing of apparel in Jordan, Egypt, the West Bank and Gaza with a minimal amount of Israeli input and allowed it to enter American markets free of duty.

Asia is conspicuously missing from all of these agreements. However, despite the cost advantages given to the regions included in the agreements, Southeast Asian vendors were in fact still able to garner a significant share of the orders placed for the C9 project based on a number of additional factors: proximity to Asian fabric sources, which reduced turn-around times; experience with the kind of garment construction techniques required; higher worker productivity, meaning more production output per unit of cost; and lower labor costs overall.

Certain trade deals with the U.S. were also dependent on the use of American inputs, principal among them yarns and fabrics. The few styles we decided to manufacture in the Americas, then, were basic garments that required the least amount of sewing time (which thus incurred the least amount of more expensive labor) and those that were made of American cotton-rich textiles. These few items were placed with in-house factories.

Some deals, such as the much-touted AGOA pact, faced multiple supply chain difficulties. To start with, nearly four weeks of ocean transit time and customs clearance delays were needed to get Asian fabric to East African ports and then to inland factories. The most impoverished nations that hoped to benefit from duty-free access to the U.S. such as Lesotho and Swaziland also had no prior apparel industry to speak of. The few regional textile mills available to source from were not cost competitive with Asia's even when factoring in shipping expenses from China or Taiwan. Productivity at newly built-up factories was also quite low compared to established global centers where sewing operators had decades of experience.

To further complicate things, many apparel and textile facilities in Africa were run by Asian investors and managers with little initial understanding of local culture and languages. This made for often-difficult relations between employees and management that took considerable time and effort to address. Years later, in 2010, the International Labor Organization's *Better Work* program would ramp up in Lesotho to help address the labor and rights issues that had contributed to much misunderstanding in the local industry, but in 2003/4 these were still nascent problems. Still, we are able to identify and collaborate with a small number of Taiwanese-owned facilities in Swaziland and Lesotho, which were the best of the available bunch to work with. We only used those facilities for our high-duty synthetic fabric garments, and, with a savings of 32 percent on the total item price, key AGOA factories with the right equipment and commitment to employee relations and training were able to carve a niche for themselves. But by far the most promising of the duty-free agreement countries — where much of the C9 business was initially placed — were later found to be some of the most ethically challenging for multinational brands to deal with. A very dark chapter indeed in the modern apparel industry's history was on the horizon.

Jordan — New Oasis or Desert Mirage?

On October 26, 1994, the official state of enmity between the Hashemite Kingdom of Jordan and the State of Israel ended with the signing of a much-lauded peace treaty between them. In that same year, a Western-educated Jordanian businessman, Omar Salah, took advantage of the newly emerging peace to sign a manufacturing agreement with Israeli textile and underwear maker Delta Galil. With significantly lower labor rates than Israel, new production units were opened across the border in Jordan. By coincidence, Sara Lee had a vested interest in the venture, having bought into the Israeli manufacturer some six years earlier to the tune of 25 percent of its outstanding shares.

In the face of what must have seemed at the time quite insurmountable odds, Mr. Salah was able to convince disparate political actors from Israel, the U.S. and Jordan to facilitate a special export processing agreement allowing goods manufactured in Jordan to enter American markets free of import duties and restrictions. The caveat was that specific percentages of added value to processed products needed to originate from within Israel, Jordan or the West Bank/Gaza territories in order to claim the duty savings. A full 65 percent of value could come from outside those regions, which boded well for apparel industries because fabric tended at the time to constitute 50–60 percent of a garment's manufacturing cost.

By 1997, the first Qualifying Industrial Zone (QIZ) in Jordan authorized by the U.S. Congress a year earlier (in an amendment to pre-existing Israeli-American trade agreements) was opened. Dozens would follow over the next decade as predominantly Chinese, Indian and Sri Lankan investors surged into the country. By 2004 nearly $US one billion in duty-free shipments left Jordan for U.S. markets, 99 percent of which were apparel. Many of these investors were based in nearby Dubai, where tax-free enterprises had been established in duty-free zones of their own, and which became the transit point for Asian fabrics en route to Jordanian and Egyptian factories. But it wasn't until I began to personally visit facilities identified by the Li & Fung team as potential manufacturing sites in 2003 that the impact of additional anomalies under the QIZ arrangements became clear to me.

Instructions from my VP back at the Winston-Salem HQ for Sara Lee's sourcing team were clear: no production commitments would be finalized until either she or I had set foot in the factories proposed by our agent. If a pre-visit determined an operable, organized factory had potential, then third-party labor auditors would be dispatched to further qualify them.

I had flown into Amman, Jordan, from Kenya via Dubai on a whirlwind fact-finding tour as the inaugural C9 program began to ramp up its pre-production phase. The hillside city was abuzz with construction as new five-star hotels went up and public works benefited from an inflow of post-peace-plan investment. Economic growth for the country was projected to exceed seven percent in the coming year. As we made our way out of the city into the dusty Jordanian countryside,

I chatted in the factory van with our agent's regional merchandise manager Ashish Malhotra, who had flown in from Dubai two days earlier. A former Gap brand merchandiser from India, Ashish was a sharp, industrious yet softly spoken apparel professional brought onto the team by Mark Agius at Li & Fung to help manage relations with the Indian and Sri Lankan factory management who were pitching us their facilities.

I was a bit puzzled when he mentioned that a new crew of sewing operators had just arrived by plane the week before and were still settling in at one of the four facilities we would be touring that day.

"Arrived from where?" I asked. It was Ashish's turn to look puzzled. "Sri Lanka."

No doubt my expression must have given away my total surprise. As this was my first trip to the region and the first time I would be assessing facilities in the Middle East, I could do little else than to claim my honest ignorance of the practice allowed under Jordan's agreement. It was an embarrassing moment for me, and, frankly, I should have been better prepared and aware.

While much of the early work done at the international level in promoting the trade deal had sold the concept based on its potential contribution to regional peace, stability and the creation of employment for Jordanians, the reality on the ground turned out to be something quite different. Instead of acting as a catalyst for local job creation, international apparel firms from China and South Asia were given the green light to import the vast majority of their factory laborers from their home countries. According to data from the Jordanian Ministry of Labour, by 2006 just over 66 percent of the 54,000 QIZ employees were foreign "guest workers."[71] And, as I was to find out firsthand, the other 34 percent, who were Jordanian nationals, were often assigned tasks in teams and multiples of three or four people, when half that number of employees would have sufficed. Job titles were being created simply to achieve quotas for local hiring and job creation.

Cultural dynamics certainly played a significant role in the underutilization of local labor; the majority of workers in QIZ apparel factories, both foreign and domestic, were women. Despite its opening to the West and the growing metropolitan flair of Amman, the Jordanian kingdom was and still is a highly patriarchal society. The

government of the country was on a clearly stated track toward mod-
ernizing the societal and political opportunities of women, but women
working outside of the home was still a contentious issue for many
households. Thus, even those facilities that sought to employ a greater number of local staff faced significant hiring problems due to local
cultural bias.

Many potential Jordanian employees vs sewing operators objected
to jobs that required doing repetitive tasks for nine or more hours a
day (such as sitting at a sewing machine carrying out the same tedious
motion over and over). They seemed to prefer less onerous jobs that
allowed for greater ongoing social interaction with their peers such
as sorting and inspecting trim inventories or end-of-production-line
packing of export cartons. Most office administrative jobs were also
reserved for Jordanians or better-educated Asians. Juxtaposed with
factory management goals of achieving high production efficiencies
and volume garment output, the practice of depending on imported
foreign labor therefore came down to economics and profit.

The individual organizational approaches to factory management
that vendor-suppliers of branded apparel take tend to vary greatly. My
own experience has been that what one finds at the shop-floor level is
most often reflective of the traits of facility owners themselves. As we
toured the locations that day earmarked for Sara Lee's production in
Jordan, the same types of management problems I had already spent
ten years dealing with were evident in varying degrees.

Our first stop was a large, new and lonely-looking facility comprised
of two massive industrial buildings in the middle of nowhere. While by
no means a manufacturing engineer, I had by this point developed my
own methodology for assessing factories based on a decade's worth of
experience. Together with the more formal management checklist and
our local agent's support, I was prepared for my standard two-hour
cat-and-mouse exercise with the factory management team. Based on
this initial review, Sara Lee's corporate compliance team would then
call in experienced auditors from one of a shortlist of external agencies
to carry out a much more thorough, two-day social compliance assessment (which I will dissect in detail in the following chapter).

Following the opening meeting customary of most Chinese factories — complete with high-grade green tea, expressions of gratitude,

goodwill and smiles all around — we proceeded outside to the factory receiving docks. The past four years in and out of Sara Lee's self-owned and contract factories across the Americas working with highly competent manufacturing leaders much more capable than myself recommended a process of following the flow of production — from the receipt of materials through to the output of finished goods. Here, this approach turned the typical two-hour "walk-through" to a visit of less than an hour.

The facility was generally unkempt and lacked indications of hands-on production and people management skills. While Jordanians were working in supplies and inventory management, there hardly seemed enough of them around to fulfill minimum hiring requirements. Fabric cutting and sewing operations, however, were fully staffed by mainland Chinese workers, who were typically brought to the country on minimum three-year contracts. Chainmail safety gloves were missing on the hands of the cutting room staff, and piles of fabric waste littered the floor. More than a few sewing operators were taking their mid-morning breaks eating leisurely at their machine stations, and fire extinguishers were noticeably absent from the walls.

Like all facilities within the QIZ zones, workers were housed in on-site dormitories. Multiple bunk beds were crammed into dingy rooms, and the sanitary conditions of shared washrooms were sub-par, to say the least. There was no evidence that the factory knew that an order was depending on this visit. With a number of possible vendor locations elsewhere in Jordan, we didn't need to go through the time or expense of in-depth labor or production-systems audits to know we wouldn't be placing any orders with the facility. The whole experience necessitated a serious discussion with Ashish; he had to be ready to present me with suppliers who were already at least most of the way toward passing muster.

As it turned out, and as was expected, he *had* previously met with facility management prior to my arrival to ensure they would take the necessary actions toward putting their house in order. That, after all, is the minimum of what any buyer expects of their in-country or regional agent. The factory manager simply hadn't taken Ashish at his word that we would be visiting the next day, nor had he taken even the most cosmetic of actions to show any intent to comply. The difference between the poorly organized Chinese facility and our next stop was like night and day.

With facilities strategically located across China, Taiwan, Dubai, Egypt and Jordan, Singapore-based Alpine Creations Limited is one of the retailing world's largest apparel suppliers. For the past 30 years, the organization led by Sri Lankan businessman Lalu Mahtani has serviced clients as diverse as Wal-Mart, Sears, Disney, Osh Kosh, Hanesbrands, H&M and Under Armour. During that time, they earned a reputation as one of the most responsible and responsive players in the garment industry. They did so by investing in technology and training, by promoting and treating their employees with respect, and by recognizing early on the growing trends in sustainable textiles and responsible manufacturing practices.

Our visit to Alpine's United Creations facility in Jordan's Ad-Dulayl industrial park ended up being the highlight of my first trip to the country (I would later make the trek to their sister factory, Alex Apparels in Egypt, as part of the negotiations for placement of C9 business through Li & Fung). We would go on to use nearly a dozen Jordanian locations, but United Creations remained in my eyes our leading supplier in the region. Their expansive facility with over 1,200 employees was the poster child for a well-run and orderly sewing operation. This proved true not only of our initial management tour and assessment, but also in the detailed results of existing and later-executed labor and technical audits, which they passed with flying colors. Such a factory setup comes with a price, though. The Alpine team did not prove to be the cheapest supplier to work with, but the old adage that you get what you pay for couldn't be truer than it is in the garment trade.

On far too many occasions coming up through the industry as an aggressive young sourcing manager, I made the mistake of throwing my vote behind the absolute lowest-priced vendor. And why wouldn't I have? For most brand and retail procurement teams, recognition and rewards have long been tied to driving down per-unit costs while increasing margins. Frankly speaking, my job, my career and the security of my family depended on it. But I learned some very hard lessons: what may appear at first to be the cheapest first cost (again, the FOB, or out of factory and on the boat price of a garment from its country of origin) very often snowballs to become a painfully expensive one by the time goods are delivered. Beating up your supplier for the absolute lowest cost is never a good sourcing strategy.

The costs of unsustainable pricing can take many forms — from vendor cash flow shortages resulting in delayed raw material purchases, to seeing your reserved production lines handed over to brands willing to pay more. Missing your sewing start date at a factory often results in delays of weeks because neither factories nor workers can afford to sit idly by waiting on your trims and textiles to arrive. Yearlong planning lifecycles that start off with sufficient time assumptions for all supply chain players can easily be spoiled. If too much time is wasted in back-and-forth discussions during the product development, design and sampling stages, by the time manufacturing actually ramps up, factories are left with a bare minimum of time to achieve their deliveries.

Missing shipment dates for ocean vessels can kill a program's profitability in one fell swoop, as brand or retail client penalties (and/or probable consequent air shipment costs) vaporize factory and wholesale margins. But for many brands and retailers, allegations of labor and human rights abuses are by far their worst fear because of the long-term costs to reputation and brand value they bring. In 2006, just a couple of years after the C9 production launch in Jordan, that country would be rocked by allegations and charges against specific factories for complicity in human trafficking and the abuse and sexual exploitation of workers.

By 2005, after six years with the organization and a number of long, heartfelt discussions with my wife, I decided to leave Sara Lee. I had become increasingly disheartened with my own role in the apparel industry. Belatedly, perhaps, I decided on taking a deliberate tack in the direction of social and environmental accountability. So the same year that the bakery and underwear giant publicly announced its intentions to spin off their apparel holdings into a new listed company, I took up an Asia-based role in labor compliance and quality management with another major branded holding group, U.S.-based Kellwood Brands.

I would go on to join the South China/S.E. Asia-focused team at one of the top three global social and labor auditing firms, Bureau Veritas, before being tapped to open the first Asia office for U.S.-based labor standard WRAP, an acronym for Worldwide Responsible Accredited Production. The timing proved fortuitous.

In May 2006, the first in-depth media report by Steve Greenhouse and Michael Barbaro at *The New York Times* hit the press, bringing to light allegations of harsh working conditions at a number of Jordanian factories. Interviews with employees brought to light stories of physical and verbal abuse and egregiously excessive working hours of 19 hours a day or more. Human trafficking practices such as the seizure of foreign workers' passports to prohibit them from leaving the country and employment brokerage fees in the thousands of dollars had been identified. Many claimed not to have been paid the full wages they had been promised, while others complained of being paid far less than employment contracts called for.

The shocking level of allegations far outweighed almost anything I had personally witnessed while working in the Americas and Africa. Yet spokespeople for a number of American brands — from Jones Apparel to Target stores and Wal-Mart — confirmed in the article that they had become aware of many of the reported issues and were taking actions to correct them. The *Times* article opened a flood of coverage on industry practices in Jordan. Until then, earlier media reports by the New York-based National Labor Committee, which had first flagged the scandal, had gone largely unnoticed. But the worst was yet to come.

Media stories continued through 2007. By 2008, the corporate responsibility consulting group Business for Social Responsibility (BSR) released an in-depth report on the role and responsibilities of global businesses in addressing the growing challenges of international labor migration. The issues faced by South Asian guest workers in Jordan were specifically referenced more than a dozen times in the lengthy document, calling attention to the general failure of host countries to adequately protect migrant laborers from a multiplicity of abuses. While noting that Jordan at the time had failed to ratify a number of key United Nations International Labor Organization (ILO) conventions regarding the treatment of migrant workers (specifically ILO Cs. 90, 97 and 143), the BSR report also highlighted the details of worker strike actions at Jordan's Mediterranean Garments factory.

The issues behind the strike by 1,400 foreign employees at Mediterranean had first been reported by labor activists from the Institute for Global Labour and Human Rights in early September 2008.

Serious allegations again came to the fore of excessive overtime hours, threats of deportation, physical abuse, passport confiscation and illegal deductions from workers' wages. In subsequent follow-ups, the Institute reported on worker charges of repeated beatings by Jordanian police called in to maintain order in and around the factory. It would be another ten days before reported efforts by Jordanian labor officials, Hanesbrands representatives and factory management would result in an agreement and the resumption of production at the factory. As international attention grew and as U.S. apparel consumption continued unabated, the United Nations' ILO committed to ramping up a local team as part of their efforts under the Better Work program.

As a partnership between the ILO and the World Bank's International Finance Corporation (IFC), Better Work projects currently operate in eight developing countries across Asia, Africa and Latin America/Caribbean. Better Work teams take a tripartite approach to resolving factory challenges by engaging with labor unions, government and the private sector. Funding comes from a variety of sources including direct bilateral governmental assistance from the U.S., Canada, the U.K., the Netherlands, Denmark and Switzerland. (We will look at this program in further detail in subsequent chapters.) Still, the bad news kept on coming.

In its April 2010 follow-up on conditions in Jordan, investigators for the Institute for Global Labour and Human Rights first identified reports of sexual abuse and the alleged rape of a young Sri Lankan woman in late 2009. International British Garments (IBG, a factory said to be owned at the time by global security firm G4S) was named; they faced additional accusations of physical abuse, 16-hour work days, illegal payroll deductions and the seizure of employee passports. However, the ILO's first compliance synthesis report on Jordan, a 21-page document published in May 2010, made only brief and passing mention of sexual harassment and reported no findings whatsoever with regards to the issue. It appeared that along with trafficking and abuse, a new evil was raising its head at QIZ facilities, even as global brands continued to ship millions of dollars of goods from them.

The Institute identified U.S. and Canadian brands as clients of the factory; big names such as J.C. Penney, Wal-Mart, and Nygard were included. This time, it would take the efforts of emergency delegations from the U.S. National Labor Committee and the United Steelworkers union to pressure factory ownership into taking action. By late May of the same year, both organizations reported on improved conditions at the IBG facility as workers were provided improved dormitories, overtime hours were cut back, and wage deductions for meals were reduced. But this limited success did not stop either Tim Waters of the United Steelworkers or Charles Kernaghan of the National Labor Committee from lobbying against Canada's efforts to join the U.S. in extending duty-free trade benefits to Jordanian factories.

On October 18, 2010, both gentlemen testified before the Canadian Parliament's Standing Committee on International Trade. Members of Parliament John Cannis (vice chair, Liberal), Ed Holder (Conservative), Gerald Keddy (Conservative), Jean-Yves Laforest (vice chair, Bloc Québécois) and Lee Richardson (committee chair, Conservative) took their testimony and politely questioned them on their opinions and findings.[78] Yet, in the face of collective reports regarding the labor and human rights abuses that had been mounting for years in Jordan, the Conservative government of the day did little to ensure that robust remediation actions would be written into the Free Trade Agreement between the two nations. The Canada-Jordan Economic Growth and Prosperity Act received Royal Assent on June 29, 2012, well after further accusations of sexual harassment at factories had surfaced.

By the summer of 2011, the offshore apparel industry was rocked by mounting stories and accusations of sexual abuse centered on the multi-unit production facilities of Classic Fashion Apparel Industry Ltd., in Jordan's Al-Hassan QIZ. From June through September of that year, media outlets including *The Wall Street Journal, The Huffington Post, Ms. Magazine, Associated Press* and *Business Week Magazine* widely reported on National Labor Committee (NLC) findings from an early June fact-finding mission to the Kingdom.

NLC interviews with the staff of multiple facilities where the alleged perpetrator had worked in Jordan, Dubai and Tanzania painted a horrific picture of repeated, predatory sexual abuse. Committee staff accompanied a young Bangladeshi woman to the Criminal Investigation Department of the Jordanian police where she swore a complaint against factory supervisor Anil Santha, identified as the culprit, and later published her full account of the incident.[82] Santha was reportedly jailed for two days before inexplicably being released, whereupon he immediately returned to work at the Classic Fashion factory.

While brands all expressed concern about the accusations and promised to investigate, evidence and testimony from additional victims who came forward over the coming months were dismissed by Jordanian authorities. Standard factory labor audits had apparently failed to turn up any such accusations. In August, Rafiq Alam, the Institute for Global Labour and Human Rights director for Bangladesh and the Middle East was preparing to head to the U.S. for a scheduled address to the international convention of the United Steelworkers union. Alam was detained by Jordanian authorities for questioning with regard to the ongoing investigations and had his passport seized. Next to nothing was done for the women involved.

In the three years leading up to these heart-wrenching events, the International Labor Organization's Better Work program, which was operating in nearly half the country's factories by late 2011, had issued four consecutive synthesis reports on Jordan's apparel industry. Not a single one of them reported on any findings related to sexual harassment or abuse. There was certainly no shortage of other serious labor rights, health, safety, freedom of association, or payroll issues to be gleaned from their efforts, as the following snapshot of findings from the second such report (March 2011) showed:[84]

Table 1

Issue of Concern	Percent of Workers Reporting Concerns
Coercion	63%
Bonded labor	29%
Payroll deductions	25%
Excessive overtime	43%
Paid leave	29%
Work contract	67%
Discipline measures	33%
Workplace safety	from 42–92%, by specific sub-issue

Yet, despite these worrying results, the Project Advisory Committee of Better Work Jordan (comprised primarily of governmental and business group representatives) praised their own efforts and called on global apparel brands and retailers to further increase their orders to the country.[85] Grassroots labor and human rights groups were beside themselves. The ILO's own data stood in stark contrast to the group's stated zero-tolerance protocol with the Jordanian government that covered issues such as child labor, forced labor and threats to health and safety.

Under increasing international pressure and calls to respond to perceived failures in Jordan and dependent on financing from foreign governments, including Canada's Department of Human Resources and Skill Development and USAID, the ILO finally took steps to tackle sexual harassment challenges in the country.

In February of 2013, they publicly released the in-depth findings of a rigorous, independent impact assessment led by researchers from Tufts University in the U.S. Bringing together experienced professionals from the areas of economics, human development, psychology and workplace practices, the report put forward startling data that had been collected from March 2010 through April 2011. The authors were pointed in their summary comments regarding the issues and allegations of sexual harassment in the Jordanian apparel industry:

"Structural features of the global garment industry make sexual harassment pervasive throughout it. The power differential between managers and workers makes workers vulnerable to various forms of abuse. Specific to Jordan, the nature of migrant workers' contracts prevents them from changing employers, as loss of work results in deportation to their home country. This results in job insecurity, which makes migrant workers more vulnerable to sexual harassment." [85]

Among their findings, the following data from over 800 workers at 22 facilities addressing issues of abuse and harassment in the workplace are particularly telling:[85]

One month later, Better Work Jordan followed up with the release of a case study titled "Addressing sexual harassment in Jordan's garment industry."[86] In it, the organization spelled out the steps it had begun to take and addressed plans to roll out comprehensive factory-level

Table 2

Issue of Concern	Percent of Workers Reporting Concerns
Verbal Abuse	50%
Physical Abuse	30%
Sexual Harassment	34%
Fairness/Respect	30%

training for managers, supervisors and garment workers. Tools, training and workshops would be reinforced by commitments to extend advisory services to factories and to better protect those workers who found themselves threatened or harassed, including counseling and legal services.

It had taken three years from the time of early allegations of sexual assault at International British Garments and nearly two years since accusations of serial harassment at Classic Fashion surfaced to achieve these outcomes. To their credit, the ILO and Better Work staff (together with well-placed individuals struggling against apathy in government agencies, at brands, and across grassroots, labor and business lines) showed meaningful leadership in supporting the need for effecting industry change in Jordan.

It came too late for many young South Asian women, and by no means has this uphill struggle yet been won against industry and cultural acceptance of abuse. But events in Jordan would serve to galvanize the opinions and efforts of a growing number of my colleagues in the apparel industry; we were long overdue in looking for the new approaches needed to humanize an industry that for far too long had profited from dehumanizing and exploiting so many of its stakeholders.

3

Alphabet Soup

From the time our young family arrived in Asia in the summer of 2005, it would take another five full years before I was able to wean myself off the teat of the industry I had grown used to benefitting from. Even then, tragic circumstances in the far-off future would pull me back into it.

I found it no easy feat to make a mid-career change that required developing a whole new set of competencies. But I had been close enough to the labor and social compliance functions of the garment trade to have a good idea of where to start. Around this time, sustainable manufacturing and ethical trade initiatives were beginning to gain wider industry and media attention, and we had planned the move to take advantage of trends that would support the direction I hoped to move in.

Most labor and environmental auditing and the remediation services tied to these practices were at this point, however, still highly dependent on textiles and apparel. The truth was also that I had excelled early on at the challenges the industry had thrown at me, and I was fascinated by the evolution of creative ideas into real-life products. My passions for travel and foreign cultures also meant that I enjoyed literally being a part of the journeys that those products took as they came together from a variety of components and communities from different parts of the world.

But like many people, before I entered the consumer products industry, I had little idea of the societal and environmental impacts that a garment, its inputs, processing and supply chains caused. When I started out in the industry in late 1994, the Internet was just beginning to become available, as some readers may remember, along with sketchy dial-up phone line connections. The great communication and information age was just being born. The Central American child labor and sweatshop scandal surrounding media personality Kathie Lee Gifford's apparel brand was still two years off. Sustainability and corporate responsibility were not yet part of anyone's jargon, and the Rio Earth Summit had taken place just a couple of years earlier. And, to be completely honest, even after I became a part of those multinational supply chains and my awareness did begin to grow, I often found excuses to push that burden of knowledge to the very back of my mind for a good long while.

The apparel industry has given me some of the most rewarding experiences of my life, but it has also taken me to some of the most downtrodden, dangerous and poverty-stricken communities on the planet. Along the way I collected my fair share of "war stories," as I made a point of living and working close to the communities that supported my career. I have been robbed at gunpoint in Mexico City and have been lost while driving the back streets of Nairobi's slums. I have had to deal with factory fires in the Middle East and hotel bombings in Indonesia. But there are few things I have ever faced in nearly 20 years of globe-trotting for multinational brands, retailers and audit firms as gut-wrenching as pulling a child laborer out of a factory.

Thankfully, I had to do this only twice, and in 20 years I have both visited and audited more than a few factories. This is not to say that child labor doesn't continue to be a serious issue, but it is measurably less so in the apparel industry today than it was 20 years ago. The practice also tends now to be concentrated in specific geographical areas and in certain stages of the supply chain process, which the vast majority of brands and retailers seldom look into.

Up until this point, we have looked primarily at issues of historical context within the industry and some specific examples of the more disturbing practices. In this chapter, we will look closely at the point where the issues of worker and human rights and supply chain transparency intersect within global garment industries. The object here is not simply to give random statistics or to elaborate on secondhand stories about the ills of the apparel trade. Lots of data does exist that could be recounted (and I have been fortunate and far-sighted enough to have collected much of it firsthand over the years).

As we look now at what concrete measures brands, retailers and key industry stakeholders have taken to address the social fallout, the goals here are multifaceted. Firstly, it is important to understand the evolution of these measures and the drivers behind them. Secondly, we need to clearly identify the systemic gaps and failures within them. Finally, by looking at best-practice experience and new outlier models of supply chain engagement, we need to understand what all of us can do to get behind and support the most promising of these trends.

Face-to-Face with Child Labor

My first personal experience with child labor took place in Mexico.

By mid-1995, the sourcing team I had pulled together at the new Mexican start-up for Wal-Mart's buying agent PREL began to come together. I worked at the time under the tutelage of a sharp senior PREL manager out of the Philippines named Chiqui Cui. When Wal-Mart later took over direct control of their agent network and established their Global Procurement Group in 2002, Chiqui would go on to hold senior roles within the retailer's buying teams. With his help, following my initial stint at Wal-Mart's home office in Bentonville, we worked quickly to get the greenfield operation up and running.

It was a skeleton crew to begin with: two sourcing managers recruited from Wal-Mart's Mexican partners at Grupo Cifra; a seasoned production engineer 20 years my senior to handle quality inspections and factory assessments; and me, as team leader. Over the course of the next year we would bring onboard an accountant and two junior managers to help identify Mexican export factories and prepare bid packages for seasonal Wal-Mart buying trips.

The multi-billion dollar factory-auditing industry that has come to dominate labor and environmental risk management services not only for apparel industries but also for most consumer goods manufactured overseas was just in its infancy. In response to growing media attention and the spotlight American organized labor was trying to throw on Central American sweatshops, the American Apparel Manufacturers Association (now the American Apparel & Footwear Association) was just taking its first steps toward the creation of an industry-wide response.

While social or labor auditing at suppliers was still a year or two years off for major brands like The Gap and Reebok, Wal-Mart's significant early presence in China had led it and PREL to begin developing factory-level assessments by 1992. These early checklist-type question-and-answer surveys, along with on-site factory tours and reviews of facilities' legal and employment documentation, became part and parcel of our responsibilities in Mexico. This was something new for Mexican manufacturers and our local team. But under constant surveillance by organized labor groups and the media, our client was deadly serious about the importance of carrying out these assessments, even though there seemed at the time to be little concern about potential conflicts of interest.

In today's sourcing world, having your agent (whose earnings are tied directly to the ability to ship products on a trouble-free and timely basis) also act as the party that validates a factory's technical and labor compliance is *not* recognized as a best practice! But in the mid-90s the rules of the game were just being written, and we were in fact at the leading edge of what would become over the next decade a standard cost of doing business offshore, though not, strictly speaking, a legally required one.

Both David Gonzalez, our team's apparel engineer, and I were put through training on the early audit process by the external consultant who had developed the methodology for Wal-Mart. This included handling discussions with factory management each time a new facility was nominated to bid on export programs, along with document reviews and technical factory assessments. We were also taught how to keep an eye open for human resource risks while walking the factory floor occupied with auditing tasks like examining the contents of first aid kits and taking note of expiry dates on fire extinguishers.

It was this peripheral-vision skill that came into play late one afternoon while making our initial assessment at a denim facility outside of Tehuacán, about 250 kilometers southeast of Mexico City, bordering the states of Oaxaca and Veracruz. Originally famous for its natural spring waters, the city had exploded with new sew and dye facilities for jeans after the onset of NAFTA. At one point, more than 700 factories there churned out woven pants for brands like The Gap, Guess and J.C. Penney.

The larger operators servicing international retailers generally took pains to ensure proper treatment plants were in place for highly polluted dye water runoff, but a host of clandestine and second-tier facilities had long been accused of ignoring legal health and safety codes. The zone also had a reputation for using young teen laborers, due to both a shortage of workers brought on by the apparel boom and the crushing poverty still typical of rural Mexico.

As David walked the factory floor and guided the facility manager's attention to fire extinguishers a few sewing lines over from me, I made my way toward the back of the open complex while scanning the faces of the operators hard at work. I was on the lookout for workers whose faces might betray their ages and if any *seemed* to be too young, would note their positions and work station numbers; later, I would review administrative files and copies of official identification in the upstairs office. The trick here was not to draw immediate attention to the worker, which could potentially add a significant amount of stress to their already stressful day. In the case of Wal-Mart, at the time, finding true child labor in a supplier's factory would be breaking a cardinal rule, one of a shortlist of zero-tolerance policies that would immediately halt any business or the placement of production orders.

At least two young men appeared too young to me to be working at the factory. I would have guessed them to be around 13 years old, which put them right on the line of legal employment under Mexico's child labor laws. Like many countries (Canada included, which incidentally has yet to ratify the International Labor Organization's Convention 138 on Minimum Age)[89] Mexico allows young teens to legally work, generally within guidelines meant to ensure a minimum of formal education has been met while avoiding employment at high-risk jobs.

What became apparent early on in my experiences with PREL and Wal-Mart was that very specific skills were needed to play the full-time role of a social and labor practices auditor; I needed more than a passing knowledge of a host of occupational health and safety laws, human rights legislation, and labor codes on a "by-country" basis. Sometimes laws would differ across regions within one country! Within a short time, these responsibilities would in fact be turned over to full-time professional auditors.

In any event, a review of both teens' human resource files noted significant differences between the two. The file of the elder, who as I recall was 15 years old, was complete — with birth, education and medical certificates. A mandatory letter from the boy's parents giving their permission for his employment was also available, and verification of time cards showed that he was working less than the six hours per day allowed by law and never at night.

The younger boy however, just over 14 years of age, was missing a number of documents, including parental consent, but was shown to be working within the same hours as his *compañero*, his co-worker.

I had mixed feelings about how to manage the issue. On one hand, the client's policies were clear. Even if the boy legally fell into an allowable age group, his documentation wasn't in order. The factory could be fined should a government labor inspector come calling; they were, technically speaking, outside of compliance.

On the other hand, no orders had yet been placed with the factory. They were just now being assessed ahead of having them cost and quote garment pricing for an upcoming buyer event. If given the chance, the boy might be able to gather the proper paperwork together. I realized then that my personal feelings about his case were not as relevant as I might have liked. It is all well and good for those of us in wealthier countries to criticize others for poor child labor management. But it is quite something else to take the responsibility of cutting off a family's sorely needed income and potentially causing conflict within a family.

In discussion with the factory owner, we decided to err on the side of caution, but to also pursue a practical path toward resolving the problem. The boy would have to be taken out of the factory and sent home that day. But not until after it had been carefully explained to him why in a calm and non-threatening manner. The fault, after all, had not been his. The owner agreed to hold the job for him for ten days (and, in any event, he most likely needed the boy back) while the teen worked to gather the missing documents. His employer promised to cover the cost of a missing medical certificate and no deductions would be made for it. The boy was understandably upset, but seemed genuinely relieved once he understood that he could return to his job once the missing paperwork had been brought in. What could have been a much more traumatic experience for him and a loss of opportunity for the entire factory was averted.

For our part, we agreed with the factory that David would return within 30 days. It was in the vendor's hands to ensure compliance with everything that had been agreed to. At the end of the day, it was the owner's facility and his decision to follow our proposal or not. Rarely have I ever heard of a foreign brand or retailer calling out a vendor by reporting factory issues to the local authorities, and at that stage in my early career I doubt I would have had the wherewithal to try that approach.

Thankfully, this turned out not to be an example of egregious child exploitation, and the story would have a silver lining because it acted as significant impetus behind the American apparel industry's efforts to agree on a common approach to tackling some of the worst practices at offshore manufacturers.

Politics, Markets and the Global Trade Agenda

The end of the global political stalemate of the Cold War between the United States and the Soviet Union around 1989 had a significant impact on global businesses and workers in both developed and developing countries. Specifically for textile industries, this would mean concerted efforts to liberalize international markets in these commodities, which had been restricted under the Multifiber Arrangement (MFA), alternatively referred to as the Multifiber Agreement. Negotiated as a series of clauses within the larger General Agreement on Tariffs and Trade (GATT) between 1961 and 1973, the MFA put in place a quota system of imports and exports among member nations. This acted essentially as a system of protectionist measures to help manage a surge of post-World War II imports into the U.S. and Europe and avoid negative price pressures on American cotton growers.

Both the growing efforts of international business to expand markets and shift manufacturing, together with increasing moves toward trade liberalization in textiles and apparel, caused significant concerns within the organized labor communities of the U.S. and Western Europe, particularly in the U.K. Relaxed trade rules would, they projected, lead to significant job losses and downward pressure on manufacturing wages as industry would seek greater profits from the use of cheap, offshore labor.

Building on its earlier work to support Central American trade unionists and political activists during the bloody violence in the region throughout the 1980s, the National Labor Committee in the U.S. became a registered nonprofit organization in 1990. Jointly formed by the Amalgamated Clothing and Textile Workers Union, the United Auto Workers and the International Association of Machinists, this organization shifted its mission toward the global protection of worker and human rights. Their investigations, among the efforts of other civil society and labor groups, brought media and public attention to the offshore sourcing activities of brands and retailers.

In 1992 and 1993, media stories began to catch the attention of politicians in Washington regarding the treatment of Chinese workers at garment facilities on the American-held island of Saipan. Part of the Northern Mariana Islands, the Pacific island chain had become a commonwealth in 1975 (a similar legal status to that of Puerto Rico) after 30 years of administration by the United States following the end of World War II. And, as with Puerto Rico, business interests had found a location where goods could be manufactured under the protection and duty-free status of the U.S. flag at near half the mainland's minimum wage. More than $US 270 million of apparel orders had shipped from the territory in 1992 destined for retailers like The Gap, Eddie Bauer, Liz Claiborne and Levi's, who had all sourced product from suppliers manufacturing there.

Conditions were sufficiently poor on Saipan that the U.S. Department of Labor brought suit against a number of manufacturers, charging that Chinese workers had been maintained in near slave-like conditions. Squalid living spaces, lengthy contracts and failures to pay either overtime on 80+ hour work weeks or the required minimum wage led to a $US 9 million settlement, most of which went to the workers who had been victimized.

During this same period, Wal-Mart had been raked over the proverbial coals by activists and media alike following an NBC Dateline investigative report in early 1992. It accused the growing global retailer of both misleading customers with "Made in America" signage placed over foreign-made goods and of contracting goods from Asian suppliers who were using children as young as 11 years old in Bangladeshi apparel factories.[93] And while Wal-Mart executive management vehemently denied the child labor allegations, the attention did little to help instill an image of ethical and responsible practices in the minds of U.S. consumers.

With the swearing in of Democratic President Bill Clinton in 1993, organized labor groups, which had thrown their weight behind his election campaign, began to leverage the growing public and political pressure resulting from reported industry activities. While a handful of brands and retailers like Levi Strauss and Wal-Mart began to draft and announce labor codes of conduct and vendor-partner standards, many activists were angered by Clinton's sign-off on the North American Free Trade Agreement in 1994. A sidebar agreement committing signatory countries to robustly enforce national labor law was included in NAFTA in an effort to appease U.S. labor groups, but any effort to internationalize standards was rejected.

Further efforts by the Democratic administration to include social clause linkages within the 1994–95 Uruguay Round of multilateral trade negotiations (which led to the founding of the World Trade Organization) went nowhere. Business interests in developed Western nations and so-called Third World country governments rejected the efforts. Arguably, business was after higher profits from unrestricted access to cheap offshore labor, while developing country elites targeted greater job creation, tax revenues and in many cases, ownership in manufacturing enterprises themselves.

Kathie Lee Gifford, the Clinton Agenda and Industry Action

The final thrust that would galvanize the American government to push apparel and textile lobbies into taking more robust voluntary actions in lieu of threatened regulatory measures came in the spring and summer of 1996. From May through July of that year, a score of activists led by the National Labor Committee's (NLC) Charles Kernaghan testified before the U.S. Congress to level charges of exploitation and child labor against the global apparel trade.

These efforts gained heightened notoriety through the press coverage of the NLC's specific accusations against the apparel brand of popular actress and television host Kathie Lee Gifford. Carried exclusively by Wal-Mart stores, the brand had proven a runaway success until investigations showed that original domestic manufacturing orders had continuously been sub- and sub-subcontracted to a variety of Central American factories while multiple intermediaries all took a cut of the action. The NLC claimed that workers as young as 12 and 13 had been laboring in Honduran sweatshops sewing garments for the brand, and they brought a young worker from one of these factories to Washington to reinforce the accusations.

Congressional sub-committees heard from a host of activist, industry and governmental witnesses including Harry Kamberis, director of Program Development at the Asian American Free Labor Institute; Jesus Canahuati, vice president of the Honduran Apparel Manufacturers Association; Robert B. Reich, then-secretary of the U.S. Department of Labor; and Ms. Gifford herself. Industry representatives from the National Retail Federation and the U.S. Council for International Business were also on hand to steadfastly reject the claims.

Most poignant was the testimony of a 15-year-old Honduran girl by the name of Wendy Diaz who had figured prominently in Mr. Kernaghan's public relations efforts to trigger such high-ranking attention. She spoke of her life at a Korean-owned facility in Honduras where she had begun working at the age of 13. She testified about the 10–12 hour work days, making $US 0.31 per hour, she described the verbal and psychological abuse and maltreatment that she and other minor-aged workers had suffered while sewing garments for American apparel brands. The statement read that day by this brave young woman makes for difficult reading, especially for industry insiders like myself.

Also testifying was a 15-year-old boy from Thornhill, Ontario, by the name of Craig Kielburger, who would go on to become another distinguished alumni of my *alma mater*, Trinity College. Craig had been driven to action by a *Toronto Star* newspaper article he had read a year earlier. It had told of the tragic murder of a 12-year-old bonded laborer who had fought against child labor in Pakistan's carpet trade. Craig, his brother Marc, and a number of friends would begin a school project that eventually evolved into *Free the Children*, now an international charity dedicated to youth empowerment and education in developing countries around the world. Through their efforts, Wendy and Craig would put many of us in the industry to shame, myself included, by vocally raising awareness of the need to fight against child labor.

Of particular interest to the apparel and retail trades, Secretary
Reich made a number of pointed comments about "disturbing" and "de-
spicable" child labor practices.[99] Referencing the often-quoted phrase
by progressive jurist Justice Louis Brandeis of the U.S. Supreme Court
that "sunlight is said to be the best of disinfectants," [100] Reich observed
that there was "no way we can solve this problem without responsible corporations backed by an informed and concerned public." [99] He
spoke seriously, giving examples of child labor in Indian glass factories
and Bangladeshi brick kilns noting that while the U.S. itself did not
face a significant child labor problem that "we do have . . . a sweatshop
problem." [99]

Secretary Reich advised the committee that he had called for meetings that same week with major American retailers and their key U.S.
manufacturing suppliers to examine what progress was being made
on the home-front battle against labor abuses in the apparel industry.
"Before we point a finger of blame at foreigners," he stated "we have to
make sure our own backyard is clean." [99]

In a stern warning to industry attendees, he informed his audience
that the Department of Labor was actively working on an industry report examining the codes of conduct and international labor practices
of the top 20 largest American importers of apparel while committing
to provide the congressional committee with follow-up testimony on
their findings. Reich insisted that the responsibility did not lay with
government alone, but that business had "to be actively engaged" [99] in
bringing an end to labor abuses overseas. As for the subject of the U.S.
trade agenda, the Secretary of Labor expressed his belief that "we cannot talk about trade without talking about labor standards at the same
time." [99] Only time would tell if these forceful statements carried the
weight of real actions.

Both directly and indirectly, the committee hearings and subsequent governmental pressure brought to bear on retail and apparel
interests led to the formation of two organizations that would shape
industry responses in the U.S. regarding offshore industry labor rights
for the next 15 years.

The first of these would be the Fair Labor Association (FLA),
which evolved out of the Clinton administration's multi-stakeholder Apparel Industry Partnership (AIP) initiative first convened in

August 1996. The second would be driven by member interests from within the American Apparel Manufacturers Association in 1998 (now the American Apparel & Footwear Association), whose "Worldwide Principles for Responsible Production" would evolve into the Worldwide Responsible Apparel Production standard, or WRAP. A further attempt to expand the certification standard to additional industries beyond apparel would see the organization change its name once again to Worldwide Responsible Accredited Production in 2007.

Certainly worth mentioning at this point is the work done by Social Accountability International (SAI) toward the development of the SA8000 social practices certification standard. Formally begun in 1997, SAI evolved from the earlier Council on Economic Priorities (CEP) founded in 1969 by economist Alice Tepper Marlin. Long before corporate social responsibility had become a business and civil society catchphrase, CEP provided research into the social and environmental practices of corporations. The group published reports on corporate behavior and pioneered an economic activist approach to social and ethical investment. While the development of the SA8000 standard did include participation by the business community, it was not an industry-driven initiative to the degree that both the FLA and WRAP were.

Meanwhile, on the other side of the Atlantic, similar issues faced by British retailers under pressure from NGOs, labor activists and religious organizations would soon bring industry together with civil society, government and labor under the Ethical Trading Initiative in 1997. From 1998, the British Retail Consortium would begin its work on common standards tied to a number of health, safety and manufacturing concerns. By 2001, a number of U.K. retailers and their major suppliers would begin the discussions around common approaches and methods of auditing factories that would lead to the formation a year later of the Supplier Ethical Data Exchange (SEDEX). Continental Europe's business-dominated Foreign Trade Association based in Brussels wouldn't release their industry standards for social accountability until 2003 under the Business Social Compliance Initiative (BSCI).

The Canadian government under Liberal Prime Minister Jean Chrétien made attempts in 1999–2000 to facilitate discussions between members of Canada's civil society and manufacturing industries. Spurred in part by the grassroots actions of groups such as the now-defunct Maquila Solidarity Network, these efforts resulted in the formation of the Canadian Partnership for Ethical Trade (CPET) in 1999. A significant number of labor, civil society and religious organizations came together under the Ethical Trade Action Group (ETAG) that same year to engage Canadian business interests represented by the Canadian Chamber of Commerce, the Retail Council of Canada and the Alliance of Manufacturers and Exporters. Direct government participation was not forthcoming however, a fact that many from the NGO and labor community felt contributed to the impasses that ensued. Unable to agree on the contentious issues of which standards to adopt or how best to construct an effective and independent monitoring system, negotiations broke down in the spring of 2000, effectively killing the effort.

Diane Brisebois, the current president and CEO of the RCC (Retail Council of Canada) believes that efforts at the time were too narrowly approached.

"From our perspective and with the benefit of lessons learned, we would suggest that it was too confrontational. Until recently stakeholders, regardless of who they were, tended to have a firm and unique position and negotiations were more about which unique position to support versus how we can all come together with a solution that satisfies all major stakeholders."

ETAG would try for a number of years to unsuccessfully reignite the discussions. The general sense of apathy that civil society believed had taken hold at the governmental and industry level has apparently continued to this day. As Ms. Brisebois puts it, the RCC leadership is in no hurry to see a legislative approach taken.

"It has always been our position to support global standards/practices [read: voluntary] *versus* trying to deal with issues such as supply chain transparency and accountability through different pieces of domestic legislation. It has been my experience that public pressure, education and joint efforts from a large group of stakeholders tend to work best. Trying to keep it out of the political realm is, in my experience, more desirable and more effective."

Since joining Sara Lee's Branded Apparel group in 1999, I had collaborated with the WRAP organization through my years of sourcing for the Hanes and Champion brands; Sara Lee, in fact, had been one of

Fixing Fashion

the original supporting manufacturers of WRAP during its formation. All of Sara Lee's apparel brands were technically required to ensure suppliers adhered to WRAP principles, though in practice this was not enforced for many vendors, especially those who served as short-term seasonal and stop-gap suppliers. Later in my career, as I continued to step back from commercial sourcing roles, I would go on to work directly with the standard as WRAP's regional director in Asia, hired to manage the start-up of the group's regional hub in Hong Kong.

That said, I have also had occasion to work with a number of suppliers and participating companies under the Fair Labor Association as well, particularly during my time as business director in Asia with the global auditing firm Bureau Veritas. Hanesbrands themselves, the company that emerged from Sara Lee's spinoff of its apparel companies in 2006, joined the FLA in 2008 after a particularly contentious battle with labor leaders at its TOS Dominicana factory in the Dominican Republic.

It is a telling exercise to look at the evolution of each of these two key initiatives — WRAP and the FLA — and the distinct paths they have followed in approaches to dealing with labor, human rights and workplace safety over the years.

Even before the congressional committees began taking testimony regarding the use of child labor offshore, the Clinton administration had been making efforts to engage U.S. business leaders in its fight against sweatshop conditions. Initiatives such as the Compliance Alliance of Southern California, started in 1995 to support self-policing in the garment trade, were representative of efforts the Department of Labor pursued. Secretary Reich was more than willing to take a carrot-and-stick approach however, publicly recognizing those companies that made efforts to engage and take responsibility for labor practices while naming and shaming those who failed to do so. His department's highly publicized "No Sweat" campaign, which also launched in 1995, focused on public education efforts, stricter domestic enforcement of workplace labor laws, and on partnering with manufacturers who signed up to support responsible workplace practices.

On the international front, as early as 1993 the Department's International Labor Affairs Bureau (ILAB) began to focus on child labor overseas and on providing funding to the ILO's International Program for the Elimination of Child Labor (IPEC). ILAB's reports would prove significant during the congressional hearings and follow-up meetings that began to take place immediately afterwards.

Just before the congressional testimony began, Reich and Kathie Lee Gifford had publicly announced the convening of an industry roundtable event, the Fashion Industry Forum, to be held in July 1996. Some 300 stakeholders across apparel supply chains — from brands and retailers to labor unions and civil society groups — met in Arlington, Virginia, outside of the U.S. capital on the 16th of the month. Thus began the contentious work of hashing out a consensus among disparate groups with separate interests who, nonetheless, recognized that some sort of collaborative effort was needed.

With the U.S. government set to introduce legislation aimed at holding manufacturers and retailers responsible for the conditions in which their contracted goods were made, business seemed ready to agree to certain of the points under discussion. The easiest was that sweatshops posed a risk to all actors in apparel supply chains. All sides would need to approach responsibility for both problems and solutions as a shared objective. For industry leaders, sweatshop practices were being recognized as what we might call today "unsustainable."

For their part, civil and labor leaders appeared agreeable to pursuing a continuous improvement approach, not wishing to be seen as supportive of actions that could arguably lead to job losses among the poor in developing countries. This is a point of view, however, that has also been manipulated on many occasions by self-serving business interests to justify their operations in countries that have offered an exponential return on profitability versus the local value of factory employment their sourcing programs have be tied to. (This is a theme we will come back to in Chapter 4 addressing aid-for-trade paradigms.)

There was also a shared understanding that the efforts of government alone could not be counted on to provide a wholesale solution — including a dependence on regulatory enforcement. The willingness and ability of many developing countries to actively pursue enforcement had historically proven shaky at best. Rather, some mix of international standards and market inducements might better effect change. Continued leverage of consumer and civil society pressure and the management of economic incentives as well as raising the reputational and bottom line costs of failure seemed to hold promise.

Throughout these discussions, one of the most significant areas of disagreement centered on the issue of who exactly was responsible for exploitive labor practices offshore. Labor and civil society groups contended that such responsibility was shared by those who procured the goods and those who held the purse strings — and that these were the actors who could best influence supplier actions. In the view of a number of the brands involved, foreign operators and industry standards were to blame; the multinationals claimed no authority in such cases.

Despite continued disagreement on this and a number of other significant issues, in August 1996 President Clinton announced that the Fashion Industry Forum's efforts had resulted in a multi-party agreement to form the Apparel Industry Partnership (AIP). The AIP would bring labor leaders from the AFL-CIO and UNITE (Union of Needletrades, Industrial, and Textile Employees), the Lawyers Committee for Human Rights (LCHR), the National Consumers League (NCL) and key American apparel brands together (Liz Claiborne, Nike, Patagonia and L.L. Bean, among others).[107] The mandate of this organization would be to create agreed-to and enforceable labor standards to combat exploitive sweatshop conditions, to develop a voluntary industry action plan to support their implementation, and to report back to the president on the group's progress within a six-month timeframe.

The effort received mixed reviews from NGO groups. Some felt it represented an important step forward, while others felt it was only a limited victory for organized labor and human rights interests. Within the apparel and retailing industries there was also significant disagreement, especially from those who had not signed up for it. Many were unhappy to see management of the agenda being taken out of business's hands. A number of those who had agreed to participate had already taken proactive steps toward embedding responsible practices in their supply chains, as was the case with both Patagonia and Liz Claiborne. But while those who weren't onboard may or may not have expected to feel additional public pressure, the fact remained that the entire exercise was voluntary and carried neither force of law nor legal repercussions for their decisions to abstain.

By the time the six-month deadline came around, rumors were rife that the members had hit an impasse. The reality was that most of the issues regarding the development of the common standards themselves

had been dealt with. They were still working on the monitoring mechanisms to oversee compliance, but two particular issues were at the heart
of remaining difficulties: wages and the right to freedom of association.

In the end, it would take a compromise to reach agreement among
the actors who had spent a considerable amount of time struggling to
build trust together through months of deliberations, internal and external discussions, and comparative analyses of international law and
existing codes of conduct. By exercising flexibility on the issue of living
wages tied to the adopted standard of paying the higher of either the
local legal minimum wage or the prevailing industry wage, civil and
labor participants were able to ensure inclusion of the rights to collective bargaining and freedom of association. Additionally, there was
wording included under the wage standard by which industry committed to meeting the basic needs of employees.

More than a decade later, the issue of living wages would once again
come to the forefront of labor's ongoing conflicts with international
apparel brands, as production continued to seek out ever-lower priced
geographies in which to manufacture. For the time being however, an
agreement in principle regarding shared standards had been reached.
The issue of monitoring took somewhat greater effort. It was here that
civil society and organized labor stood firm on the need for external,
independent monitors to ensure a credible and transparent process.
Either professional auditing firms hired by brands and manufacturers
in collaboration with local NGOs, or local NGOs themselves might
be used, though any applicant would need to be accredited by the AIP
to carry out monitoring.

The agreement would finally be delivered to the White House in
April 1997, but not before AIP member Nike was forced to confront
a scathing public report by the Vietnam Labor Watch in March of
that year deriding the brand for well-documented and glaring gaps between its written code of conduct and actual factory practices on the
ground.[109]

On April 14, 1997, President Bill Clinton announced the AIP's
historic agreement between apparel industry stakeholders, needed because "as has now been painfully well documented, some of the clothes
and shoes we buy here in America are manufactured under working
conditions that are deplorable and unacceptable — mostly overseas,

but unbelievably, sometimes here at home as well."[110]As part of the accord, the members of the AIP had recommended the formation of a new and independent nonprofit body to oversee members' adherence to the adopted workplace code of conduct.

That initial optimism was soon quashed as members of all stripes got down to the brass tacks of sorting out exactly how to implement the code and structure the organization that would be responsible for managing the program and monitoring adherence. By November of that year, *The New York Times* was reporting on the serious level of divisiveness that had gripped the AIP's proceedings. For the next year, labor and civil society members remained deadlocked as the situation around them continued to evolve.

A number of the largest American apparel firms would approach senior leadership at the American Apparel Manufacturers Association (AAMA) to push for an industry solution as they watched what seemed to be a deteriorating situation at the AIP. These players were also concerned with an overly aggressive labor and NGO agenda, as both stakeholder groups had begun to push for greater concessions within the talks. By this time, Social Accountability International had also launched their own effort at creating a labor standard that threatened to further dilute a consolidated industry approach to common standards of practice.

Even as the National Labor Commission and union forces continued to hammer at leading AIP brands, in the summer of 1998 a smaller number of the working group pulled together to attempt to break the impasse and deal with the issues still on the table. Representatives from Nike, Liz Claiborne, Reebok, the BSR and Phillips-Van Heusen together with the RFK Center, National Consumers League, the Lawyers Committee for Human Rights and the International Labor Rights Fund had hammered out an agreement by late October. In it, they committed to the formation of a new independent body, the Fair Labor Association, and for the rules governing monitoring of the group's standards. The plan was presented to the balance of AIP members. Patagonia, L.L. Bean, Nicole Miller and Kathie Lee Gifford seized the opportunity and agreed to join in November.

The Interfaith Center on Corporate Responsibility and both union participants of the AIP rejected it, though the AFL-CIO left the door open to future collaboration with the new organization. There would be many hard years yet ahead for the Fair Labor Association, but the tremendous effort at multi-stakeholder collaboration over more than two years had produced a significant outcome that continues to impact markets today.

One measure of the difference in approach that industry-dominated efforts toward common standards by the AAMA indicate can be found in the lack of transparent, widely available information regarding its early development, especially as compared to the very public history of the AIP/FLA. What is certain is that fallout from the Kathie Lee Gifford ordeal and the consequent congressional investigations into the offshore practices of many American firms had jolted the industry wide awake. Secretary Reich's notice to the garment trade that his department was looking into the labor practices of the largest garment importers must have certainly made for some sleepless nights for a good many U.S. apparel execs.

Clinton administration efforts in April of 1996 to send new anti-sweatshop legislation to the floor of the House spoke to the seriousness of their intent. If passed, the proposal would have held U.S. retailers and apparel manufacturers liable for ensuring the labor practices of their contractors no matter where they might be located. While there was little expectation that the Republican-dominated legislature would have passed the bill, it still served to put industry on notice once again.

It was certainly enough of an incentive to push the AAMA to begin looking into ways they might best mitigate potential risks, political or otherwise. By the summer of 1996, they began looking at external database services that might help their members to track labor, health and safety infractions at contractor facilities. In an effort to help major apparel manufacturers "steer clear" of bad publicity, as AAMA execs put it,[113] they inked a deal with OSHA-Data Services for just such support. Meanwhile, a good number of the Association's members, particularly those dedicated to the manufacture of low-cost, mass-produced goods like Sara Lee, were taking greater advantage of offshore operations even while downsizing domestically. According to AAMA numbers, there were still some 770,000 apparel manufacturing jobs in the U.S. in 1998, which represented a reduction of 43 percent since the mid-1970s. Industry kept up the pressure on job costs and by late

1997, Sara Lee had launched its three-year "Project 2000" plan, which would lead to the closure of some 100 facilities by the end of fiscal 1999.

On September 25, 1998 AAMA President Larry Martin sat before Representative Pete Hoekstra's Congressional Subcommittee on Oversight and Investigations of the Committee on Education and the Workforce to lay out his members' plans. The 300+ brands and manufacturers represented by the AAMA garnered an astounding $US 85 billion in annual wholesale sales at the time, controlling 85 percent of the U.S. apparel market. The balance was in the hands of the retailers themselves and tied to offshore manufacturing of their private label brands.

Mr. Martin testified before the subcommittee's inquiry into the inner workings of the garment industry that a number of prominent members of the association had approached them more than a year earlier with the idea of spearheading an industry-wide effort to create a comprehensive effort to deal with industry labor conditions at home and abroad. Referring to sweatshops as "immoral and dishonest," he stated categorically that it was his industry's job to put their own house in order.[114]

Martin further added that the AAMA membership had expressed frustration at the lengthy delays and scope of existing attempts at collective engagement (presumably referring to the AIP's efforts), and that it was time for manufacturers themselves to take a leading role. The organization had participated in the earlier Fashion Industry Forum that had led to the AIP's formation, and had been highly critical of the 1997 AIP agreement announced by President Clinton.

Since 1996, in fact, an AAMA taskforce, chaired by Steve Jesseph, executive director of Global Workplace Values at Sara Lee from 1997 to 2003, had spent considerable time amassing a large amount of data and market knowledge on international codes, practices and labor law. (Steve would later go on to serve as president and CEO at WRAP from 2005 through 2011.) Their work was primarily supported by external consulting firms. Efforts were also made, it was claimed, to include the recommendations and input of a number of academic and civil society groups, but there was no formal announcement of who they were or what explicitly they added to the discussions. As the current head of the AAFA recently confirmed, in fact, it has never publicly disclosed the taskforce's membership, and despite a number of requests to release the material for inclusion in this book, it was never forthcoming. Among those organizations that did publicly support the effort early on were a number of foreign industries' manufacturing associations, including those in Mexico, South Africa and the Philippines.

In any event, Mr. Martin's testimony committed the organization to have their program up and running by 1999. The taskforce plans called for a pilot of their factory certification model built around a core set of standards under the Responsible Apparel Production Program (RAPP). Some 30 facilities in Mexico, Central America, the Caribbean and Asia were targeted to participate in the initial start-up phase. To reinforce their seriousness, the AAMA board had already moved ahead to unanimously endorse RAPP the week before the committee's proceedings. The voluntary program (no industry group has yet recommended a legally binding one) promised to provide three key components:

+ Clear and verifiable standards.
+ Factory evaluations carried out by industry-knowledgeable and independent monitors.
+ Oversight of the organization by an entity independent of the AAMA, which included a commitment to invite stakeholder members from NGOs, academia and elsewhere.

One particularly interesting issue raised during Hoekstra's questioning of the AAMA president had to do with the legal responsibility to disclose any compliance discrepancies to manufacturing country authorities. Mr. Martin was pointed in his response.

"That," he replied "is a law enforcement question. We don't want to do law enforcement."[114]

This, consequently, is indicative of where much of the industry still sits today. Essentially, and in contravention of most brand and retailer codes of conduct, business knows full well that a good many of its suppliers are breaking the laws of the countries where they manufacture.

Aside from the moral and ethical obligations to be considered, this was, in my opinion, a legal slippery slope. Each country does have its own laws, after all, and responses would need to depend on the jurisdiction in question. Knowledge of illegal activities might well impel an executive or auditor to report them. It was the argument of the Association however, and to some extent agreed to by Mr. Hoekstra, that the program shouldn't aim to frighten off manufacturers from the potential impacts of liability but rather to help guide them toward in-cremental improvement.

These points tied directly to another significant difference from the AIP/FLA's structure in that the RAPP (soon to be termed WRAP, Worldwide Responsible Apparel Production) proposal centered on certification at the individual, in-country facility level. In this way, they believed responsibility would be put into the hands of the manufac-turer in the country of production and not necessarily rest with a U.S. brand or apparel company. And, as evidenced by the AAMA's testi-mony, responsibility and liability were closely linked in people's minds.

It wouldn't be until October 1999 that the WRAP program was ready to be publicly announced during the opening of the Bobbin Americas industry trade show in Atlanta, Georgia. A year and a half after Larry Martin had first disclosed the project, the AAMA was ready to unveil the program's principles regarding basic labor prac-tices, factory conditions, environmental law and customs compliance. Missing still at this point were the operational details of the program's monitoring mechanism, which AAMA leadership expected would be handled by accounting and safety and human rights NGOs in-country.

Although accounting firms may not have seemed to many in the industry or civil society to be the most appropriate or competent of bodies to carry out manufacturing-level health, safety, labor and en-vironmental assessments, in 1999, the firm PricewaterhouseCoopers (PwC) carried out over 6,000 such audits for brands and retailers globally, principal among them Wal-Mart, Nike, The Gap and Disney. Their execution of the social audit process was roundly criticized by MIT Professor Dara O'Rourke in a September 2000 research study for the Independent University Initiative (IUI) supported by Harvard, Notre Dame, Ohio State, the University of California and the University of Michigan.[117] This was not a simple desktop analysis of previous reports. Dr. O'Rourke had accompanied PwC's auditors personally and found many of their practices to be sub-par; yet major multinationals were depending on them, wholesale.

By 2000, WRAP had truly pushed into its operational phase, and the second of two major U.S. industry efforts hit the market fast on the heels of the FLA program: the latter clearly and publicly built out of cross-industry stakeholder negotiations with government's encouragement, and the first put forward by the manufacturing industry with substantially less publicity and transparency to the proceedings or participants.

Labor and Factory Auditing: The Good, the Bad and the Ugly

Within these and most major apparel and consumer goods accountability programs (as the industry refers to them), the role of external auditors became central to ensuring compliance to each given set of standards. Perhaps this started out logically enough in the early days of attempts to wrestle with factory-level challenges, but over time the practice evolved in rather negative ways. In a slightly modified take on the Iron Law of Oligarchy[118], or what James Hyland has called the "tactical and technical necessities"[119] of managing organizational responsibilities, the "elite" role of the audit process overtook the real intent of many programs.

Probably the most valuable benefit of having taken on a wide range of responsibilities myself across a variety of supply chain positions with brands, retailers, auditing firms and factory standards can best be defined as *perspective*. And over time this unique point of view, acquired as a result of wearing many different hats in the industry, led me to some troubling conclusions.

The first is that, not unlike the different communities of stakeholders that various standards and factory compliance programs serve, an intense sense of competition has historically existed between accountability programs. This was one challenge I ran up against during my time with WRAP in Asia, as my own approach had by then led me to seek greater collaboration and brainstorming exchanges across party lines, if you will. Those at the very top of the food chain at the time seemed to believe wholeheartedly that WRAP was the greatest thing since sliced bread and that no other program was worth the paper it had been written on. Cross-program engagement was frowned upon and not to be encouraged.

As a sourcing decision-maker, I had long heard either directly or by proxy through the grassroots organizations that supported one standard or another, what was so unique and preferential about the approach of any one of a variety of standards versus the others. All of the major programs seem to have their benefits and drawbacks, but many share some of the same challenges that for one reason or another senior decision-makers I have worked with either didn't get or preferred to ignore.

The auditing industry that has evolved over the past 20 years or so to serve the outsourced needs of international brands and retailers is now a multi-billion-dollar goliath. While there are literally dozens of medium and smaller-sized companies that have developed geographical and product-specific niches, the field continues to be dominated by a troika of European-listed firms with global reach.

Between them, the combined incomes of Bureau Veritas of France, Intertek in the U.K. and Swiss-listed SGS (formerly, the Société General de Surveillance) reached $US 14.24 billion in 2013, and they employed over 180,000 people around the world. To be sure, all of these earnings did not result from factory auditing, which as a category includes a range of environmental, technical capacity and labor evaluations. To one extent or another, they all offer a range of health, safety and risk management services — from laboratory testing of products to quality inspections, industry certifications and factory auditing. But even as a representative ten percent of their total business, this is an incredible sum, which doesn't even include the dozens of SME (small and medium enterprise) firms operating mostly in the developing world on their own programs and niche projects.

To cheaply and effectively offer competent monitoring services requires scale, systems and on-the-ground teams that most brands and retailers simply don't wish to invest in owning. For many, this would also result in some difficult conflicts of interest. But organizations the scale of these three giants and perhaps another six to eight second-tier competitors of still-significant size also face potential conflicts. By far the largest segment of risk management firm business with retailers is in product testing. And relationships tied to this more profitable business line are often leveraged by both sides of the equation: one to push for more competitive costs, and the other to leverage their services to gain access to more business. The entire dynamic is, of course, financially driven, as auditing firms are by nature for-profit enterprises. This results in often-unhappy outcomes for many directly employed in the auditing field.

The audit itself as an exercise of evaluation and monitoring has be-come a commodity. It is not quite as cheap a commodity as the exercise of factory quality inspections has become, but it is nonetheless a unit of work that many brands and retailers have continuously attempted to re-value downwards. Both audits and inspections are sold to clients in so-called Man-Day units, based on the amount of time it takes on average for one auditor to execute the work. (There are, of course, vari-ations, but I am using widely accepted industry standards here.)

In the largest global apparel production region of Asia, on average a quality inspection of export-ready production from the factory rep-resented as one man-day costs approximately $US 280.00. Depending on the client's buying power, volume, and negotiation tactics, this may range from $US 85.00 to $US 350.00. Audits, on the other hand, re-quire a set of human technical competences and experience still more difficult to find than those of a quality inspector. So much so that the major firms often sub-contract work to smaller local companies during seasonal spikes of demand. The relative shortage of qualified auditors and the past decade's increasing demand for their skills has meant audit firms have been able to maintain rates at around $US 1200.00. Again, this may range plus or minus a couple of hundred dollars depending on the brand, and certain country costs run lower than this average.

Needless to say, locally hired auditors in China, Bangladesh, Cambodia or Vietnam do not make anything near that daily pay rate. Maintaining the cost of a large, global workforce and Western-based sales, account management and marketing staff do also contribute sig-nificantly to operational overhead. But auditors are still driven quite hard to ensure a high rate of utilization — which simply means they are working nearly all the time.

Typically on the road at dawn to spend a long day in the factory, they won't arrive home or back to their local hotel digs until evening sets in. From there they may then continue, submitting their reports online until late in the evening, pulling in overtime hours that are rarely paid as such. I recall more than one conversation with senior audit firm staff about the counter-logic of labor compliance auditors working outside of legal com-pliance themselves while auditing brand labor-compliance standards.

Of significant concern to those with an eye on liability issues is the standard industry practice (a term that does not indicate either a legally or morally correct one) of retailers implementing a home country "Code of Conduct" stating that overseas suppliers *must* be in compliance with their own local health, safety, environmental and labor laws — while being fully aware that many suppliers simply are not. This is the epitome of hypocrisy, yet day in and day out, brands who swear by the strength of their codes to critics at home follow this practice.

As those on the manufacturing side of the business will know, social or labor audits (the terms are generally interchangeable) focus on a range of management practices and adherence to any combination of legal requirements, internationally adopted standards or standards mandated by brand compliance (see Table 3). Most audit systems will then rank the results (referred to as "findings" in audit-speak) in terms of their risk or severity: low, medium and high for example; or minor, medium, major and critical. Typically, major or critical risk findings are tied to clearly defined legal requirements in the country of production. Or at least they should be. Any resulting non-compliances (audit-speak for practices that break local law) are then summarized and provided to the factory and back to the brand or retail "*client*" with a recommended corrective action plan, or CAP. Let's come back to that highlighted term in a few moments.

A CAP will typically provide a calendar against which the facility should or must — depending on the severity of the brand/retail code of conduct — take corrective measures to become compliant. Again, this means the time by which they *should* commit to then becoming

Table 3

Leading Ethical Labor Standards and Schemes
Fair Labor Association (US)
Fair Trade Certification (US/EU)
Worldwide Responsible Accredited Production (US)
Business Social Compliance Initiative (EU)
Ethical Trade Initiative (UK)
Fair Wear Foundation (Netherlands)
SEDEX / SMETA (UK)
Social Accountability International SA8000 (US)

a facility operating with due regard to the laws of the country where they operate. To spell this out even more clearly, it is the time a brand or retailer accepts or allows that their vendor factory will continue operating illegally.

Minor issues, say, an incomplete first aid kit, might be given a week to correct. More significant findings that require time and money to put in place, perhaps a missing fire escape or the widening of a stairwell, might take a month or more to address. Missing operating licenses or incomplete environmental impact assessments, which are a common occurrence in many offshore production countries, will take considerably longer. As an example, from the recent thousands of follow-up audits at factories in Bangladesh following the tragic collapse of the Rana Plaza facility there in 2013, an overwhelming number of facilities were found to be operating without fire safety licenses, occupancy certificates or construction permits. All the while, Western brands were churning out millions of dollars' worth of apparel exports from the country.

Policies vary from client to client as to when and whether orders may continue to be placed and produced while these "non-compliances" are corrected before a re-audit takes place to then verify the corrections. Having worked with, for, and on behalf of, some two dozen brands over the past 18 years, I can say without a doubt that many clients allow business to continue as usual in these circumstances.

There is certainly, in most buying organizations, a short list of cardinal rules that would immediately halt orders or prohibit them from being placed. Typically, these are out-and-out child labor, forced labor in slavery conditions, or fully locked-down facilities without any means of escape in case of fire, earthquake or other emergency situations. Short of these, many brand and retail customers allow for ongoing orders within the timeframe of a CAP. This may be news to the average consumer and those outside of the industry, but it is no secret to those in sourcing, social compliance, or legal teams at retail HQs.

More nefarious is the fact that this practice allows brands and retailers to profit from ongoing illegalities throughout the CAP timeline. To arrive at such a conclusion, one only has to examine the reasons why factories continue in their non-compliant ways. I say "continue" because the average offshore apparel facility is probably audited upwards of two dozen times per year, often by the very same auditing firm, for a variety of client codes and programs. Chasing corrective action plans is a game with often tragic consequences.

By looking at the specifics of what type of legal and code infractions happen most frequently, one quickly gets to the gist of the matter. A typical labor/social audit that examines a host of health, safety, human resource, environmental, payroll and business operational issues might run 300+ questions or data collection points. These are grouped into logical categories (see Table 4) for tabulation. By far, the largest two areas of non-conformity are:

1. Wages and working hours, including mandatory deductions for benefits.

2. Health and safety issues, ranging from low to medium risk.

That is not to say that more significant issues are not common; simply that statistically speaking these have been the largest and most problematic areas for a number of reasons. *The single largest driver of these issues is cost.* Overtime pay, holiday pay, days off, social insurance, medical benefits, maternity leave, etc. all carry a direct cost to the factory that manufacturers in Europe or North America or countries with

Table 4

Social/Labor Audit Categories of Focus: What Brands/Retailers Measure	
Labor Management	Forced Labor Child Labor Discipline, Harassment and Abuse Discrimination Employment Contracts Freedom of Association
Wages & Working Hours	Working Hours Wages & Benefits
Management Systems	
Health & Safety	Work Facility Conditions Emergency Planning Occupational Hazards Equipment and Machine Safety Chemical Management On Site Living Conditions
Environmental Management	

robust implementation of the law are obliged to pay. The same holds true for safety system costs for proper fire sprinklers, safe chemical-handling equipment, extinguishers, firefighting gear, escapes, stairs, fire doors, etc.

Thus, in order to remain competitive with a host of other developing countries in a cutthroat industry where an overabundance of factories exist, factories simply fail to invest in proper systems and pay practices, which would price them out of the market. Most brands and retailers know this and are aware of the deficiencies because the vast majority of them audit on an ongoing basis. They then put in place corrective action plans that allow for ongoing cycles of audit and re-audit, all the while realizing financial benefits because of these gaps in health, safety, labor, environmental and business practices.

If, as is being proposed here, these gaps are legal infringements (which depend on the law in the country in question) and these financial benefits are then realized across international borders, then the question might legitimately be raised: *Is this not transnational crime?* To date, few labor or civil society groups have dared to take this issue on, in part because they lack the financial resources to do so and in part, also, because of the difficulty in gaining access to documentary evidence to support such claims and importantly, of finding legal jurisdictions willing to allow such cases to be tried.

This brings us back to the earlier highlighting of the term *client*. Much like the use of buying agents by some brands to provide a layer of distance and potential liability between themselves and actual manufacturing facilities, many auditing relationships have been constructed with similar intentions in mind. While in most cases major retail and brand players have direct online access to audit documentation that monitoring firms upload in platforms that only end users have access to, contractual paper trails often show something quite different.

In a very common organizational scenario, monitoring firms maintain administrative hubs in Hong Kong while their operational country offices are logically scattered among key production countries. A brand compliance decision-maker sitting in New York or London or Toronto routes the request for a factory audit directly to their supplier or buying agent in country X while advising their nominated auditing firm to proceed with scheduling said audit. In-country suppliers and monitoring offices then communicate directly to sign a local agreement on service pricing previously negotiated with the foreign retailer. The supplier or their contract factory pays directly for the audit, and the client relationship is established locally. Legal responsibility and ownership of the audit file and results are retained in-country. The factory then provides approval for the given North American client to have access to the results they "own," but the reality is that the entire process is driven and directed by the brand/retail client.

Regardless of how the paper agreement has been structured, however, the fact remains that end client brands and retailers maintain full visibility to the fact that the factories that have been contracted to produce goods under their brand names are in breach of local laws on an ongoing basis. This flies in the face of both the spirit and intent of codes of conduct. If brands believe this process to be a legitimate method for addressing factory conditions, then they should both rewrite codes of conduct to remove the requirement of suppliers to follow the law and publicly release their audit results.

In some retailer home-country jurisdictions, knowledge of supplier illegalities may well pose potential issues for publicly listed companies. An argument could be made in the Canadian province of Ontario, for example, that under Ontario Securities Commission rules for Continuous Disclosure Obligations, any undue risks to business operations should be publicly declared to markets and shareholders. It is not a huge leap to assume that the use of supplier factories in foreign jurisdictions that are in breach of health, safety, environmental, labor or human rights laws may well pose significant undue risks to a business. If management is aware and being kept in the loop, why shouldn't shareholders and investment funds be as well? This may well provide further justification for the public disclosure of factory audit findings.

Another serious operational challenge for many monitoring and inspection firms and their end clients is the ongoing issue of auditor and inspector corruption. A September 2013 investigative report by *The New York Times* brought to light much about the issue, which is a well-known challenge within the monitoring industry itself. The risks are obvious when one considers that audit employees in China, for example, now earning on average between $US 1,200–1,500 per month, often hold in their hands the power to make or break a facility's approval for use by foreign buyers. Factories often see the offer of a "little red packet" (an envelope stuffed with cash) as a less costly way to achieve positive audit results while avoiding significant cost upgrades to systems and infrastructure, not to mention the ongoing payment of proper legal wages and benefits. The potential for corruption works both ways of course, and auditors looking to supplement their incomes can hold a factory ransom simply by fudging audit results.

To their credit, this is an area where major auditing firms have made serious attempts to respond in recent years by implementing internal quality controls and rotating staff within geographical areas. They have also raised base salaries and carry out surprise re-assessments by specialized monitor-audit staff on an ongoing basis — essentially, auditing the auditor. The challenges are equally present for quality inspection programs; high-value shipments can get held up while a corrupt inspector and the factory manager haggle over "lunch money."

Even having a large in-house team may not necessarily negate the risks of corruption, as Wal-Mart apparently found in China in the summer of 2008. On the back of industry rumors predicting mass firings due to internal trust issues that were swirling around Shenzhen at the time, inspection firm Intertek announced a substantial new inspection program aimed at enhancing the retailer's handle on quality issues. According to Intertek's press release in July of that year, 180 Wal-Mart quality staff would be "displaced" by the move to shift to an outside firm.[122] Industry gossip put the number at closer to 300 who were let go.

In my experience, however, it has often been the brand and retail clients of monitoring firms who fail to take strong action against their supplier facilities when accusations or proof of attempts at auditor bribery are brought to their attention. "Commercial consideration," as it is often called, the need for getting goods in production out the door and shipped on time, often overrides the ethical concerns of a factory's attempts to pay off auditors and inspectors. Most receive a slap on the wrist and a stern warning, but rarely in 18 years have I ever heard of a factory being cut off after offering an auditor a bribe.

The more sophisticated monitoring firms have also invested in robust IT systems in an effort to provide valuable data-mining capabilities to their clients. Conceptually, this was a brilliant move, allowing sourcing and social compliance teams to benchmark their own facilities' performance and gaps against peers, regions and industries. Actionable, hard management data about where the greatest failings occur in which audit areas at which suppliers over time should allow a focused, cost-efficient effort at meaningful improvement. Unfortunately, not nearly enough brand and retailer sourcing teams I have worked with made meaningful use of the information.

Often this is because sourcing teams are under pressure in their day-to-day roles to hit pricing and keep production moving without spending too much time on strategic thinking. Many teams are simply not staffed up with sufficient bodies or the expertise to deal with these issues; lacking their own "boots on the ground," they may have to rely on far-off buying agent relationships to keep a handle on things. Canadian retailers have been particularly reluctant to make the investment in staffing up robust compliance, supply chain and sourcing associates offshore. Whirlwind sourcing team travel to overseas factories to negotiate pricing on a seasonal basis is simply no match for having one's own professional, technically qualified audit and engineering resources in facilities on an ongoing basis.

This was certainly the case I found at Canada's Joe Fresh brand when I first arrived at their downtown Toronto offices on a consulting assignment late in the summer of 2013. Aside from not having a single employee on the ground prior to the 2013 Rana Plaza collapse (as was widely reported by Canadian media), there were no qualified compliance associates at brand level whose full-time tasks were to evaluate factory assessments with any practical criteria or experience in auditing or corrective action planning. Issues were either dealt with on an ad hoc basis by sourcing and administrative staff or were pushed back up to the corporate compliance team of food retailing giant Loblaw Companies Limited, which owns the Joe Fresh label. This team sat at Loblaw headquarters some 35 kilometers away from the Joe Fresh offices, and, while they provided a good level of oversight and desktop reviews themselves, they did not at that time have anyone on the team with either a social auditing or apparel manufacturing background.

As auditing itself has grown into a significant industry, some countries (most notably China) have seen the growth of parallel efforts to circumvent and cheat the system. Factories and a host of in-country consultants have been very industrious at finding ways around labor monitoring. Double sets of payroll books, software systems designed to provide sophisticated false paper trails and former auditors hired to coach facilities on stop-gap methods all keep brands, retailers and their monitoring firms on their toes. It does not take much effort at all to carry out an Internet search on any number of Chinese online forums or websites to find these systems and services. It is a continual cat-and-mouse game that has led many both inside and outside of the industry to question the efficacy and logic of the entire audit process.

Over the past few years it has become an accepted axiom for many of us working on the social compliance side of the industry that auditing is not working — not on its own, at least. It is now widely stated that auditing is but one tool of many and should not be relied upon as a panacea for dealing with everything under the umbrella of "corporate social responsibility." (I prefer the term "responsible supply chain practices," which more narrowly defines the role I have tried to mold for myself.)

The trouble is that most brands and retailers do rely principally on factory social audits to deal with these issues because they have become the industry status quo response to the increasing demands of customers, markets and critics. They are also a relatively cheap way to be seen as doing *something* while avoiding the more significant costs of actually re-engineering the system-wide changes so sorely needed. Given that we have allowed global apparel and footwear industries, targeted to produce revenues in the $US 2 trillion range by 2018, to evolve into the current mass production modeled monstrosity that it is, turning back the clock now will be no easy thing.

But beginning on the labor engagement front, there are certainly existing benchmarks, models and strategies open to us. Front-runner organizations have been steadily implementing some of the more promising models. While these efforts have required a considerable amount of trial and error along the way, the most critical ingredient has been acceptance and support from companies' very top leadership that sincere, pragmatic change was needed.

In the following chapters we will look more closely at the recent on-shoring trend of bringing production back to home markets as one way to ensure improved transparency into labor and human rights.

But let's first examine a more innovative and human relations-driven engagement approach to dealing with factory workplace issues that offers, in my opinion, the greatest opportunity to re-set the game — if we can reproduce its example successfully.

Getting it Right: How Verité Sets the Benchmark

Based in Amherst, Massachusetts, labor rights consultant Verité is a highly respected nonprofit group working with brands, NGOs, retailers and researchers dedicated to legal, fair and safe working conditions globally. The firm got its start in 1995 as the brainchild of Heather White, a former sourcing agent with strong on-the-ground experience in China. Ms. White is one of a small group of ethical supply chain professionals whose passion and example have deeply influenced my own commitment toward driving change in the apparel industry due, in part, to some similarities in our experiences.

Aside from her practical sourcing background, which is not all that common to find in accountability and auditing professionals, she is also an accomplished academic. A recent fellow of the Edmond J. Safra Center for Ethics at Harvard University, Heather completed her Master's in international political economy at MIT following her earlier undergraduate work in East Asian Studies at Harvard. At the time of this writing, she has been collaborating as producer and co-director on an upcoming documentary film addressing the human costs of off-shore electronics manufacturing titled, "Who Pays the Price?"

What sets Verité apart from the work of commercially motivated monitoring firms is their worker-centered approach to driving responsible supply chain activities. Dan Viederman, CEO at the firm since Heather's departure, was forthcoming when I asked about the roots of this approach:

> "This emerges from our recognition that workers are a
> key stakeholder in workplaces and no honest assessment
> of workplace conditions can ignore their viewpoint, nor
> could any gaps or problems be solved without worker
> involvement."

Their structure as a consulting firm versus that of a volume-driven audit provider means that they approach work on a customized basis in lieu of following a cookie-cutter, one-size-fits-all model. Ensuring sufficient management commitment exists from potential corporate clients and that multiple stakeholders have a voice within projects are key to their taking on engagements. The organization's stated goal is to make sure that they can contribute in a meaningful way toward resolving the most pressing human rights and labor relations issues within supply chains and manufacturing environments. Thus, they look holistically at a range of tools to best address real root causes in greater depth than any quick in-and-out, man-day audit ever could. Audits alone, after all, are simply a snapshot in time, which (potentially) provide a glimpse into management practices on the day the audit was executed.

In Verité's experience, training of production employees, factory management and clients' supply chain teams, combined with policy and practice gap analysis, industry research and yes, audit assessments, all make for a more comprehensive approach. But even their audits are weighted differently than those used to determine potential risks from a brand/retailer point of view. True to their worker-centered model, assessments are heavily dependent on input directly from production-line employees. Significantly, more emphasis is placed on human interactions, employee contributions, observations and input than what the black-and-white of forensic-document audits or brief, in-factory interviews might.

As Dan puts it: "The credibility and depth of our assessments is our distinguishing feature, and drives much of the value we provide to our client companies. We gather information directly from workers as the most credible source of information about workplace conditions."

Consultants work across a number of issues-related initiatives high on the team's agenda, from forced labor and trafficking to civil society capacity-building to gender equity, all of which have contributed to the firm's reputation as an innovator in their field. Verité has built exceptionally deep knowledge in the areas of forced labor and human trafficking. Within this core competency they have broken down their value approach to provide tools and services including open access e-learning modules, in-depth sector-specific research into labor and human rights risks, supply chain accountability guidelines and a unique focus on migrant recruitment practices.

I was curious to learn which geographies in the apparel world were prone to forced labor abuses (besides Jordan, which we looked at extensively in earlier chapters).

"We have conducted assessments and intervened on behalf of workers in apparel facilities in locations as diverse as Mauritius, Madagascar, Jordan, Taiwan, Malaysia and Saipan," Dan says. "Anywhere there are foreign migrant workers has the risk of forced labor as a result of debt-bondage and unethical labor recruitment. We are working extensively in Southeast Asia, including Malaysia, Taiwan and Singapore."

What the Verité model offers is a practical, value-added and financially sustainable benchmark, which civil society, social enterprise funds, organized labor and government might get behind in searching for equitable ways to address the current industry malaise. Approximately 95 percent of the group's income is generated by fees for services, with the remainder coming from small grants and contributions. Investing in the setup and roll-out of various such firms on a geographical basis, perhaps by retailer home markets or trade blocks, would be a start.

Lessons learned from commercially driven audit firms should dictate the avoidance of multinational, monolithic organizations beholden only to shareholder returns. Profit-driven, business-first models have had their chance and have generally been shown to have failed in achieving meaningful, measurable and lasting change. It is time for them to step aside, with regulatory intervention if need be. At a very minimum, Western brands and retailers who claim to operate as good corporate citizens upholding ethical business practices in all their operations must be held to the same legal standards of performance regardless of where they source their goods. It is preposterous and frankly immoral for any corporation to claim to follow ethical, sustainable sourcing practices while knowingly procuring goods from facilities that systematically break the law to the detriment of their workers and surrounding communities.

I might extend the following sentiment beyond its American reference while sharing this quote from a recent U.S. president during his 2002 speech to business leaders in New York City. "America's highest economic need is higher ethical standards — standards enforced by strict laws and upheld by responsible business leaders."[125] Amen, George W., Amen!

4

Unsustainable

Hong Kong: Out of the Frying Pan into the Fire

BY THE SPRING OF 2006, Angélica, the boys, and I were settling nicely into Hong Kong's expat lifestyle. Mike and Ben were making the daily trek from our place on Lantau Island to their school in Kwai Chung, and my wife had begun to teach Spanish in the local public school system. I had just taken on a new start-up role for Canadian ladieswear retailer Tabi, with an eye on building out a robust social and environmental road map for their existing vendor base.

Tabi International had been part of a long and storied history in the Canadian retail trade as one of two national brands created by Japanese-Canadian entrepreneur Luke Tanabe. In 1989, Mr. Tanabe sold both Tabi and his department store-targeted Ports labels to Chinese-Canadian businessman Alfred Chan's Etac Sales Ltd., a China-based contract manufacturer. After a rapid spate of expansion in Canada, Etac went bankrupt in 1994. Mr. Chan was able to maintain the rights to the Ports name for a cool $CND 6 million and rebranded the company with a focus on China's fashion markets. Listed in Hong Kong in 2003, the new Ports 1961 label went on to become a fashion world success story. Tabi, meanwhile, went through a number of ownership changes, together with sister brands under Canadian retailer Cotton Ginny, including a management team buyout supported by U.S. private equity group Catterton Partners in 2001.

By the time I had joined to set up Tabi's Asia team, Andrea Weiss, a sharp-witted, capable retailing exec with leadership experience at Ann Taylor, Guess, Limited Brands and Disney under her belt, was running the show. Sophisticated styling, competitive but hardly cheap price points, and quality textiles were key to Andrea's positioning of the brand, which had maintained a strong core customer base throughout its many years of ownership handoffs. Within a few months of my start and while the Hong Kong office was still being fitted out and staff being interviewed, that tie-in to textiles would see me scrambling to head off yet another industry failure from impacting my employer's reputation.

On June 16, 2006, a brief paragraph in Hong Kong's *South China Morning Post* carried reports from the mainland's Xinhua news agency that a South China textile dye mill owned by a major Hong Kong-listed company was being accused of dumping excess industrial wastewater into a nearby river. A spokesperson from the mill's parent company, textile giant Fountain Set Holdings, denied details of the report's allegations that a clandestine drainage pipe had been installed to dispose of the untreated dye runoff. The news registered with very few people.

By the following week, further details began to surface attributing earlier reports to a number of mainland newspapers known for their investigative stories, including the *Nanfang Daily* and *Southern Metropolis News*. Local buying and quality control offices of major international brands began to sit up and take notice. The *Who's Who* of the apparel industry were all clients of one or another of Fountain Set's 13 or so companies, among them Macy's, Nike, Marks & Spencer, Liz Claiborne, NEXT, Levi's, Nautica, Tesco, J.C. Penney, J. Crew, Reebok, Sara Lee, Polo, Eddie Bauer, Target, The Gap, Wal-Mart ... and Tabi International.

The outrageous details of the story that continued to surface would cause millions of dollars in fines, facility upgrades and cancelled orders for the firm that had billed itself as the world's largest manufacturer of circular knitted fabrics. As Daryl Brown, vice president for ethics and compliance at Liz Claiborne stated in a 2007 follow-up interview with the *Wall Street Journal*, "We certainly don't want to be associated with a company that's polluting the waters."[128]

With vertically integrated operations including spinning, knitting, dyeing, printing and finishing facilities in China, Indonesia and Sri Lanka and nearly $US 1 billion in revenues for 2006, this was no backwater, second-rate fabric supplier. These were the "big boys," and they certainly should have known better. But that didn't stop management at the conglomerate's Dongguan Fuan Textiles industrial park from reportedly flushing some 47,000 tonnes of untreated wastewater *per day* into village water supplies.

They were licensed to officially dispose of 6.7 million tonnes annually; investigators alleged that for the previous two years they had, in fact, flushed more than 15 million tonnes of untreated facility water a year into the nearby river system. Local government's attitudes weren't exactly aligned, nor were they helpful. While Dongguan's mayor called for harsh penalties against the firm, representatives from Hong Kong's Guangdong Economic and Trade Office confirmed that they had been recommending to Hong Kong companies in highly polluting industries that they had best relocate their businesses to more remote areas. One would assume this was to avoid the tightening environmental scrutiny in the south of the country.

To my relief, none of Tabi's fabric orders had been placed with the facility at the center of this escapade, but the fact that I had needed to verify the documented dye lot trail only served to demonstrate the lack of transparency in global supply chains. Many branded apparel retailers who opt for full-package, turnkey garment sourcing have little information about the origination of raw material inputs or where their garments' textiles are actually made. This poses significant risk. And while industry leaders and environmental activists have sometimes collaborated and sometimes clashed over how best to move the ball forward, a small but growing band of them have begun to see the promising results of their efforts. We are still, however, a long way off from seeing the seismic industry shift needed to reduce generations of detrimental, planet-wide impacts.

Sustainable Trade and the Better Cotton Initiative

I first became aware of the Better Cotton Initiative (BCI) in the fall of 2012 while interviewing with Joost Oorthuizen, CEO of the Netherlands-based Sustainable Trade Initiative, which oversees the program. The Sustainable Trade Initiative, often referred to by its Dutch acronym IDH (*Initiatief Duurzame Handel*), was founded in 2008 as a collaboration between the Dutch Ministry of Foreign Affairs, organized labor, NGOs and the business community. The organization's mission was to drive sustainability innovation into global agricultural commodity supply chains and trade relationships with developing nations. Beginning with an injection of $US 140 million in public funding and private sector matching contributions, the IDH has since built its model to focus on a number of key commodity crops and natural resources — from cocoa, timber, tea and soya to coffee, cashews, aquaculture and cotton. Additional projects expanded the effort beyond agro-goods into tourism, electronics, mining, and pulp and paper.

My own interests at the time lay specifically in the group's apparel industry involvement with the Better Cotton program (currently, BCI operates in 12 countries across North and South America, Africa, the Far East and Central Asia.) Joost and I spent two months discussing a possible role for me with their India team; while this particular contract didn't come to pass, I remained engaged with him and other key BCI staff over the next few years, including unsuccessful efforts to bring Canada's Joe Fresh onboard.

Cotton remains by far the most widely used of all fabric raw materials in the apparel trade, accounting for about one third of total global textile production. It is an extremely difficult agricultural commodity to manage because its cultivation requires large amounts of water and the crop is susceptible to pests and insects; it is also highly climate sensitive. Together, these difficulties place a slew of environmental demands on the communities that cultivate the crop.

Statistics vary depending on the resources consulted and on the particular growing geography in question, but leaning on those data compiled by textile recycling group USAgain, (fig. 4) one third of a pound (0.15 kilo) of pesticides is used on average to cultivate the cotton for one t-shirt, and up to 700 gallons (almost 3,000 liters) of water are used from growth through manufacture. In the neighborhood of 20 percent of all industrial water pollution globally is tied back to apparel and textile manufacturing. Untreated wastewater disperses not only saline and metallic compounds, but also trace residues of the highly carcinogenic chemicals used throughout various stages of processing.

There are literally thousands of chemicals used in the lifecycle of the average garment, and, as the European Union found when launching the 2007 implementation of their REACH program (Registration, Evaluation, Authorisation and Restriction of Chemicals), the actual compound components of the vast majority were unknown to industry users. As we have seen in the above-noted story out of South China, even the largest global players can get caught with their pants down.

Fig. 4.

Beginning first as a small project team in 2005, the Better Cotton Initiative got its official organizational start under the IDH umbrella in 2009. It was launched as an ambitious program, not to create another niche fiber (as many in the industry perceive organic cotton to be) but rather to provide the catalyst for system-wide change in global cotton markets. Two principal drivers were targeted, and these would also provide the key beneficial outcomes of the effort. The first of these was *the producers* themselves, the millions of small shareholding farmers who account for the bulk of the world's cotton cultivation. The second was a mix of several elements that fell into the bucket of *environmental impacts*, principally those to do with water and chemical management. Ensuring a sustainable financial model was also a critical component of the effort, which rested on the successful management of both these principal factors.

With the initial brand support of Adidas, The Gap, IKEA and H&M, the team began the task of building an operating model founded on a classic three-pillar sustainability commitment to *people, profits* and *the planet*. What evolved was the Better Cotton Standard System, structured to reinforce the initiative's credibility, the exchange of best practices and the promotion of collective actions. The end goal was to use the Standard System to position Better Cotton squarely within mainstream supply chains.

The system consisted of the following building blocks:

1. Production Principles and Criteria
2. Capacity Building
3. The Assurance Program
4. Chain of Custody
5. Claims Framework
6. Results and Impact

The goal of the **Production Principles and Criteria** was to ensure that measurably better cotton would be produced (better, for both producers and the environment). Further, the principles would help to clearly define Better Cotton's promise:

1. Better Cotton is produced by farmers who minimize the harmful impact of crop protection practices.

2. Better Cotton is produced by farmers who use water efficiently and care for the availability of water.
3. Better Cotton is produced by farmers who care for the health of the soil.
4. Better Cotton is produced by farmers who conserve natural habitats.
5. Better Cotton is produced by farmers who care for and preserve the quality of the fiber.
6. Better Cotton is produced by farmers who promote Decent Work (a recognition of the ILO's focus on equitable, fair employment standards.)

Capacity Building refers to the in-country training and practical skills support for farmers that BCI contracts out to ensure that experienced, local service providers help deliver on the program's water and chemical reduction efforts. Country-level branches of the World Wildlife Fund, U.K.-based CottonConnect and the Dutch NGO Solidaridad are all strong players, but BCI rules allow for any number of service providers to participate, including private market companies, governments and industry associations. For example, Brazil's implementation is handled by association group ABRAPA (AssociaçãoBrasileira dos Produtores de Algodão), while Mozambique's is by private operators OLAM and SANAM.

The Better Cotton **Assurance Program** provides ongoing, self-executed, BCI team and third-party assessments against specific criteria tied to pesticide use, water management, decent working conditions, record keeping, training and so forth to ensure producers are learning from and following the standards. Because employee and cultivation methods differ based on the size of a producer's holdings, participating farmers are sorted by size into small, medium and large farming groups for management.

Chain of Custody (CoC) is a methodology for establishing documentary traceability of Better Cotton as it moves along the production supply chain, ensuring credibility in the entire process while validating volumes of production. In 2013, the CoC was updated to improve on the process while establishing two distinct pathway mechanisms:

1. From farm to ginning stage: by the physical segregation of goods.

2. Post-gin level: calculated using Administrative Mass-Balance (MBa), an engineering and environmental analysis method for gauging the mass of a material flowing through a given system.

The **Claims Framework** sets out the communication strategy rules concerning economic, environmental and social benefit claims, while providing verifiable data sets for BCI members' effective marketing and communications.

Results and Impact refers to the ongoing measurements and monitoring of both positive and negative outcomes that the Better Cotton program delivers. These are geared toward addressing the three critical areas of environmental, social and economic impact and are gathered each growing season from across all farm size-groups. External case studies and independent impact reports have also been commissioned by the program's leadership to gain possible new understanding and ensure a critical evaluation of their work.

BCI's management team, together with IDH, had set some aggressive goals from the get-go, expecting to grow from an output of zero in 2010 to 2.4 million metric tons of Better Cotton lint by 2015 and impacting the livelihoods of some 1 million farmers within that same timeline. This would help bring approximately 2 million hectares of land under BCI cultivation and account for nearly ten percent of worldwide cotton production. Results by the end of 2014 show where the group's challenges lie, having achieved 770 thousand metric tons grown by almost 280,000 producers.

Behind this performance gap lay a shortfall of brand and retailer uptake of Better Cotton. As I discussed with BCI's former senior program manager in India, Anita Chester, this probably had much to do with the fact that a great many brands have no visibility into their fabrics' origins, let alone the source of cotton. Many frankly didn't want the added burden of deeper supply chain transparency. With that said, brand and retailer membership in the BCI has grown significantly from the original four supporting brands to 32 members at time of this writing. Collectively, they represent a full ten percent of global cotton consumption. But of that number, just five are non-European organizations, with four from the U.S. (Nike, VF Corp., Wal-Mart and Carter's) and one from South Africa. Not a single Canadian brand or retailer is a member, though a number of multinational brands who are members do operate in Canada. The team remains upbeat about the opportunities still ahead though, as program Director Ruchira Joshi and I discussed: "The most exciting thing will be getting retailers to buy more of what is being produced as Better Cotton," Ms. Joshi told me. "We are projecting over 2 million metric tonnes produced from the 2014 harvest. It would be a very meaningful step forward to have at least 20 percent of this procured by retailers."

Taken as a whole, the BCI has achieved remarkable structural growth in a relatively short period of time. To IDH and the BCI team's credit, they have continuously evaluated program gaps and been quick to identify critical areas of needed improvement and strategic shift, particularly with regard to entering the developed markets of Australia and the U.S. But, as Ruchira puts it, there's always more to be done.

> "I still think we are moving too slow. Better Cotton offers a standard for sustainability in cotton production, but standards and certification alone cannot be the Holy Grail. Real change takes real collaboration and more open dialogue. It can't be accomplished by carrying out a box-ticking exercise [instead of] changing behaviors, because at the end of the day, that's what sustainability is about — education that leads to behavior change."

For environmental purists Better Cotton may not achieve their impact expectations in the same way organic cotton seems to. However, given that global organic output has seen recent declines (in 2013, it represented less than one percent of world cotton markets), the benefits of Better Cotton should be obvious. The improvements sought are much easier to achieve on a large scale for farmers and program managers, and they do include real societal and environmental benefits. As critical as the reduction of fertilizers and pesticides are, the water-utilization savings the program has wrung out has been even more impressive, especially when one considers that cotton is grown in many countries with threatened water supplies — threats that will only become more acute as the effects of climate change manifest themselves. In the BCI's three largest production countries — China, India and Pakistan — average performance resulted in a 20 percent reduction in water use,

22 percent less pesticide and synthetic fertilizers, a 40 percent increase in organic fertilizers, 15 percent yield improvements and a 40 percent increase in farmer profits. The business, environmental and societal case for program support has been made. For Ruchira, the strength of that case provided the motivation behind her own participation in the initiative: "It is a real example of an entire sector coming together to make change that can be felt at field level. This approach and the equal rights of stakeholders enshrined in the statutes is what made me get behind the initiative."

In my own opinion, there are three key things that need to happen to move Better Cotton's current 4.5 percent market share past the 2015/16 goal of 10 percent toward the program's stated goals of achieving 30 percent of world market by 2020. The first was just announced at time of this writing: the expansion of the program and traceability into fabric mills. This is where it is easiest for brands and retailers to leverage their buying power and the impacts of their own CSR efforts. The second is for significantly more brands and retailers to get on board. The U.S. has some strong momentum considering the volume potential of the American participants to date, but providing financial support in order to share in some of BCI's local environmental and development claims is not the same as ensuring bulk uptake of Better Cotton lint into their supply chain.

More critical mass is needed, and progressive brands and retailers need to step up their game. There is negligible cost impact for them to do so, and, with current cotton prices at about where they were ten years ago, there is little reason not to act. Greater participation will require concerted efforts. A major first step will be to find vendors who will produce their product in accord with the goals and objectives of sourcing departments, which will guarantee fabrics incorporating BCI cotton. Having managed numerous sourcing departments myself, I see no reason why senior management teams cannot, with foresight, easily tie annual performance plans and bonuses to sustainability goals in support of greater Better Cotton commitments. Such commitments do, however, require clearly communicated and continued support from the top of branded retail organizations.

Finally, consumer buying power is what drives retailer action. If you refuse to buy cotton apparel that is not of organic or Better Cotton, if you continually ask for it at the store level and online through social media and company websites and make mention of either organic or Better Cotton when making your purchasing decisions, brands will sit up and take notice. Get behind your values. Small steps such as these do have an accumulative effect. Any one of us, if asked individually, would deplore the use of toxins, the waste and ecological impacts involved in the manufacture of the items we buy. But remember that you make your own buying decisions. You may surprise yourself with your power, but you must first choose to exercise it.

White Gold, Child Labor and Industry Reaction

When most of us hear the term *sustainability*, there is an automatic tendency to think first of environmental impacts, of "green" initiatives and ecology. But in the world of cotton there are also very real human impacts and social outcomes attached to unsustainable industry practices. No case more aptly confronts this reality than in the issues surrounding the battle against child and forced labor in the annual cotton harvests of Uzbekistan.

The Republic of Uzbekistan is a landlocked country in Central Asia with a population of nearly 30 million people. It has an abundance of a handful of resources that have contributed to its relatively high per capital GDP of $US 3,500: minerals, cotton and young people. Along with holding the world's fourth largest reserves of gold and claiming the number five spot for global cotton production (at just under 1 million metric tons collected in 2013), approximately 34 percent of Uzbeks are under the age of 15. Such a youthful population would present monumental challenges to any country.

The cotton crop has been central to the economy of the region since the times of Tsarist Russia, when American supplies of cotton were severely restricted as a consequence of the U.S. Civil War. The pre-Soviet independent khanates of Khiva and Kokand as well as the Bukhara Emirate were literally forced to make up for the disruption and to supply Russia's needs. Since then, cotton has never lost its preeminence as a cash crop in the region.

In recent years, wheat farming has been steadily replacing cotton as the primary agricultural activity of the country, which is a vital sector of the economy, providing nearly 30 percent of all employment in

Uzbekistan. But it is the conflux of cotton — Uzbekistan's "white gold" — and a large, available pool of young people that have put the republic at the center of an ongoing international movement to boycott the country's cotton output.

In its 2014 report, the U.S. Department of Labor's "List of Goods Produced by Child Labor or Forced Labor" details no fewer than 18 countries in which cotton supply chains make significant use of underage workers.[133] Uzbekistan figures prominently in those reports and has appeared on the U.S. State Department's Tier 2 Watchlist of forced labor countries for the past six years. In 2013, a higher, Tier 3 rating was applied.

It was a BBC news exposé in late 2007 that first brought these practices to wide public attention and galvanized the efforts of an amalgamation of responsible investors, labor leaders, civil society and businesses to form the Cotton Campaign. The group's mission since then has been to leverage its advocacy with governments, brands and retailers to pressure the Uzbek government for labor reforms while just as forcefully lobbying consumers and brands to boycott the country's cotton production. A more recently formed group, the Responsible Sourcing Network (RSN) in North America is dedicated to similar goals.

What particularly stands out in Uzbekistan, in comparison to any number of countries with significant child labor abuses, is the extent to which state-level involvement is systemic. The campaign's focus on children is not meant to detract in any way from the horrors of forced labor practices that victimize adults. But the abuse and economic exploitation of children is something that most modern societies find particularly unnerving, though frankly, as we have seen earlier in our reading, it was quite commonplace in both Western Europe and North America up to and even beyond the turn of the century.

The ability of the Uzbek government to forcibly mobilize millions of citizens over the years has rested on the structure of the country's cotton industry. (This included, not inconsequently, upwards of a million children between 12 and 18 years of age.) The government has dominated the entire value chain of cotton production in Uzbekistan in large part to maintain a grip on tax revenues generated by the trade. These have provided a good deal of the funding for key national development efforts focused on food and energy security.

The Cotton Campaign had already spent three years working tirelessly on brand and government advocacy efforts by the time Patricia Jurewicz, a former manager at The Gap, took her first steps toward getting the RSN off the ground in 2010. She had, in her own words, left the corporate world and "decided to work on the for-benefit side, the term I prefer to use over nonprofit, because outside of a single corporation I have the opportunity to influence and shift an entire industry."

Patricia had spent the previous four years working on corporate responsibility programs with As You Sow, a California-based shareholder and civic advocacy group dedicated to the promotion of environmental and corporate social responsibility. RSN operates as a program under As You Sow's engagement initiatives. Earlier in her career she had leveraged her project management skills at the Institute for Agriculture and Trade Policy into a role with The Gap. There, she led internal efforts at the brand to rewrite their vendor handbook, providing guidance to some 3,000 supplier facilities.

With the support of a small research team and an advisory board of execs from Calvert Investments, The Gap and "1% for the Planet," RSN has built on Cotton Campaign's earlier efforts to educate the market and hold brands more accountable. For the past five years, she and her colleagues have worked to position the "Company Pledge Against Child and Adult Forced Labor in Uzbek Cotton," known as The Pledge, as the principal market vehicle for documenting clear commitments from brands not to use Uzbek cotton. To date, more than 130 brands and retailers internationally have signed off on The Pledge.

This effort added significant weight to building multinational condemnation against the regime in Uzbekistan; the ILO, the U.N. and European trade bodies had already registered their censure. Additionally, in 2013 both the American Apparel and Footwear Association and the Retail Council of Canada, representing a broad membership of American and Canadian retailers, had signed onto a letter directed to the Bangladesh Garment Manufacturers and Exporters Association (BGMEA). The letter expressed concerns about media reports regarding major purchases by Bangladesh of Uzbek cotton. These concerted marketplace pressures, taken together with Uzbekistan's requests for multilateral financial assistance in support of its development agenda, have achieved some important progress — if only recently.

"There are millions of people in the world working as forced laborers or child laborers under abhorrent conditions," Patricia told me. "Consumers, as well as companies, do not want their clothing or other everyday goods to support this type of exploitation."

From 2013 through the 2014 cotton harvest season, gradual yet measurable reductions in the use of children below the age of 15 were noted. The government's earlier conscription efforts however, were shifting the burden onto other levels of society. High school children as young as 15, teachers and public servants in a variety of state enterprises were still being forced to work long hours throughout the harvest season for very little pay. To add insult to injury, deductions were made for the meager food and transportation provided to the gangs of pressed labor. Aside from the direct negative effects of harsh working and unsanitary living conditions, tens of thousands of hours of education had been lost, with 50–60 percent of school teachers absent from classes while attending to compulsory harvest quotas, which ranged from 30–60 kilos per day per person.[135]

Signing up to the RSN's pledge is a good first step for retailers and brands who want to ensure their garments don't contain cotton from unethical sources in those 18 countries cited by the U.S. Department of Labor, but it is, admittedly, a limited step. The Pledge itself only asks for signatories to "not knowingly" procure goods with Uzbek cotton in them. As the vast majority of brands don't pre-select preferred fabric suppliers or purchase textiles directly for their manufacturing vendors, most don't have the level of visibility needed to verify origin. Even this minimal commitment was initially dismissed by the senior execs I reported to at Joe Fresh in the late summer and fall of 2013 when, on two separate occasions, I recommended signing up as the first step of a wider sustainability strategy I had tabled. It wasn't until the Canadian press reported on the 2013 harvest later in October of that year that explicitly called out Joe Fresh's parent company that they reacted and agreed to sign up.[138] Beyond that step, however, there was little interest in making any further efforts at looking more deeply into cotton or supply chain transparency. I was, in fact, warned against it. There are still a good many brands and retailers across North America, Europe and Australasia that have yet to take even this simple step.

Patricia was guardedly optimistic about the shifting sensibilities in the industry when we talked about the continuing challenges beyond this first level of recognizing the problem.

> "I am optimistic, but the change is taking much longer and is less widespread than what is needed. I am optimistic because we have seen *some* changes over the years and there are a few examples of companies that *really* know how to do it right. Unfortunately, there is still excessive forced overtime, which is typically underpaid. Factory workers continue to work in unsafe buildings and are exposed to toxic chemicals. Beyond the first-tier supplier and in some cases the second tier, labor conditions deteriorate drastically. If a factory, facility, or farm cannot be directly tied to a brand name and is not part of an accountability or certification scheme, there is minimal accountability or verification of basic labor standards."

In response to concerns with this lack of visibility and given the reality that so many brands simply don't make the effort to look beyond the garment factory, RSN has been working to provide business the tools they need to expand their assurance and minimize risks.

> According to Patricia, "Right now we are underway to create a platform to verify that cotton yarn spinners and mills are only using ethically-sourced cotton. This will give assurances to home goods and apparel brands that their cotton products are clean of slave-labor. I am committed to creating transparent and accountable systems in the middle of the value chain that will drive the market away from cotton or other raw materials harvested or mined with immoral and foul practices."

There are good reasons to be concerned. Let's first of all recall that the majority, if not all, of the brands and retailers that have now signed The Pledge have both codes of conduct and CSR programs in place, which they claim make them ethical, responsible corporate members of society. Yet to claim so and know that your primary source of product raw materials may well carry inherent risks from environmental degradation or child and forced labor without taking any action whatsoever to verify a "clean" source of supply is simply disingenuous. And if we, as the purchasing public, turn a blind eye or plead ignorance to these practices, then shame on us.

To better understand what brands do or know with regard to visibility into cotton sources, RSN carried out a membership survey intent on laying bare the level of transparency in cotton supply chains. Or, it would perhaps better be said, to lay bare what members were willing to share and what they weren't. Of 130 brands and retailers who signed The Pledge, only 50 companies returned the survey. This is a less-than-stellar number of companies (only 38 percent) who were willing to disclose information on their cotton visibility practices, even after having signed on to The Pledge.

The following data summarizes the findings of the 28-page survey report:[139]

Company Policy on Uzbek Cotton:
+ 20 percent have no policy at all.
+ 32 percent have a well-defined public policy.
+ 48 percent have signed The Pledge and have an internal policy.

Supplier Code of Conduct:
+ 4 percent have no Code of Conduct at all.
+ 75 percent have a code that applies to garment suppliers.
+ 21 percent have a code that applies to garment and mill suppliers.

Disclosure of Uzbek Policy Progress:
+ 67 percent do not publicly disclose policy progress.
+ 2 percent fully disclose policy progress.
+ 31 percent provide limited disclosure on progress.

Disclosure of Company Suppliers:
+ 45 percent disclose country-level information only.
+ 43 percent do not disclose any supplier information.
+ 12 percent disclose country/name of cut and sew suppliers.

Active Stakeholder Uzbek Engagement:
+ 35 percent not engaged in any stakeholder engagement.

+ 43 percent participate in RSN's Economic Leverage Workgroup.
+ 22 percent have signed onto industry letter, attended one event.

Active Cotton Spinner Engagement:

+ 71 percent do not have any spinner-level engagement.
+ 10 percent participate in RSN's spinner engagement efforts.
+ 19 percent engage individually or through other initiatives.

Policy Communications Regarding Ban on Uzbek Cotton:

+ 29 percent have not communicated their policy to suppliers.
+ 57 percent have sent a policy letter to suppliers.
+ 8 percent require supplier compliance/provide training.
+ 6 percent require compliance by contract/provide training.

Require Cotton Origin Declaration

+ 60 percent do not require suppliers to provide origin data.
+ 40 percent require suppliers to provide origin data.

Traceability/Spinner Verification:

+ 70 percent have no type of traceability/verification in place.
+ 24 percent are in the process of implementing a system.
+ 6 percent have fully implemented traceability in place.

Spinner/Mill Audit Program:

+ 80 percent do not require any type of spinner/mill audit.
+ 2 percent require spinners/mills to provide self-assessment.
+ 6 percent perform their own audit of spinners/mills.
+ 12 percent accept independent spinner/mill audits.

Disclosure of Audit Data:

+ 53 percent provide no disclosure at all.
+ 47 percent publish aggregated audit data.

Assuming, first of all, that survey data of this type is factual, the summary paints a rather bleak picture of fabric and raw material visibility. The following takeaways are most telling:

+ 80 percent of respondents carry out no auditing of any sort at the spinner/mill level.

+ 70 percent have no traceability or verification system in place at spinner/mill level.

+ 60 percent do not require spinners to disclose origins of cotton.

+ 29 percent do not communicate their policy on Uzbek cotton to suppliers.

+ 71 percent have no engagement activities with spinners/mills.

+ 88 percent do not disclose any information about their suppliers.

+ 67 percent do not address progress on Uzbekistan policies/practices.

+ 80 percent do not extend their Code of Conduct down to spinner/ mill level.

+ 20 percent have no policy on Uzbek cotton at all.

Remembering that only 130 brands and retailers worldwide have taken even the first step of making The Pledge's low-level commitment to not *knowingly* use Uzbek cotton, and considering that China, Bangladesh and India are among the largest of the country's export clients, chances are very good that Uzbek cotton has made its way into mainstream European and North American markets. This is even more likely with the active participation in Uzbek cotton industries of some major global commodity players. According to Cotton Campaign, these include OLAM (Singapore), Cargill Cotton (U.K.), Otto Stadtlander GmbH (Germany), Daewoo International Corporation (Korea), ECOM Agroindustrial (Switzerland), Dunavant S.A. (Switzerland), and Paul Reinhart AG (Switzerland).[140]

As important as addressing systemic issues in Uzbekistan is, we should be as deeply concerned with cotton supplies from *all* countries that have been documented and identified as users of child and forced labor. From multiple perspectives then — human rights, reputational risk, international labor agreements, financial market risk, environmental impacts — the logic of extending stakeholder traceability and assessments into fabric, yarn and cotton supplies is overwhelmingly self-evident.

Considering all the levels of verification, assessment and auditing — of sew factories, cotton plantations, working conditions, fabric mills, dye houses, etc. — being expected of brands and retailers, it is a fair question to ask whether outsourced manufacturing can ever *really* be cost-effective, beneficial and risk-free.

It is a very good question, and one we shall come back to in the closing chapter of this book as we look in detail at a number of initiatives, innovations and leadership approaches to resolving the growing web of difficulties threatening to catch the apparel and textile trades in its trap. For the moment, let's just say that these expectations *are not just now* being demanded by society. They are the same rules of the game that any responsible manufacturer operating within developed markets must play by. They are the same ones that those people who purposefully shed jobs, closed down factories and decimated communities ran away from, arguably for the simple reason of unburdening themselves and their margins from the true total costs of production. I emphasize *people* here over *companies* for good reason. Corporations, which have been given the dubious legal fiction of being recognized as persons independent of shareholders or management,[141] do not in fact make any decisions at all; real people do. As I did. And by dealing with individuals, we stand the best chance of driving real change in existing systems. Recognizing personal responsibility can be a strong motivator, indeed.

Turning over a New Leaf: Supply Chain Transparency

For Lisa Drewe and the team at New Leaf Practice in the quaint Wiltshire village of Bishops Cannings, some 40 kilometers from Bristol, England, as the crow flies, driving those system changes means getting an early start on the day.

"We wake up to emails and calls from the Far East from the suppliers of our European clients. Before breakfast, we wade through details of factory locations in China, ethical audit reports and delivery notes and certificates supplied to endorse a chain of custody," Lisa told me when I asked about the typical work day for the team. "Before coffee, our European retailer and supplier clients get to work. They want to know how their suppliers are performing, what claims they can make about their products, how many are meeting their sourcing requirements, when is a good day to train their staff or suppliers, or information on emerging trends in legislation, materials and supply chains."

New Leaf is one of a very few sustainability consulting practices with a focus on responsible supply chains that has developed a deep, web-based transparency platform for ensuring product traceability. As part of a full range of responsible supply chain services that help track some 30,000 products from over 300 suppliers, New Leaf's data systems help their client base to track real-time ethical and sustainability data globally against regulatory and voluntary standards. Lisa explained the next evolution of their system for me:

> "We are currently testing our market-leading digital platform that manages all sustainable supply chain data for organizations striving to gain full transparency and understand the stories of their products. Once we have road tested this with multinational organizations and specialists teams, we will be launching it later in the year. We are excited because for the first time companies will be able to gather information from their suppliers, upload it, analyze it and use the dashboard reports and visualized supply chain maps to truly bring the information to life and make it relevant to the operational and strategic business decisions in sourcing, suppliers, product portfolios and marketing."

This is part of what New Leaf refers to as "natural intelligence" — the data sets and actionable information clients use not simply to follow products from raw materials to customer shelves, but more importantly to drive problem-solving and better business planning. I asked Lisa to talk more about the drivers behind this understanding of data.

> "We do this through providing greater transparency by tracing products and their components back to where they came out of the ground or ocean and following them all of the way to where the life of the product ends. Along this journey, we identify the real impacts on the environment and people — both good and bad and provide the evidence to support it. We call *this* natural intelligence. The big realization for me was that where nature is being destroyed, so are cultures, people's livelihood and their quality of lives. I now feel as passionately about the social

and ethical side of our work as I do about the environment. It is all connected."

Their clients run the gamut, from government entities like the
U.K.'s Department for Environment, Food & Rural Affairs to NGOs
such as the WWF and Global Forest & Trade Network, to leading
retailers Marks & Spencer, Sainsbury's and B&Q. New Leaf founding
directors Charles and Lisa Drewe head up a team of communications,
training and project management professionals dedicated to making
an impact on commercial supply chains globally.

As Lisa put it, "We love the natural world, we are part of it, we
play in it, and are alive because of it. We want to protect it, and after
we thought hard about the greatest threats to the natural world, we
distilled the root-causes down to overconsumption and irresponsible
sourcing and supply chains. We felt that we could and should focus
on the latter and support others who are picking up the gauntlet and
wanting to do something about it too — the responsible retailers and
manufacturers, the NGOs who are highlighting the issues and the
legislators."

The range of their consulting efforts aims at closing the loop on
addressing these challenges and is built around supplier and strategy
management, business intelligence and product lifecycle management.
The New Leaf team begins by targeting critical sustainability hotspots
in a client's supply chain through the successive stages of a product's
life. They can drill down on a product's specific issue-type challenges,
such as water or carbon footprints, or approach the project's impact
from a macro-level evaluation of challenges like pollution, ecosystem
services or land usage. And, like some of their peers in the industry,
they are cautiously optimistic about the direction business is moving
— something heard with growing regularity in the past three to five
years.

Lisa puts it this way, "When we see our clients reporting a 750 percent increase in products verified as meeting a positive environmental
attribute after five years of working with them, we know that our journey so far has been worthwhile. We are cautious optimists. Optimistic
because we love the promise of the circular economy and net-posi-
tive, along with an explosion of standards, policies, legislation and

innovations. Cautious, though, because we are running out of time, and this new way of thinking and designing products has a long way to go before they are mainstreamed. *The starting point, though, is always transparency.* Before any business can understand the impacts of its supply chains and products and what it can do to remove or reduce them, it firstly has to know what's in its products, where they have come from, who made them etc. *To be honest, currently so few businesses do have this information.* If we are to continue sourcing from faraway places using complex supply chains we do need this transparency — before, back in the day, we knew where our stuff was coming from and who made it within a few miles' radius because we could see it with our own eyes. With our longer supply chains, we need different tools. Of course the length and complexity of supply chains does raise a much bigger question about future opportunities."

Based on the findings of the Responsible Sourcing Network's brand and retailer survey as one small starting point for the apparel industry, there would seem no lack of opportunity or need for just such a supply chain traceability tool. What has been missing more than anything to date has been the will of senior decision-makers to address visibility and risk gaps. This is perhaps an area where the responsible investment community, risk-adverse financial markets and government regulatory authority might best be applied. Looking only at the knowledge that we as end users and customers of brands have accumulated throughout this book, we cannot simply assume that business decision-makers are always doing the right thing. Certainly, they cannot even be aware of issues if they aren't looking at them!

Global Shipping's Case for Action: Sustainability = Survival

Those longer supply chains Lisa made mention of also come with challenges that we might not consider to be a large part of the sustainability equation when talking about consumer products like apparel. Transportation factors, for example, are sometimes left out of the equation, but they offer some interesting opportunities — not only to reduce petroleum use and carbon emissions but also to generate substantial cost savings, thus incentivizing business to take action. A focus on shipping may also help to lower adverse environmental fallout on marine life in the oceans, which provide the highways for much of the global apparel trade. Both macro-level shipping industry initiatives aimed at addressing these types of impacts as well as company-specific efforts are worth reviewing as benchmarks of what is possible.

About 90 percent of the world's international trade takes place across oceans, making the global shipping industry a key stakeholder in addressing sustainable solutions for a wide range of consumer products, from bulk grains and foodstuffs, to automobiles and oil, and our textiles and apparel. Estimates put the impact of CO_2 emissions alone from the more than 100,000 ocean-going vessels currently in operation around the world at three to four percent of global output. This is nearly double the amount produced by the aviation industry, and comes as a negative result of the significant recent growth in global trade patterns.

Between 1990 and 2008, total ton-miles of international cargo (literally, tons of goods per mile moved) doubled, adding significantly to carbon, sulfur and nitrogen air pollution. Among the other negative impacts of global shipping identified by the WWF are the transfer of invasive alien species into new ecosystems, the dumping of waste and sewage at sea, risks from accidental spills and threats to natural habitats in and around ports.[142]

In 2011, Forum for the Future, the U.K.-based nonprofit behind the London Sustainability Exchange; Farming Futures; and Green Futures magazine released their Case for Action report on behalf of the newly formed Sustainable Shipping Initiative (SSI). In it, they put forward a compelling case for the global shipping industry to collaborate on sustainability initiatives within the SSI's framework, bringing together leading shipping lines, the WWF and the Forum. This was not simply a philanthropic or communications-driven exercise but rather a pragmatic effort to help ocean transportation leaders to look beyond the current state of affairs to a distant point some 30 years away.

A number of significant ship owners and operators are now members of the group, including Maersk Line, Carnival Corporation, China Navigation Company, Bunge, Gearbulk, IMC, Rio Tinto Marine, and U-Ming Marine Transport Corporation. According to Alastair Fischbacher, chief executive with the Initiative in London, shipping line interest in getting behind the organization has been picking up steadily since its launch: "Yes, there has been increased interest. We are having a lot more enquiry and a far wider dialogue with companies large and small, with other associations and organizations and with entrepreneurs since we launched the Case for Action and Vision 2040. We are open to approaches from leading companies and organizations that not only subscribe to the vision but are also willing to actively work toward it and share knowledge and experience."

The SSI is also actively on the lookout for additional partnerships that can add value to ongoing discussions within the industry including NGOs, academics, entrepreneurs and technology providers. While the organization itself hasn't put forward a particular standard for sustainable shipping, its website offers tools that enable stakeholders to compare a variety of existing schemes online. Among the better known are Business for Social Responsibility's (BSR) Clean Cargo Working Group, the North American Green Marine certification standard and the Clean Shipping Index.

Projecting global trends that were likely to affect the industry's operating sphere well into the future, the SSI's Case for Action identified critical challenges to the shipping industry community. Their hope was that through foresight and collaborative efforts, leadership companies would be able to begin a genuine discussion on how best to agree on a coordinated agenda of action.

Global Impact Trends

The Global Economy and Shifting Patterns of Trade. Relative power within global trade relationships was beginning to shift toward the developing world. SSI projected potential risks to recent growth that might well threaten ongoing trade, including increased protectionism, closed-loop economies and increased online trade in digital products.

New Models of Ocean Governance. The changing rules of the game with regard to multinational ocean management had led to a complex network of regulatory and voluntary standards — and things may well continue to gravitate in that direction. Without a robust international maritime organization able to firmly take matters in hand, SSI's fear was that a multi-class system would emerge of high and low performing companies.

Operational Transparency. The increased rapidity of modern communications, social media and technology was putting pressure on clients and stakeholders outside of the shipping industry to adapt to new expectations for supply chain transparency. The SSI advocated for early engagement with civil society, government and client networks because that would allow leaders to help define how deep these expectations for transparency might go.

An Uncertain Energy Future. Future growth within the industry could not be staked on easily available, low-cost fuel. Price variations were becoming increasingly volatile and unpredictable. Tensions were on the rise in geographies that had historically provided much of the world's oil, as pressure also mounted to bring alternative energies on line.

Increased Sustainability Regulation. A host of issues over and above traditional regulatory ones may well impact operating environments — from greater social and labor accountability to closed-loop resource systems and recycling efforts.

Making Technology Pay. Technology was highlighted as an area that offered opportunities to significantly drive sustainability improvements in everything from efficient ship design to transparency, energy and materials. It is also an area of great potential for the generation of cost savings tied to high tech.

Climate Adaption. A drive to reduce emissions is a logical first step for the industry. Additional climate adaption challenges also emerge when considering potential climactic effects on coastlines and port areas. Changing ocean currents, flooding and the increased number and severity of hurricanes and tropical storms all have the potential to impact the industry.

To address the challenges that Forum researchers had identified for SSI members and leadership meant that the organization would need to first develop and then articulate a way forward. They seem to have recognized this in the Initiative's publicly stated vision: "Radical changes in the external operating environment explored in our Case for Action indicate an urgent need to reshape the way in which shipping business is conducted."[144]

The values and aspirations tied to this vision statement offer some powerful commitments from the shipping community members who stand behind the statement. SSI members followed up with their

Vision 2040 document, projecting the group's goals and objectives for the future. It speaks to the energy mix changes that are needed to dramatically cut greenhouse gases as well as the importance of working to earn reputations as trusted members of the communities within which they operate. They have commited themselves to the safety, security and health of their workers. Depending on the oceans for their livelihoods, SSI members accept responsibility for their proper governance while recognizing the value that transparency and accountability in operating practices provides. And importantly, they have focused on the critical role that developing financial models holds in the arena of much-needed investments in technology and innovation.

Mr. Fischbacher mapped out the Initiative's near-term focus for me: "In the context of the progress to Vision 2040, we are just a couple of years down the path and we are on track. However, we cannot assume that this is good enough, and we are still looking to accelerate progress toward our Vision 2040 so that, if anything, it is achieved earlier.

"We review our activities in the context of the Vision, the megatrends that we identified in the Case for Action and against the roadmap that we have developed. We also are scanning the horizon, both in the shipping industry and other industry sectors, for the weaker signals of change that may affect the shipping industry, and we are reviewing the development of the mega-trends to track progress — again, information on both of these will be made public during this year."

Their commitment to keep members and the public apprised of progress and their awareness of the importance of such transparency is laudable as a benchmark that other industry associations might learn from. And, in the short term, by announcing a program clearly tying financial benefits to the retrofitting of older vessels along with environmental objectives, they have validated the adage for members that doing good is indeed good for business.

The potential financial benefits are certainly one reason why a number of brands and retailers have made transportation an area of attention within corporate responsibility plans. Hard sustainability benefits as well as bottom line savings can be wrung out of a focus on shipping practices, be they by land, sea or air. It is also an area in which most apparel and retailing organizations have at least some level of direct control and responsibility.

That said, the international transportation and store-level distribution of apparel products is complex (especially for fashion-driven brands with a limited full-price sell-through date). The supply chain is fraught with conflict between least impact and cost on the one hand and quickest turn time on the other. Resolving these conflicts is no easy feat, but for those brands that do it best, the rewards are two-fold: credible sustainability claims and improved bottom lines. H&M is one retailer that has been able to manage this dynamic with a good deal of success as part and parcel of their wider responsible supply chain strategy. U.S. and Canadian brands that have recently targeted entry into European markets would do well to closely examine H&M as the benchmark they will be measured against.

A Distinctly Scandinavian Approach

With 132,000 employees worldwide and some 3,500 stores across 55 markets at the end of 2014, Sweden's H&M has positioned itself as the sustainable fast-fashion leader. It had proved a stellar year for the retailer; it added 16,000 new jobs while opening 356 new stores as aggressive expansion pushed it into China and the U.S. This drove sales increases of 18 percent from the year before, to just over $US 18.3 billion.[145]

That growth also puts the organization under the spotlight, and so it has worked hard to integrate social and environmental sustainability into its operating strategy. From opening its skills development Centre of Excellence in Bangladesh (together with the ILO and the Swedish Development Agency [SIDA]), to rolling out the H&M Conscious campaign with activist actress Olivia Wilde, it has also proved a banner year for the group on the engagement front. CEO Karl-Johan Persson spoke eloquently as keynote speaker at that year's Business for Social Responsibility's conference in New York; he spoke about the importance of transparency in the industry's efforts toward transformation. He committed H&M to taking an active and engaged role in supporting that change and has followed up words with actions.

He met personally with heads of government in two key H&M production centers, Bangladesh and Cambodia, to move discussions ahead regarding living wages for offshore workers. The company's much-reported move into Africa and Ethiopia specifically committed significant resources to the region's development, while the H&M Conscious Foundation targeted youth and women's opportunities there with funding for social entrepreneurs. They are also one of a very small handful of global brands that openly publish their entire supplier list by country, facility and address on their website. Transparency is not just a sound bite for them.

On the materials front, they maintained their spot as the world's number one consumer of organic cotton while also continuing their hands-on participation in the Better Cotton Initiative. The recent launch of the Better Mill project in collaboration with European brands Bestseller, Primark, C&A and New Look, and the active participation of Dutch NGO Solidaridad, continue to leave U.S. and Canadian retailers in the proverbial dust when it comes to pushing on-the-ground change.

Emma Goodman, with Solidaridad's U.S. team, filled me in with further details: "In partnership with H&M and other major retailers, Solidaridad developed the Better Mill Initiative (BMI) as an integrated sustainability improvement program for the textile wet processing sector in China. BMI promotes sustainable production in 50 mills in the key textile sourcing areas of the Yangtze and Pearl River Deltas. The initiative builds upon and contributes to existing standards and tools, specifically the (Sustainable Apparel Coalition's) HIGG Index and ZDHC (Zero Discharge of Hazardous Chemicals)."

The wet processing facilities targeted in South China are in areas that have suffered significantly in the past due to poor enforcement of industry environmental standards. (Remember the Fountain Set story?) Energy and chemical management, water use, solid waste reductions, emission and effluent flows have all been targeted in factory-level improvement projects that joint teams are already tackling.

"The core of the program," according to Emma, "is improving the production process through the 'cleaner production' paradigm, including resource efficiency, pollution prevention and control, chemical management and social needs. It identifies challenges that cannot be overcome at the factory level alone, and facilitates dialogue to address common challenges."

H&M's focus on logistics and supply chain operations specifically targets reductions in greenhouse gas emissions, as do efforts within

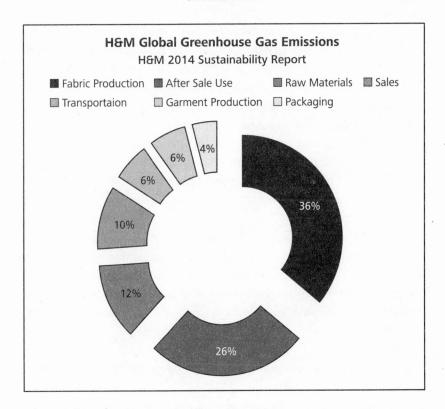

H&M Global Greenhouse Gas Emissions
H&M 2014 Sustainability Report

■ Fabric Production   ■ After Sale Use   ■ Raw Materials   ■ Sales
□ Transportaion   □ Garment Production   □ Packaging

their stores and head office locations. Product lifecycle assessments have provided the retailer with a clear understanding of where these emissions originate.

In earlier assessment years, it had been surprising to find that nearly one half of all carbon emissions were coming from transportation stages — getting goods from overseas factories into the H&M stores. This drove changes in the configuration of shipping methods toward a greater focus on the use of ferry and rail services versus trucking. More intelligent transportation planning and IT systems also allowed for more goods to by-pass intermediary warehousing and thus ship floor-ready direct to retail locations. Requirements were also put in place calling on ocean shipping partners to be registered with the Clean Shipping Index, one of the voluntary standards listed on the Sustainable Shipping Initiative's website.

In those cases where trucking was still used, the company provided driver training and ensured than no vehicles older than ten years old were being used. U.S. roadway logistics providers must now be partners under the U.S. Environmental Protection Agency's SmartWay program as well. The cost savings and CO_2 reductions have been significant.

More recent efforts have now pushed down into manufacturing with the advent of the Supplier Energy Efficiency Programme (SEEP). Both vendor contracts and financial incentives are being used to motivate participation in the effort, as H&M moves deeper into their supply chain (and they have plans to fully map and audit fabric mills as well). So far, vendors representing nearly 40 percent of purchases now participate in SEEP, reducing energy requirements (as measured per piece of apparel) by 12 percent over a three-year period. H&M is keeping up the pace of vendor engagement, and results from this attention to detail begin to add up. While bringing down emissions and energy utilization, the retailer drove a 17 percent increase in its gross profit for 2014, which finished the year at an enviable 40 percent. As I have long argued with colleagues in top-line sales-driven companies, I'll take an additional point of margin wrung out by efficiencies over increased sales any day. We just need to be sure than an equitable share of profits goes back into manufacturing investments and living wages for those who do the "heavy lifting."

This focus on the reduction of emissions, derived primarily from petroleum-dependent energy is no doubt a good thing. But, at time of this writing, global oil prices have fallen to levels not seen since 2009 (though still well above 2001 lows) as the Middle East and Western producers engage in a price war. This has provided the average citizen with benefits at the gas pump, but it challenges sustainability efforts by making oil cheaper for us all, with the result that we tend to use more of it. From an apparel and textile perspective, oil is a significant contributor to environmental problems — beyond the direct use of energy. It is also embedded in many of our everyday fabrics, most notably in manmade ones, like polyester and nylon.

Oil, Emissions and Energy

Counter-intuitively, it seems that yoga and casual sports aficionados have helped propel 100 percent + growth in the use of manmade textiles over the past 15 years, exponentially driving environmental degradation while pursuing their healthy activities. Polyester and nylon, two of the most widely used activewear fabrics, are petroleum-based plastic polymers, which are non-renewable, non-biodegradable crude oil byproducts. But the impacts don't end there. Energy consumption multiplies over the lifecycle of such fabrics, beginning with the extraction of oil. If the resource is tar sands or shale-based, the emissions generated during extraction and processing of the material increases by 12–22 percent.

Global polyester fabric production alone uses 70 million barrels of oil annually. To put this in perspective, one standard domestic barrel of U.S. crude contains some 42 gallons (159 liters) of oil. According to U.S. energy giant Chevron, this is enough to provide base material for 39 polyester shirts.[149] So, when wearing your favorite poly golf shirt or wicking tennis tee, you're wearing about a gallon of crude oil derivative wrapped about your body.

Even more energy gets used and emissions generated in processing into the actual fibers. According to data from the U.S. Energy Information Agency, the domestic textile industry is the country's fifth largest emitter of CO_2, producing approximately 20 pounds of the gas per ton of fiber versus the 3.7 pounds per ton tied to cotton production. In the case of nylon, processing also gives off significant amounts of toxic nitrous oxide, a greenhouse gas byproduct that is 300 times more potent than CO_2, with a lengthy atmospheric life of 120 years.

Significant amounts of lubricant-heavy wastewater are also produced during the finishing of both fabrics which, if untreated, have detrimental effect on local hydrological systems. And other downcycle water impacts may have even more serious repercussions. The base plastic polymer used to produce polyester is polyethylene terephthalate, or PET, the same material used to make plastic bottles. A rather unfortunate part of the chemistry of PET production is the use of a catalyst called antimony. This substance is a highly carcinogenic toxin, especially dangerous to the liver, lungs, skin and heart which, if inhaled over prolonged periods, causes chronic bronchitis and emphysema. Through the processing of PET, the antimony becomes chemically bonded to its polymers. According to the chemical industry and the U.S. Agency for Toxic Substances and Disease Registry, the antimony becomes so deeply locked to PET polymers that it cannot be absorbed into the body, and so does not cause a risk concern to human health.[150]

One needs a very strong belief in the science of chemistry to buy into such reassurances.

A greater risk, however, presents itself earlier upstream, during dyeing and finishing stages, when antimony is exposed to extremely high temperatures, which can cause it to leach into processed wastewater. If not properly treated before being expelled into local watersheds and river systems, this industrial waste can cause irreparable damage to ecosystems and human or wildlife drinking water. And all this to perspire a little easier when reaching for that "downward dog" or a rapid backhand!

There is, unfortunately, almost no end to the examples and anecdotes reflective of the negative community and ecosystem impacts that industry in general has wrought on our shared planet. And in the sizeable wake left by globalization, it seems inevitable that these physical environments are overwhelmingly those of nations still struggling with often profound political, societal and economic development issues.

Yes, there are those in the mainstream fast fashion and branded apparel world who have mapped a better way forward and those who have had, like me, their own moments of epiphany leading them to challenge the status quo, but they are for the most part still a group of outliers. Industry cannot and should not do this on its own, though to some extent I do agree with those who say it is only the organizational power and expertise of global business that can move the market to change.

But depending on and surrendering responsibility and power to profit-driven markets cannot be the chief drivers of change. And when organizations of any type — governments, unions, businesses, religions — grow too large, the individual ceases to matter as they once did, ceases to claim responsibility and power for their own decisions. For that reason, I believe that just as important as it has been to understand the historic context of these industries, to dissect recent challenges and examine what industry programs have begun to do to block and tackle some of the most pressing needs, it is just as important to look with hope and expectation at what might happen if we put people — ourselves and those around us — back at the center of responsibility for our actions. There are many inspirational stories, individual and collaborative, to tell.

5

Aid for Trade

ON DECEMBER 19, 2003, only weeks after I had visited the facility, Kenya's President Mwai Kibaki and His Highness the Aga Khan, spiritual leader of the world's 20 million Shia Ismaili Muslims, presided over the inauguration of the Alltex EPZ apparel facility just outside of Nairobi. As chairman of the Aga Khan Fund for Economic Development (AKFED), His Highness had attended to give a speech reinforcing the history and logic behind establishing the fund's local operating arm, Industrial Promotion Services (ISP), back in 1963.

I had spent considerable time over the previous months working with a small team at Sara Lee Branded Apparel discussing polo shirt production with ISP's managing director for East Africa, Lutaf Kassam. The new factory effort was a joint venture between ISP and Qatar-based Global Readymade Garments, who had purpose-built the $US 7 million export facility to take advantage of the AGOA (African Growth and Opportunity Act) trade deal and duty-free access to U.S. markets. A specific brand within Sara Lee's stable was looking to partner with Alltex and allocate significant volumes of knitted polo shirt production as the facility geared up. If a deal could be struck, they would get big volumes from the get-go to help get sewing lines up and running at full capacity, and their potential U.S. client would be strategically securing a new duty-free supply.

As President Kibaki would speak to at the opening, which occurred only a week following the celebrations of Kenya's 40th year of independence, Alltex would bring local Kenyans 2,000 new jobs, daycare and medical facilities and new industrial training opportunities. But it would be the Aga Khan's comments that I would pay closest attention

to that day. He spoke of the developing countries in which his foundation was operating and of what constituted, in his viewpoint, true
quality of life. This was something, he insisted, beyond the measures
typically used by economists and aid industries: World Bank indica-
tors, economic welfare, GDP rates, longevity and the like.

"'The meaning of quality of life," he said "extends to the entire ethical
and social context in which people live, and not only to their material well-being measured over generation after generation. AKFED,
the entity that oversees and invests in projects such as Alltex, is neither a charitable foundation, nor a vehicle for the personal wealth of
the Ismaili Imam of the time. It is a for-profit, international development agency that, because of its institutional background and social
conscience, invests in countries, sectors and projects, on criteria far different from those of a straightforward commercial investor. Investment
decisions are based more on the prospects for better lives for the con-
stituencies of people that will be impacted by the investments and
their results rather than on bottom line profitability."[151]

It was a moving and impressive speech, and I had no doubt it was
very sincerely given. But it struck me as at odds with what was actually
transpiring in many developing countries at the time — and which
is still at play today. My question was, was Aid for Trade (discussed
below) simply a misrepresented concept being used as the window
dressing for expanding international trade agreements that on the surface seem to benefit wealthy country companies and consumers at the
expense of the poor?

Winners & Losers: NAFTA's Experience

In April, 2014, coinciding with the one-year anniversary of the Rana
Plaza collapse, the U.S. Congressional Research Service published
"NAFTA at 20: Overview and Trade Effects"; it was meant to high-
light the trade pact's benefits.

The report did a fantastic job in giving economic data on a host of
measures, among them foreign direct investment positions, NAFTA
trade partner volumes by manufacturing category, and trade balances
in private services among the three nations that signed the historic agreement. Historic, as the report noted, because it was the first
example of a major trading-nation agreement with both labor and

environmental sidebar commitments written in. But what was not included in the report was something more telling. Within its 36 pages, there was no hard or measurable data whatsoever regarding the employment impacts and relocation of millions of Canadian and U.S. manufacturing jobs south, into Mexico. To be fair, slightly more than half a page of the report was allotted to detail these side agreements themselves (the Agreement on Labor Cooperation and the Agreement on Environmental Cooperation), but there was no analysis committed to real people, community impacts, dislocation and social erosion.

The report did discuss the failures of NAFTA to achieve what had long been sold as one of its primary goals and benefits: helping to close the growing gap of income disparities between Mexico and its northern neighbors. The often-spoken-of economic convergence simply did not materialize; the trade benefits touted by NAFTA proponents had failed to significantly improve life for the average Mexican. There were certainly some economic and social benefits realized, but these were, as it often the case with such trade deals, unevenly distributed to far too few people.

In principle, the policy of Aid for Trade (AfT) offers some significant benefits for developing countries by promising long-term improvements in the capacity of local businesses to take advantage of foreign trade opportunities (read: export more goods) by applying short-term structural and economic assistance from the governmental level on down, meaning opening one's markets in exchange for development assistance and the promise of those greater export jobs and governmental income. As the 2006 WTO Task Force on Aid for Trade put it, "Aid for Trade is about assisting developing countries to increase exports of goods and services, to integrate into the multilateral trading system, and to benefit from liberalized trade and increased market access."[152]

Aid and Apparel: Unlikely Bedfellows

The logical question is this: have increased levels of foreign trade between a growing number of countries significantly contributed toward not only economic growth (as is the policy's mantra), but also *equitable* economic growth and distribution of benefits, and if not, then who *has* benefited? Have levels of poverty dropped and education, health and welfare improved?

There are more than a few people in the apparel and fashion industries who roll their eyes at such questions, and frankly, these are questions beyond the scope and care of most people involved in sourcing, sales, marketing and merchandising. They make for great talking points in annual CSR reports, certainly. But aside from a very small number of nontraditional apparel brands, my own experience has shown that the localized development benefits of trade agreements are never the deciding factor behind either the support for such pacts within the industry or for the placement of production orders in a given country. Support for and use of such pacts is driven almost wholly by the cost-benefit offered to buyers. This is a logical decision for businesses that have placed financial gain and profit at the center of their missions. Although it's rare for a corporation to make public statements declaring this drive for profitability at near any cost, far too many of us have worked at companies where this is the norm, certainly within the U.S. and increasingly so in Canada, as well.

If we look specifically at the very short list of current sourcing hotspots for globally sourced apparel, we may well learn some surprising facts. Such a list would include Haiti, Jordan, Lesotho, Cambodia, Vietnam and last but not least, Bangladesh. There are another dozen countries that might well be added, depending largely on a given brand's sales country and the socio-economic profile of their target customers. For example, Banana Republic can afford better tailoring out of Turkey, perhaps, but Joe Fresh cannot. I have explicitly left China out of the mix, even though it continues to be most WTO countries' largest supplier, because they have for all intents and purposes been integrated into global trade patterns — and they now drive many of them. In any event, while regional Asian trade has given duty-free access to Chinese goods, this is not yet the case for the West.

By the Numbers: Select Country Statistics

We have looked briefly already at a significant list of multinational and regional trade agreements and at specific issues within a number of them. It's time to now look at others to see if the agreements have been followed and how any gains made, in both export and import nations, have contributed to meaningful human development. So, a few statistics to start with that will be helpful in providing some context to the value of apparel and textile exports versus the next top four categories of goods (based on the latest available data from the U.N.'s. Comtrade website):

Table 5

Export Values from Key Developing Country Sources ($US)		
Bangladesh	**Jordan**	**Vietnam**
Apparel 2009 thru end 2013 12 Billion → 26 Billion	**Apparel** 2009 thru end 2013 726 Million → 1 Billion	**Apparel** 2009 thru end 2013 8 Billion → 18 Billion
Seafood 636 Million	Fertilizers 896 Million	Electronics 38 Billion
Fabric 613 Million	Pharma 720 Million	Machinery 12 Billion
Footwear 500 Million	Vegetables 476 Million	Seafood 4.2 Billion
Leather 280 Million	Stone/lime 446 Million	Coffee 3.9 Billion
Haiti	**Lesotho**	**Cambodia**
Apparel 2009 thru end 2013 600 Million → 900 Million	**Apparel** 2009 thru end 2013 350 Million → 400 Million	**Apparel** 2009 thru end 2013 2.3 Billion → 4.7 Billion
Cosmetics 17 Million	Precious Metals 300 Million	Printed Books 2.2 Billion
Fruit/Nut 16 Million	Electronics 71 Million	Vehicles 415 Million
Seafood 10 Million	Footwear 27 Million	Footwear 361 Million
Iron/Steel 9 Million	Milled Grains 26 Million	Cereals 259 Million

There are a number of issues that might grab one's attention from even a cursory look at this data. What I note (in no particular order) is that Bangladesh, the country with the lowest labor costs and free-market access to the E.U. and Canada, is by far the largest supply source of apparel. In fact, it is almost equal to the rest of the countries combined ($US 26 billion of apparel exports in 2013, more than double those from 2009). I also note that all but Vietnam have duty-free access to Canadian and U.S. markets, though when the pending Trans-Pacific Partnership trade agreement goes into effect, Vietnam will be able to join the growing club.

It is also worth noting how the AGOA pact's Lesotho has been left near the bottom of the pile, and that Jordan's apparel exports, significantly farther away from North America than neighboring Haiti, has grown in near tandem with the Caribbean country's trade. There also seems to be an interesting story behind the US import market share and dollar value of apparel sectors between Vietnam and Cambodia. But most telling about a particular country's evolving trade profile is the size and importance of garments to the total economy.

Countries taking advantage of increased trade have been promised the residual effect of widespread growth and wealth creation cascading into other sectors: employment, wages, human development, etc. In Bangladesh, Haiti and Cambodia, export economies are overwhelmingly dependent on one sector: apparel manufacturing. In these cases, we have not seen wide industrial or manufacturing benefits, not even over the past five years. Little has been developed with regard to local supply-side industries. Both Cambodia and Bangladesh have actually become *more* dependent on the apparel sector by doubling their value over five years. Haiti has grown somewhat, but not anything like its peers, though one must recall that the country suffered a massive magnitude 7.0 earthquake in 2010 from which it has still not recovered. Just maintaining business was perhaps a feat unto itself.

Lesotho's apparel exports have grown only marginally over the past five years and together with mining far surpass any other export industries. The country's small population and landlocked nature would both seem to negatively impact its potential to grow. There have been some residual industries starting up there (primarily in textiles) that created additional employment, but not additional exports. Most of the production has been consumed by garment manufacturers as inputs to final manufactured goods.

In Jordan's case, it would seem that the country has successfully built up additional sectors to reduce its previous over-reliance on apparel exports. But with 70 percent of garment manufacturing employment tied to temporary foreign workers and overseas ownership of most factories being the norm, there has arguably been little local development benefit other than inflating Jordan's export values on paper.

Cambodia has depended significantly on foreign aid tied to development objectives ever since the signing of the 1991 Paris Peace Accord, which brought the Cambodian-Vietnamese war to an end. With funding from the World Bank, IMF and Asian Development Bank a corrupt political elite that derived its original power from the same Pol Pot regime that had ripped the country apart in a bloody civil war took control. Since then, the international community has waged a difficult campaign of trying to leverage that aid in exchange for political, social and economic liberalization in the face of much cronyism. In its 2014 international rankings of corrupt nations, Transparency International rated Cambodia #156 out of 174 countries. This is not a fact lost on many brands and retailers sourcing there, and the additional "out-of-pocket" export expenses per container simply to clear customs and leave the country are well-known in sourcing circles.

In Transparency International's rankings, Haiti sat at 161, Bangladesh at 145 and Vietnam at 119. Jordan sat well above the class of peer off-shore manufacturing states, at 55. Denmark, by the way, topped the list, and Canada held a respectable 10th-place ranking. The United States finished in the #17 spot. It seems the apparel trade has a penchant for locating itself within the most corrupt and corruptible geographies.

Prime Minister Hun Sen and his clique have now ruled Cambodia for 24 consecutive years — during which time he has successfully played off Western concerns about China's growing influence in the region. When pressure from Western donors gets too hot, as recent efforts by Australia have shown, he turns to China to make up the difference. This seems a practical strategy considering, after all, that the majority of apparel factories in Cambodia are not built or run by Americans, Canadians or Brits, but by mainland and Hong Kong-based Chinese, Malaysians and Singaporeans. Interestingly enough, few of the apparel factories have been built or run by Cambodians themselves. In a not very modern version of colonial economics, the means of production are largely in the hands of foreign interests.

The garment industry has certainly added to the country's rapid growth as its near-only legal export industry of any size — to the tune of 11 percent annually from 2004–08. While this has slowed to seven percent for the past five years, Cambodia's fight against poverty has only seen reductions of one percent on average per year in that same timeframe. Meanwhile, and as we have reviewed earlier, the value of apparel exports has doubled, growing by $US 2.4 billion dollars from 2009–13. It would seem apparent that the great majority of benefits generated by this additional duty-free trade, which saved importing brands and retailer margins literally hundreds of millions of dollars, were not seen by average Cambodians.

Vietnam also stands out due to the growth of both the electronics sector and machinery. Apparel remains the country's number two export earner and employer, far more than either coffee or seafood, which have both gained greater attention from trade experts as of late. Much of the discussion around Vietnam's successful climb up the rungs of the economic ladder rests on its investment ties to Korea, Taiwan and Japan. All three have turned to the quasi-Socialist country to help prop up the margins of their automotive and mobile phone companies, which provide significantly better salaries and working conditions than the average sew factory might. Central planning by a generally well-disciplined cadre of the state apparatus has no doubt helped drive much of the development planning linkages to general aid, but free trade with the West has not yet come. There is no doubt either that the large influx of ideas, experience and money — especially into southern Vietnam by Vietnamese Americans — helped drive rapid growth there since the late '90s.

Mixed Results, Disastrous Outcomes

In terms then of a residual sector growth effect, it seems either not realized or perhaps achievable only under a given set of circumstances, such as an autocratic government or free zone manufacturing such as Jordan's, which generates little tax income for government social programs or employment for locals. The costs and challenges of depending on foreign labor can lead, as we have seen earlier, to some rather dark outcomes. A look at Bangladesh offers another troubling example.

The tragic events surrounding the collapse of the Rana Plaza complex in Savar, Bangladesh on April 24, 2013 brought the Southeast Asian nation to the attention of many in the West for the very first time. Since then, a steady stream of media attention has been keeping us up to date. The massive industrial accident that resulted in the loss of more than 1,100 lives and thousands more injured and maimed, called into question the efficacy of earlier business and governmental efforts to support the country's long-term economic and governance development.

For those of us more familiar with the country due to work, study or research experience, that such a tragedy could occur was not surprising. As a sourcing manager, I had long been wary of the country's ability to cope with the significant expansion of the sector that took place over the past decade or so. For numerous reasons I had been able, throughout my career, to resist the purely economic benefits of placing or recommending the placement of production there. But for many people in the industry, the pressures to maintain margins while off-setting rising costs elsewhere in the region seemed to have proven too great. And once your brand's financial viability has been built around unsustainable labor costs and the accompanying lack of social benefits, it becomes very difficult to extract from such a scenario.

Cambodia and Vietnam have also been primary beneficiaries of incremental production outflows from China due to these same cost factors over time. Industry growth in these two countries, while mean-ingful, has been limited due to the relatively smaller human resource base and, in the case of Vietnam, the country's focused development policies that have allowed it to successfully shift its industrial base over the past 20 years. High tech, pharmaceutical and automotive sectors have helped to bring the country greater levels of income, skill devel-opment and prosperity, albeit with their own set of social costs and challenges, not least of them a lack of political freedom.

One of the questions some of us involved in trying to manage these significant industrial shifts into Bangladesh over a relatively short period of time have had is, was the effort of some governments in collaboration with the apparel industry a concerted one aimed at replacing direct, bilateral development aid with industrial wages? As I've stated previously, I've never known of businesses placing factory orders in a given country to explicitly support international develop-ment aims. They will, however, move quite quickly to take competitive advantage of trade policies allowing for improved margins and operat-ing efficiencies. This has been the historic pattern of the apparel and textile trades since the early days of the Industrial Revolution, and, as I've argued, it is in the nature of the capitalist economic system. I also firmly believe, however, that business can and will change and adapt to the expectations of wider society, be they driven by governmental, consumer or responsible investment market pressures. But not, most likely, if simply left to their own devices.

According to Professors Abdur Razzaue and Abu Eusuf of Dhaka University in their 2007 study, "Trade, Development and Poverty Linkage: A Case Study of Ready Made Garment Industry in

Bangladesh," the participation of direct foreign aid and garment-led exports as a percentage of the country's GDP have essentially reversed positions since the early 1980s to land, at the time of the study, around three percent and 17 percent respectively. That is to say, where once direct aid flows represented nearly 20 percent of GDP, they now represent only three percent. Garment exports have since taken the lead, as we have seen, and remain far out front of any other sector. This explosive growth has led to the creation of nearly 4 million jobs in the industry in the span of just 20 years, most of them held by women, providing second incomes to countless families while improving accessibility to education, medical care and skill development opportunities. But this has come as part of the cost of shifting huge profits to brands and retailers.

In Canada's case, this shift in aid contributions has meant a real purchasing power reduction driven by inflationary impacts of nearly 23 percent between 1998 and 2011. This projected loss is based on an analysis of CIDA's (the now-defunct Canadian International Development Agency, which was absorbed into the country's Department of Foreign Affairs and International Trade in 2013) budgetary reports of the same time period. Consequently, Bangladesh dropped in priority and ranking from second place in CIDA spending in 1998 to tenth place by 2011, while in actual Canadian dollar terms, allocations changed very little from the approximately $CND 90 million of combined bilateral and multilateral aid extended in both periods. Over time, the same dollars obviously buy and represent significantly less benefit.

One might think then, from the above, that both Bangladesh and international aid donors have realized a net benefit by the exponential growth of the ready made garment industry. The country successfully put millions of poor people to work while donor nations, at least in Canada's case, realized a 23 percent cost savings of contributions to Bangladesh's development. But considering the billions of dollars in apparel exports that have flowed out of the country over the past few years, how is it that the robust industrial infrastructure and development policies one would expect of such success was so wholly lacking at the time of the Rana Plaza tragedy?

Simply put, the vast majority of factory owners failed to invest in robust buildings that had integrity, proper fire and safety systems, or industrial infrastructure, and they failed to provide employee training. (These are the same factory owners, by the way, who prefer terms of payment not to their Bangladesh business but to offshore company accounts in the City of London, Hong Kong and Mauritius.) Results of initial structural and electrical systems auditing by both the E.U.-led Accord on Fire and Building Safety in Bangladesh and the U.S.-led Alliance for Bangladesh Worker Safety (http://bangladeshaccord. org/; www.bangladeshworkersafety.org) have shown a stark failure of the industry to secure construction permits, occupancy certificates, operating licenses and fire inspections by competent authorities.

The Canadian and E.U. governments in particular had been loath, pre-Rana Plaza, to look beyond the paper legislation demanded of Bangladesh in order to achieve duty-free access to Western consumer markets. What is law on paper and what has been documented as actual industry practices are as different as night and day. The Institute for Development Studies outlines four key components of effective aid-for-trade programs including:

+ Technical assistance in the development of trade policy and negotiations.

+ Infrastructure (which one might logically assume would be inclusive of a particular industry's regulatory and institutional needs).

+ Productive capacity (which is where government and industry seem to have put all their eggs).

+ Adjustment assistance (with declining terms of trade — read: lower and lower commodity prices).[154]

Seen in this light, the failure of Bangladesh can thus be seen as a failure of pre-Rana Plaza engagement by Western donors with the government-led burgeoning apparel trade (more than a few members of government in Bangladesh have also been successful garment manufacturers, as is also the case in Hong Kong) — all to the betterment and increased profitability of multinational brands and retailers.

Managing Trade Better

The trend doesn't just belong to Bangladesh. If we look where for example, the International Labor Organization has expanded its Better

Work programs over the years in response to pre-existing challenges and serious, structural issues regarding labor rights and workplace safety, we're back to the same shortlist of places where brands and retailers seek to place their business in the first place: Bangladesh, Cambodia, Haiti, Jordan, Lesotho and Vietnam, with Nicaragua and Indonesia thrown in for good measure.

Aside from, perhaps, Cambodia's model, which grew up as a structural part of multinational development goals to support the garment trade (and thus parallel to it), these programs have all been after-the-fact efforts. Each of these countries' garment industries have faced significant localized labor conflict and many well publicized scandals. From Lesotho to Haiti to Cambodia, industry has been shown time and again to be ready to exploit and disregard laws that aim to ensure the rights of workers defined as part and parcel of trade negotiations and pacts.

So it would seem, based on this discussion, that we have now gravitated away from the expectation that managed trade opportunities should be *accompanied by* respect for environmental and labor rights, to a norm where it is a de facto given that they don't really exist and that at some later date, tag-on efforts will be allowed to Band-Aid the systemic failures.

Far too often, the Aid for Trade model has simply meant shifting the lion's share of economic benefits toward industry at the cost of increased health, human rights and safety risks for factory workers the world over. The way around this is not necessarily to reinvent the wheel, but rather to improve on it. We can start by actually holding all parties accountable to bilateral and multilateral agreements that:

1. are negotiated openly with full public disclosure.

2. include robust guarantees that are measured against well-identified standards for labor, health, safety, environmental and human rights, *with required reporting mechanisms* and incrementally open markets *only upon the delivery of results against a prescribed calendar.*

According to the ILO's own in-depth studies on the effectiveness of labor requirements as part and parcel of global trade pacts (outlined in the 2013 ILO paper "Social Dimensions of Free Trade Agreements"), there has been a growing trend in this direction. By 2013, some 58 trade-related treaties included one form or another of labor issue amendments for example, up significantly from just four in 1995. Of these, only 40 percent included conditional requirements spelling out economic penalties for a failure to comply with or enforce such clauses. The E.U. in particular has tended toward legally binding provisions dealing with labor protections and assurances but, as with the U.S., these tend to focus overwhelmingly on institutional, legislative efforts with less follow-through on practical implementation and capacity building.

Some limited successes can be reported, however, and they offer proof that when enforcement follows through on legislative intent, improvements on the ground lead to real change. This has been the case in American agreements with Peru, where labor inspectors were given additional powers to sanction manipulative contract practices; and in the case of Panama, where regulatory amendments resulted in greater protections for short-term contract employees and improved freedom of association statutes. Interesting benchmarks may also exist when looking to South-South trade relationships, as exampled by MERCOSUR's (the South America common market, or *Mercado Común del Sur*) Regional Plan on Labour Inspection, which has led to cooperative, multilateral monitoring efforts among member states.

In any event, the ILO could certainly be given strengthened powers as a U.N. body to hold members accountable for their failure to meet conventions they have signed onto or to pursue punitive actions against those countries that fail to uphold their own health, safety and labor laws.

If countries require capacity building, infrastructure development, and the hiring of safety inspectors and industrial engineers, this should not come about well after the fact, as we have seen in Bangladesh at the cost of thousands of lives, but must be clearly written into trade agreements from the start and enforced. A failure to do so only validates the premise that Aid for Trade is simply window dressing, built on false promises. There is far too much at stake for us not to challenge the current status quo.

6

Redefining Fashion

EDUCATORS, FINANCIAL MANAGERS, SOCIAL enterprise entrepreneurs, designers, salespeople, film makers, social justice activists,
marketers, supply chain managers, labor auditors — the apparel and
textile industries are made up of people from every walk of life pursuing many different careers. They encompass a host of trades and skills
and competences, some old and some new. Many of those that were at
one time truly *trades*, in the old hand-tool-and-apprenticeship meaning of the word, have become automated and industrialized beyond
recognition. Certainly a handful of *ateliers* remains in pockets of old
world Europe; but these are staffed by either very old craftspeople or
an elite class of younger artisans working within the very small world
that is *haute couture*.

But for the most part, the service-dominated post-industrial age
of globalization, and business's often-blind drive to achieve scale and
efficiency have killed much that was once creative in our everyday lives.
(I was born in the mid-1960s, and so still have some vague memory and inkling of how things were.) There are, however, people from
across the apparel industry spectrum in organizations large and small
who have broken free from the industrial mold, along with those who
have always been outsiders and rebels who could not or would not
"fit in." In this closing chapter, we will look at the people, enterprises
and efforts that represent the real, best chance for change within the
industry I have spent nearly 20 years now in a love-hate relationship
with. They are people like you and me who have simply decided to do
something about what they didn't like happening around them. They
are representative of those who inspired me to begin my own journey

toward a more equitable and fairer world, to think a bit more of others and a little less obsessively of myself. I have no doubt they will inspire you as well.

The Educators

Being married to a teacher and having spent most of my life as either a formal or informal student, I believe there is no more important starting point when thinking about the deep changes needed in apparel and textile trades than in the area of education. Certainly, my sense while writing this book was that, based on the great number of industry people that I have worked with, there must be some significant gaps in the curriculum for merchandisers, marketers, fashion and textile designers. Most — though of course, not all — of the people I dealt with were generally unaware of the social, community and environmental impacts of their roles. I'm still not sure if this is a generational issue, truly one of curriculum, or simply my own limited perceptions. It did, after all, take me quite a while to come around!

I should also clarify here that I am not speaking of those who directly work on labor and environmental issues. As a percentage of fashion and apparel industry employment, we are a very small bunch indeed. Within the typical brands and retailers I have worked with or for, such roles are probably outnumbered 100 to one, and in some organizations it is a much higher ratio. I am talking here about the larger pools of people whose efforts day in and day out revolve around planning merchandise assortments, selecting materials, planning ad campaigns and creating designs — from either a creative or technical viewpoint. I thought it important to talk to a few people who might best be able to shed some light. One comes from a top Canadian fashion school, another from a leading Italian academy and the third from an outstanding school on the west coast of the U.S. One of the largest and best known fashion schools in New York was also contacted, but sadly failed to respond to inquiries for their input.

Lu Ann Lafrenz, Ryerson University

Originally from the U.S., Lu Ann Lafrenz completed both her Masters in Textiles and Clothing, and her PhD in Education and Training at Ohio State University. She has been an associate professor with

Toronto's Ryerson University for 16 years and programme director of the Masters in Fashion degree for the past three years now.

The School of Fashion at Ryerson offers Canada's preeminent degree programs for industry students, offering undergraduate studies with a focus in either communications or design. The Master of Arts in Fashion is the first to be offered in the country, and is built around a two-year interdisciplinary research and studio program. The program's core theoretical and practical courses are further augmented by a hands-on internship component.

Lu Ann is also a fellow board member at Canada's *Fashion Takes Action*, a Toronto-based sustainable apparel group focused on industry education and awareness issues that also works to raise the profile of local, ethical designers in Canada. We talked about the challenges in formal education settings. Getting a sense of the changes she has seen in fashion education from her early years as a student until now seemed a good starting point.

"When I went to university in the '70s and '80s, social and environmental issues related to the fashion industry were not even on our radar. There was no mention in any of my textiles classes about the impact textile production had on the environment. Our exposure to ethical issues was limited to studying the 1911 Triangle Shirtwaist Factory fire in New York, with discussions around sweatshops, concluding they were still prevalent at that time.

"As an undergraduate I went on a NYC fashion tour where we visited a garment factory, but that was not the emphasis of our experience, perhaps concentrating more on the design and retail aspects of the industry. Later, as a university instructor, I took numerous groups to NYC where we visited manufacturing plants, but of course never saw 'sweatshops.' Now, students have conversations about these issues and question the impact our industry has on people and the environment. Students are exposed to retailers introducing eco-lines, or they themselves shop at vintage stores; they have experienced recycling their entire lives and through the expansive information on the Internet are exposed to documentaries about these social and environmental issues surrounding the fashion industry.

"Now, as educators, we include these topics in courses beginning in first year and throughout many of our courses. The students most passionate about social and environmental issues have created their capstone projects around some aspect of sustainability in fashion."

Did that mean students were coming in with a heightened sense of industry issues?

"Every year, students are coming into our program with more awareness of the impact the apparel industry has on the environment. They are certainly aware of the retailers that have introduced 'green' lines, and in many cases they want to know more about the social and environmental issues surrounding the industry they are entering."

Many people seem to still interpret sustainability as largely an environmental quest. I was keen to know if this greater awareness was translating into a real demand for curriculum dealing with all the issues.

"Certainly, students today want to know more about both social and environmental issues surrounding the fashion industry. During the past decade, very passionate students have questioned the impact the production of textiles has on the environment, the waste of materials, and the problems with overconsumption. Their questioning has resulted in incorporating even more of these topics in our curriculum.

"One of the events the students organize outside of their coursework is an annual fashion production where students showcase their sustainable designs for the education of their peers, the university, the community and the industry.

"Over the past approximately ten years, the demand also for research and teaching presentations about sustainable fashion issues has exploded at the International Textile and Apparel Association (ITAA) annual conference. Prior to this time, there were no real sessions in this academic conference dedicated to research and teaching social and environmental issues. Now, multiple industry publications like the *Journal of Fashion Marketing and Management, Clothing and Textiles Research Journal, Fashion Theory* and *Textile: The Journal of Cloth and Culture* have all included special editions related to these issues."

I wanted to know where Lu Ann thought the gaps in industry education might be.

"In general, more colleges and universities *are* including specific courses such as ethics, social responsibility, and sustainable design in their fashion programs. However, it is difficult to tell how many are really creating a more inclusive approach of including these topics throughout their curriculums in all programs."

I had to admit, I was heartened to hear of the interest and growing awareness from younger people looking to come into the industry. Based on my own experiences, they would need that passion and curiosity to make headway in a trade that on many fronts has been dominated by a group of rather elderly white men for quite some time. This topic of existing industry challenges was the starting point for my discussion with Amy Williams, chair of Fashion Design programs at California's prestigious California College of the Arts (CCA) in San Francisco.

Amy Williams, California College of the Arts

A graduate of the renowned Parsons School of Design in New York, Amy has been at CCA for 14 years and continues to be an active designer and illustrator herself. Her studio specializes in fashion development for contemporary and young designer/active sports in sweater and cut/sew knits, which often finds her consulting on design direction and business development for a variety of labels. She was quite frank and practical in her assessment of the challenges up-and-coming fashion students faced.

> "In my opinion, the biggest educational gaps are in the industry. For the most part, it's made up of traditionally educated people — those holding the decision-making purse strings. While the younger student of today may have the knowledge, they do not yet have the voice to advocate or activate new actions. Our students are all required to do two full courses in sustainability education; however, most of our graduates enter the traditional industry for first jobs. They need these to prove themselves and their talent, and to pay off their student loans. Their ability to make a difference is not yet fully known. The corporate structures have not yet embraced sustainability at all levels; some companies have, and we are also excited as they share their findings and the good news for their bottom lines . . . Levi's for example!"

Amy made good points about the new generation's conflict between the need to deal with financial realities and gain entry-level experience on one hand and to feed their hunger to drive change. We were talking about California after all, which has built a reputation as a forward-thinking state on sustainability issues. I wanted to know if she was convinced this awareness of social and environmental impacts came with the students to class every day.

> "Absolutely! Today's student has been trained to pay attention to their waste — be it elementary students learning to pick up their trash, use reusable lunch pails and to properly recycle paper in the classroom, to fashion students redesigning clothing in the classroom from Goodwill donations; the entry-level student is aware of their daily choices at all levels.
>
> "Students are also more concerned about their future 'footprints.' They know that their actions will put into action some sort of reaction, and most of these students are eager to learn how to do more with better environmental/

societal citizenship embedded. Our college has folded sustainability into its mission, but it has been a part of our fashion design program story for over a decade now."

What did that mean, practically speaking, from a program design and curriculum point of view, I wondered?

"Specific to the Fashion Design undergraduate program, two full semesters in the junior year, for a total mandatory six specific units, are required; however, we also have targeted projects that are in sophomore and senior level coursework. Our design courses are two mandatory courses per level — so to have two of the six dedicated courses deliver this information with support from the five construction studio courses is outstanding. Our health and safety coursework also involves much education around sustainable subject matter. Science has been taught in the studios across the college's 22 undergraduate programs. All health and safety courses are for the support of the programmatic work but carry equal value to the final degree. Our students learn for their industry training, but also for their full educational training."

Based on earlier comments from Lu Ann, I was sure that Amy's own observations regarding changes within formal fashion education would be equally interesting.

"What a difference there is today! Back in the '80s the focus was on product development with regard to a set of inspirations and color stories that were being adopted worldwide — presented at PV [Premiere Vision trade show] and trickling into all levels of fashion creation. The concept of environment, societal or cultural affect/effects were not discussed or considered back then. We were not chasing the cost to the bottom penny, mark-ups still had keystones, and manufacturing could happen on a local platform in many U.S. cities.

"Our industry is *finally* acknowledging that its actions have lasting long-term effects, that we are very seriously depleting our resources — human and nature resources alike. The fact that this is being discussed now in board rooms and classrooms gives our industry hope."

Francesca Romana Rinaldi, Bocconi University/Milano Fashion Institute

I was happy to hear this sentiment echoed by an educator in Europe when I talked with Francesca Rinaldi, director of the Master's program in Retail & Brand Experience Management at the Milano Fashion Institute. I had just finished working my way through her new book *The Responsible Fashion Company*, by far the best academic reference out yet on the subject, and was keen to pick her brain.

"Companies are now turning from a 'tactical' to a 'strategic' approach, going from special projects that are not involving the value chain to projects that involve sourcing, manufacturing and retail.

"The big change will take place when demand and supply will work in synergy for a better world: the virtuous cycle requires customers that are well informed and demand a better product with a higher transparency of the value chain, and companies that are working to answer the needs of the different stakeholders — Environment, Society, Art, Culture and Territory, Institutions, Media — integrating ethics and aesthetics in the value chains. Technologies could be the catalyst of this change, they can help to increase the transparency of the value chain, help customers to get closer to the companies, make the shopping experience very special or just make the process more efficient . . . and more sustainable."

Did that also hold true for, say, Italian high fashion?

"Until the last decade, there was complete silence around the topic of responsibility in the fashion industry; there were just a few pioneers that were leading the way in Italy. In the last ten years a large percentage of fashion companies, also Italian, began this important journey, and many CSR departments are now a reality.

"In the last years, my teaching has been focusing on how to integrate ethics and aesthetics in the value chain and on which tools managers may use to answer the needs of the different stakeholders, to reach several objectives: increasing sales, working on their brand image and reputation, and building the sources of a sustainable competitive advantage."

Might it be, I proposed, that the next generation working their way now through fashion programs where ethics and sustainability are beginning to take hold, will be the ones to get us there? Francesca agreed.

"I must admit that, more and more, students are now expecting to have courses on corporate social responsibility when they study fashion management; they are the future generation of managers! Generations X, Y, Z have the willingness to learn more and more about responsible fashion, and I find them very open to discussions and sharing of different opinions and even skeptical points of view."

Sass Brown, Academic/Activist

When I asked Sass Brown for a hit-list of the latest and greatest in inspired eco-fashion, she responded with a flurry of names: Swato Kalsi's embroidered luxury collection, New York-based Chilean designer Pola Thomson, Stella Jean, mYak's yak hair accessories, Karina Kallio's upcycled childrenswear, Brit-Brazilian bag creations from Bottletop, and Venezuelan-Brooklynite Susana Colina.

There seemed to be a preponderance of Latino names in the dozen or so that this prolific author of books, blogs and academic papers offered up. I can't say that I know Ms. Brown well, though anyone who has done their homework on the topics of upcycling, heritage crafts or global artisans will certainly know a lot *about* her and her work. I had heard tell of her experiences in Latin America, and she kindly elaborated.

"When I was teaching, I was fortunate enough to be able to spend up to four months a year, over more than five years volunteering and working with COOPA-ROCA in Rocinha, Rio. I subsequently advised and worked at several other cooperatives and creative industry collectives around the world, but COOPA-ROCA was the first, and it holds a special place in my heart. The work that they were doing with luxury designers and artisans in the *favela* (a Brazilian shantytown or slum) was ground breaking and a complete eye opener for me on what is possible through the collaboration and partnership between tradition and contemporary design. That experience changed my life."

Hers certainly seems to have been, true to the trade, a globetrotting life. Originally from the U.K., Sass has lived and worked in various parts of the world both within the apparel industry and its related educational institutions. Her earliest fashion studies took place in the U.K. From there she went on to earn her Master's at New York's Fashion Institute of Technology (FIT), and she recently completed her PhD studies in Artisanship at the Swedish School of Textiles.

Prior to landing on a more-or-less full-time basis in New York, where she has held a number of roles at FIT over the past seven years (including four years at the school's campus in Florence), Sass spent more than a dozen years in Canada. There, she spent time as a patternmaker before launching her own boutique label; she later moved on to an executive merchandising role with Perry Ellis, Canada. According to Sass, her time here didn't contribute anything of real note to her outlook or philosophy regarding ethical fashion

Her most recent book, *Refashioned: Cutting-Edge Clothing from Upcycled Materials*, was well received in 2013 and provided a visually stunning collection of global designers whose upcycled creations from the discards and textile waste around us captured beautifully the essence of post-modern slow-fashion. The topic is one of her favorites; she addresses it often online at the hub of all things upcycled and eco-conscious: ecofashiontalk.com, which she started over ten years ago. I asked her, all things considered, did she expect that the movement would gain sufficient traction to displace any sizeable volume of today's imported apparel?

"Absolutely. The slow fashion movement isn't something confined to the U.S.; it is a global regional movement

fueled by independent designers around the world committed to producing locally and ethically. I do see them
collectively building sufficient mass to offer a viable op-
tion for consumers, but not to produce on the same mass
scale as High Street; that would be antithetical to everything they stand for."

Indeed!

Market Mover

At the time of this writing, here in Canada the media has been awash
with news about money managers specializing in investment options
that take account of social, environmental and governance issues; these
managers now hold over $CND 1 trillion in their funds. Responsible
investment markets are one of the tripartite stakeholders I often mention when asked about the best ways to influence business practices.
(The other two are regulatory action and civil society engagement.)

Kevin Thomas, Shareholder Association for Research and Education

I first met Kevin Thomas in the summer of 2013, just after I had
approached Canada's Joe Fresh brand with a plan of responsive, responsible actions in the months after the collapse of the Rana Plaza
factory in Savar, Bangladesh. He was just coming to the end of a
five-year stint with Toronto-based labor activist Maquila Solidarity
Network (MSN) and would soon be making an exciting move. As director of engagement with the Shareholder Association for Research
and Education (SHARE), Kevin would find himself in new territory,
looking at social justice issues from a financial market perspective.

With a background in resource management and international
business law, Kevin's previous corporate engagement work with MSN
and as political advisor to the Lubicon Lake First Nation in Alberta
dealing with lands rights and resource protection, he certainly seemed
well suited to just such a role. Since 2000, SHARE had been working with a range of clients that included mutual funds, foundations,
pension fund managers and faith-based organizations, and provided
services such as education, policy advocacy and investment research.

I was curious about what had first motivated Kevin to choose the often-thankless path of an activist. I was surprised to learn that his social justice journey had begun just a few hundred kilometers from CFB (Canadian Forces Base) Cold Lake, where I had spent a number of years as a boy. I remembered the region as one of pristine northern forests and unbelievably cold winters.

> "My uncle introduced me to the plight of the Lubicon Lake First Nation in Alberta when I was in high school. Their lands had been overrun by oil and gas companies in the early 1980s, and I was inspired to get involved in helping to fight for a land rights settlement with our government. The oil and gas sector in Alberta in that era was like the Wild West, and it was my first instance of seeing the terrible impacts unregulated resource exploitation could have on both the environment and the people who depend upon it. Their lands and way of life were irrevocably destroyed.
>
> "I still believe very strongly that we need strong legal structures and governance to protect environmental and social values, but that where governments aren't playing that role, companies still have to act responsibly for their own part. Many years later, I ended up working as chief negotiator in their land negotiations with the government, and also negotiated with oil, gas and forestry companies over environmental and economic development matters."

Although his new role at SHARE deals primarily with larger financial organizations, I was hopeful that Kevin might have some insight into what the average small investor might do to help leverage the growing trends in responsible investments that the media had grabbed a hold of.

> "Small investors have a collective action problem" he told me. "They're too small on their own to move a company and too dispersed to organize easily. So a lot of the push has come from institutional investors like pension funds that are larger in scale. However, we do work with some

asset managers that sell mutual funds, like Qtrade with its Meritas mutual funds, and we engage with the companies in those funds to improve practices, so there are some options out there. And while I've been working largely on behalf of institutional investors, the retail investment side is growing every year — more and more options are out there even for individual investors."

Heartening to hear.

For the five years before moving to SHARE, Kevin had been deeply embedded in ongoing responsible supply-chain engagement with global apparel companies — well before the Rana Plaza tragedy. I asked him to share a bit of the history leading up to the negotiations that led to the European-spearheaded Bangladesh Accord on Fire and Building Safety.

"At the time, I was working with the Maquila Solidarity Network. We worked with an international network of NGOs and trade unions that had been focused on the horrifying conditions in the Bangladesh garment industry for years. After the earlier Spectrum factory collapse in 2006, we began working with Bangladeshi trade unions and this informal international network to look at how to fix the problem of unsafe factories in that country.

"One of the things we arrived at early on was an action plan that mirrored many of the steps that are now being carried out under the Bangladesh Accord. From there, a small group of five or six of us worked with a couple of companies to turn that into a formal and binding agreement. I was most closely involved in drafting that agreement, working on the mechanism to make it legally binding internationally, and trying to bring companies on board. The sad fact is that we signed what was basically the Bangladesh Accord with PVH (owners of Calvin Klein, Tommy Hilfiger, IZOD and Arrow, among other companies) more than a year before Rana Plaza happened, but only one other company was willing to get on board at that time. Only after 1,100 workers died at Rana Plaza were other companies willing to act. Those workers didn't have to die. The solutions were available, but the will on the part of the other companies was not."

As outcomes of such a horrific event, both the E.U.-led Accord and the U.S. Alliance for Bangladesh Worker Safety have built on tripartite structures that folks like the Ethical Trade Initiative and the ILO's Better Work programs had been modeling for years. Kevin was cautiously optimistic that lessons learned by the brands in Bangladesh were leading to systemic change.

"I'm an optimist of the will, as they say. I think that we can make ethical sourcing a norm for the industry, but it won't happen without sustained involvement and support by all concerned — consumers, investors, regulators and those within the business itself."

Collaboration Counts

And speaking about the Alliance and Accord efforts in Bangladesh . . .

Much has been written and said about both the European-led Accord and the U.S. Alliance efforts to address factory safety issues in Bangladesh (myself included, most recently in an op-ed piece for Canada's *National Post* on the one-year anniversary of that somber tragedy. The day that article ran would be the last I would find myself working for any major Canadian brand).

To its credit, Canada's largest retail group, Loblaw Companies Limited, moved quickly and decisively to put its money behind the Bangladesh Accord on Fire and Building Safety (The Accord), but that doesn't necessarily mean the brands it owns shared the same level of commitment. It remains, unfortunately, the only Canadian company to have done so to date.

Keep in mind that Bangladesh is the second largest provider of apparel to all Canadians after China, having shipped us just over $CND 1 billion worth of garments in 2013, a 50 percent increase over the country's textile business with us since 2009. Only an additional four Canadian companies have joined the U.S.-led Alliance for Bangladesh

Worker Safety (The Alliance). I hardly believe that just six companies in the entire country account for this volume, which would indicate a significant lack of responsible engagement by a good number of Canadian brands and retailers. It seems that our long-held self-image as a nation that believes in fairness and equality might be a little oversold.

The Accord is by far the larger of the two schemes, with 190 brand members accounting for some 1,600 factories and affecting the livelihood of nearly two million workers. Canadian connections have been strong, aside from the fact that there is only one retailing member. The group's chief safety inspector, Brad Loewen, is a Canadian, and the now-defunct Maquila Solidarity Network was instrumental in negotiations between Loblaw and The Accord.

As I recently had the opportunity to chat about an Alliance role with associates at corporate diplomacy firm Albright Stonebridge Group, it seemed *à propos* to take a closer look at what the Alliance had been up to. Joyce Wong was kind enough to fill me in.

The Alliance for Bangladesh Worker Safety

As senior project lead at the Alliance with ethical engagement consultants Elevate Global, Joyce is a highly regarded professional with solid research and policy experience. Following her BA in Rhetoric from Berkeley, she went onto tackle roles with BSR, Fair Trade, CARE Peru and the World Bank before completing graduate studies at Columbia University's School of International and Public Affairs, earning a fellowship in Global Health Practice along the way.

I wanted to know what the next year and a half held in store for the Alliance and its members.

"The major focus over the next 18 months will be on remediation. Now that all factories have been inspected and we know what the deficiencies/risks are, the next step will be to ensure that factories are remediating them correctly and in accordance with specified deadlines. We have recently increased our staff to bring on a team of remediation case managers, who will be following up frequently with each individual factory to make sure they're progressing and verify that progress through site visits.

"We'll be monitoring remediation very carefully, as there's risk that factories will purchase non-certified safety equipment or implement solutions in ways that don't meet the standard — this is due to a lack of availability of equipment and local service providers that can design and install plans that meet the standard, and lack of awareness among factories regarding where and how to procure it. We're pursuing opportunities to increase access to credible product and services, increase access to affordable finance for remediation, and build local capacity for fire protection longer-term.

"In addition to remediation, we also will be continuing and expanding our training and worker empowerment programs. On the training side, we'll continue the basic fire safety training that all factories have completed and develop a refresher course/requirement based on the recommendations of our training impact assessment, and launch additional fire safety trainings that target specific audiences/areas of risk. For example, this spring, we'll be rolling out training for security guards, which we piloted in November 2014, and will later focus on other high-risk positions. To further our goals to empower workers to raise safety concerns, we'll continue expanding our worker helpline (called Amader Kotha) and will also begin to pilot and scale approaches and training for establishing democratically-elected, credible OSH committees in factories."

The business-led Alliance (versus the governmental and union-led Accord) had earlier been criticized for leaving worker engagement and the labor voice out of their efforts. It seems to me that they are effectively addressing these shortcomings. Industry chatter, especially among civil society groups, suggested that the time was ripe to take some of the knowledge from both of these multi-stakeholder initiatives. Building a model on the prototype that Bangladesh was proving to be, would it be possible to introduce these safety-driven initiatives to additional offshore hotspots at early stages of their development? I put it to Joyce.

"The models and levels of commitment and resources seen in the Alliance and Accord are truly unprecedented. We've heard interest among some of our members in transferring this approach to other countries where sourcing is increasing and fire safety risks, in particular, are also relatively high, but no concrete plans yet."

And progress depends on what?

"Whether a model like this does roll-out in other geographies will likely depend on our impact and sustainability, as well as the measures that individual companies take to integrate some of the tools and learnings into their own programs.

"We've heard some interest in Cambodia, in particular, but not yet enough to catalyze an expansion or replication. In the meantime, companies that are the most concerned are starting to integrate some of the learnings from the Alliance and Accord into their other audit tools and programs. What's happening in Bangladesh — from both a risk and a momentum perspective — has drawn buyers' attention to other geographies, which, on one hand, is encouraging. We're seeing measurable progress in hundreds of factories. On the other hand, it's important to appropriately assess the level and nature of risk in other countries, and to allow that to guide the approach taken."

Based on discussions with numerous people, I understand that for many working at the social, safety and sustainability fringes of the apparel trade, collaborating on the inner workings of either The Accord or Alliance has been a frustrating and rewarding experience. Joyce has already spent a considerable amount of her life thus far working for equality and justice. Understanding what motivates people like her from a young age often makes me quite ashamed that it took me so long to look beyond myself. I find no end of inspiration in listening to their personal stories.

"Personally, I grew up hearing about sweatshop scandals in the '90s and became fascinated with garment factories and workers as a teenager. At that time, I knew nothing about the codes of conduct or social compliance audits that were getting off the ground, and will admit that I thought the solution was to boycott the companies I saw in the newspapers — but, as an adult, I've been drawn to working with those very same companies to improve conditions in their supply chains, and have found much greater opportunity for impact and innovation. I've been passionate about improving the lives of the workers that make our jeans and sweaters, and have spent the last 12 years working mainly with apparel companies on CSR and building sustainable supply chains.

"After working in CSR for over a decade, the Alliance seemed to offer an unprecedented opportunity to go beyond traditional CSR to catalyze change in garment factories in a country that urgently needs it — for its 5 million workers, to sustain the growth of the industry, and for the country's overall economic development. The rapid growth of the garment industry has brought economic opportunity to millions of workers, the majority being women, but there's still a lot to be done to ensure that they feel safe in the workplace — no worker should feel that they are risking her/his life simply by going to work. In the Alliance, I saw the opportunity and the mandate, really to work with companies to reach ambitious and meaningful goals within a relatively short period of time, and to make Bangladeshi workers feel safer when they go to work every day.

"There is certainly much to be said for the efforts now underway in Bangladesh. It is unprecedented, certainly within the region, to have successfully brought together the range of stakeholders at the scale we've experienced

over the past two years. But sometimes perspective is
everything, and just as it's been of value to capture the
points of view that we have so far, it is just as important,
if not more so, to hear from local people themselves on
the ground in production hotspots about how this work
is advancing."

And, as many people on the ground will tell you, getting to a place
of trust and collaboration across cultures is often no easy thing to
achieve. Relationships between foreigners and locals, workers and employers, haves and have-nots are fraught with half-truths, stereotypes
and prejudices. People will often tell you what they expect you want
to hear. They may also tell you things you don't want to know that
may be reinterpreted out of ignorance, fear or self-interest. No one in
Bangladesh is without their criticisms, even those who work on behalf
of organizations like the Fair Wear Foundation, an Amsterdam-based
nonprofit working toward improving the conditions for garment industry workers around the world.

Shatil Ara, Fairwear Foundation, Bangladesh

Shatil Ara has been the country representative for Fair Wear
Foundation in her native Bangladesh for the past two years, a role she
took on after spending the five previous years with Germany's *Deutsche
Gesellschaft für Internationale Zusammenarbeit* or GIZ (much less of a
mouthful for non-Germanic speakers!). GIZ is the highly respected
technical-support arm for international development projects run by a
number of the German government's ministries. Their expertise runs
quite deep, helping to manage and staff projects in economic development, governance and reconstruction, civil conflict transformation,
education, and environmental protection.

Ms. Ara breaks the preconceived mold of what many Westerners
expect of a woman from Bangladesh. She is certainly no victim, which
is how media sources often portray South Asian women from developing countries, particularly Muslim ones. She is articulate and well
educated with a background in business studies and the recipient of
a Commonwealth scholarship. She holds five degrees across business,
population studies, governance and public policy and has written widely

on these subjects; all of this is in addition to her extensive practical, field-level work in the country. She is often conflicted between these areas of interest and the role of civil society in the apparel industry.

I wanted to know, considering all the attention and efforts of the past two years, if she was optimistic that the results so many people seemed to expect of Bangladesh would come to fruition.

> "Big question! I have written 17,000 words on this; therefore, I can't give a straightforward, short and crispy answer. I am neither optimistic nor pessimistic. The question is, 'will the civil society movement be capable enough to challenge and supersede market power?' If yes, then how? If not, then why?
>
> "Currently the path [we're on] looks like it is neutralizing market risk (in favor of the market) by creating segmentation among civil societies and by absorbing more immediate risks, thus hinders creating a system that is both enforceable and accountable. Right now it is a complete mess. If I take the current situation as a starting stage, then a 'norming' phase should come in the near future, unless some new trend out-powers the current one.
>
> "The market and ethics have followed *Das Capital* [referencing Marxist theory] to neo-liberalism. Both words have been omni-present. Therefore, I see the current trend is a civil society movement, but not a rise of ethics. The words are just old wine in a new bottle."

This rather somber introspection seemed to reveal a deeper conflict between the results of her own ongoing efforts as part of a civil society movement on the one hand and the expansion of opportunities for those working in related fields.

> "I have considerable criticism about all multi-stakeholder initiatives. My interests in politics and in the global business context have brought me into this field. [It offered] direct contacts with garment workers, trade unions and manufacturers ... this is my poker chip to play with ... I'm an activist but I can't claim to be a human rights

activist, I have my own interest involved. I'm not Mother Teresa. I'm just trying my best in different ways, but I'm not sure how far can I go."

That being the case, I wanted to know what were the immediate needs and risks.

"I'm hoping that garment manufacturers will begin to think differently; they might want to move upward toward middle-ranged fashion items and will be inclined to learn from better management systems. Manufacturers will [continue to] be frustrated with the level of offered price from big discounters and retailers. As manufacturers' overhead cost is going up, due to investment in fire and building safety, they will be expecting better business. On the other hand, giant retailers, who have paid a lot of money to be members of The Accord or the Alliance, will want to adjust their investment in pricing, so there is a bigger possibility that retailers would either offer lower prices or offer loans to factories adjustable with the order over time, like forward purchasing with a flat rate offer, keeping the market risks a constant.

"I think The Accord will soon be in a political crisis and will be subject to media attention both nationally and internationally. Brands will not keep paying them just to shut the mouth of the ILRF, ITUC, etc. [The International Labor Rights Forum and International Trade Union Confederacy]. The Alliance is expected to have a longer life."

That seemed a rather dark and realist assessment of things for someone working within civil society to effect change, though perhaps not unexpected from someone with her political studies background. Shatil's final comments were reflective of the conflicting realities she and peers in countries from Bangladesh and Cambodia to Haiti and Lesotho have had to come to grips with.

"I'm just trying to be a good mother. Soon, I'll be trying to develop garments, less cost, yet with a nice look.

Maybe next I'll appear in the market as a businesswoman.
Enough with the ethical game."

In spite of her frustrations, Shatil and others in Bangladesh who
have been neck deep in these issues for longer than media's attention
span seems to last, recognize that new collaborations are providing real
benefits to local communities. Solidaridad, who we talked about earlier when looking at efforts to address water pollution in China, are also
active in Bangladesh.

Solidaridad/The Bangladesh Water Pact

The Partnership for Cleaner Textile (PaCT) is a multi-stakeholder
initiative focused on the textile wet-processing sector in Bangladesh.
Implemented by the IFC (International Finance Corporation) and
Solidaridad, with support from the Dutch Embassy, and with the
collaboration of H&M, C&A Inditex, KappAhl, Lindex, G-STAR,
Primark and Tesco, PaCT aims to engage 200 wet processing facilities
in Dhaka.

Emma Goodman and her colleague Marieke Weerdesteijn from
Solidaridad explained that PaCT partners are collaborating to
incorporate environmental aspects of textile wet processing in product development, design and sourcing. In its first year of operation,
PaCT has already worked with over 100 factories, conducted Cleaner
Production Deep Dives in 19 factories, completed service provider
training, and launched a Textile Technology Business Center (TTBC)
to support the roll-out of Cleaner Production to participant factories. Together with fellow no-profit group MADE-BY, Solidaridad is
developing decision-support guidance for buyers to reduce the environmental impacts of design and sourcing decisions in the wet processing
stage of garment manufacturing. As of 2014, 1.6 million cubic meters
of water has been saved and 3,000 tons of GHG emissions avoided.

Solidaridad is encouraged by initiatives that foster convergence,
transparency and scale beyond individual projects. Emma clarified.

> "We believe in continuous improvement by mapping im-
> pacts on people and planet, throughout the supply chain.
> For that, it is essential that brands and retailers know

their supply chain and collaborate to achieve that continuous improvement.

"However, there is a risk the industry will shift to new producer countries and repeat mistakes from the past. Sustainability must be part of daily business decisions. In upcoming sourcing markets like Ethiopia, there is now an opportunity to demonstrate that through collaboration with all stakeholders, we can achieve sustainable economic growth."

SEDEX (Supplier Ethical Data Exchange)

Collaboration is at the core of what SEDEX stands for and does, or has been doing, to more properly state it, since 2001, when the organization was first founded by a number of U.K. retailers seeking to build a common approach toward social auditing standards and practices.

At its core, SEDEX is a database platform built to facilitate the management and sharing of health, safety, labor, environmental and ethical practice data among its membership. Those members now include more than 30,000 factories, farms, growers and retailers worldwide — and not only in fashion and apparel categories. The organization has grown to include global players in health care, food and beverage, banking, industrial goods and real estate sectors. This all keeps Tom Smith, acting general manager and executive director at SEDEX on his toes.

"SEDEX is a fast-paced, dynamic business constantly in flux to the changing business landscape in CSR. Currently, my focus is on the operational elements of the business including our global team structure and future growth strategy. Many forget that roles in CSR often require as much knowledge in CSR as other areas of business such as sales, account management, human resources and marketing."

One of the newer hats Tom has been wearing lately is as director of SEDEX China, an area where the organization has long been imbedded. Their release last year of a Responsible Sourcing Briefing update on the country dealt with issues such as child labor, migrant workers, new anti-corruption laws, and human trafficking. I asked Tom what his most important takeaway from China had been thus far.

> "I am far from being an expert on China but do see much misunderstanding on this rapidly developing market. My advice would be for people to experience the business environment themselves to get a better understanding of the ways of working."

Considering that advice and the depth of experience many global businesses have already had in China, I wanted to know if he remained optimistic as to the near-term direction CSR efforts were taking.

> "Overall yes, but admittedly [I am] increasingly cynical. Businesses need to be careful not to lose concentration now that we are on the path of change. I felt, and still do, that business has a *huge* potential to bring about both social and environmental change. I studied politics and then worked at a Latin American political think tank before coming across this area. Where many of my friends and colleagues were looking at careers with political parties and the civil service, I was frustrated by the politics *in* politics and saw 'CSR' as the vehicle that could bring about real change."

One of the key developments that the team at SEDEX had to bring about was the practical development of (and agreement on) a common approach to social auditing across its membership. Considering the variety of sectors that members come from and the wide range of industry-specific initiatives that they pursue, this was no easy task. The resulting tool was SMETA, the SEDEX Members Ethical Trade Audit. Along with its accompanying Best Practice Guidance and measurement criteria, SMETA does not attempt to create a new standard for member brands and factories to follow. Rather, it provides a best-practice tool to help drive convergence of efforts while reducing duplication of cost and efforts.

These types of collaborative efforts, over time, provide their own rewards in terms of highlighting the cross-industry knowledge that

SEDEX team members have hung onto. Tom identified some of the most critical areas.

> "Patience; real change needs deep adjustment that won't happen overnight. 'Good things come to those that wait,' so to speak. Professionalization — when I joined this space there was no 'industry'; we have gone a long way to professionalize and improve our practices. Also, don't try to reinvent the wheel, working in geographical or industry silos will not support change.
>
> "We all face similar challenges, collaboration is the key. Bottom line; there is still plenty of work to be done to make this 'the new norm.'"

The Big Brands

After many years of in-country work and dealing hands-on with some of the same challenges Shatil Ara (Fairwear Foundation, discussed above) has struggled with, I can both understand and appreciate her pragmatism. For people who are so close to the issues day in and day out, it is often difficult to step back and appreciate just how much has been done. And while there is no end to this journey, it is recommendable and good for our collective sanities to recognize that many good people, hardworking and dedicated people, have been working from within brands large and small to effect change. Some brands have even started out with that goal in mind.

Eileen Fisher, Amy Hall

A case in point is the privately held U.S. apparel company Eileen Fisher. There have been few other major American casual wear brands quite like the one Ms. Fisher started in 1984 with a few hundred borrowed dollars to her name. She started out with a vision to create what she called in a 2003 interview for *Fortune* magazine "simply comfortable clothing and a simply comfortable environment."[152]

Since then, she has built a reputation for great clothes and a commitment to sustainability throughout her team's operations. This began with how the core management team that built the business treated each other, as their goal was to build a place their team and associates *loved*. What speaks most to me about any company's efforts and intentions are how passionately its people, one on one, speak about not only their "company" but about their commitment and belief in its mission. This is a value that many companies have only recently begun to look at more closely. Tapping into this level of "give" from an employee requires only one thing to build from: sincerity. The rest grows only with this firmly in place.

Of the many people I have met over the years through the global apparel industry, Amy Hall is just about the most sincere person I have met. I originally connected with her during my time in Hong Kong. She was recently in Toronto for the country's first multi-stakeholder ethical apparel event WEAR2014 (World Ethical Apparel Roundtable) to speak with Canadian brands, nonprofits, media and educators about some of the company's experiences and practices. I followed up with her again recently, for starters because they provide a fantastic benchmark to discuss here, but also to know what had kept her more than 20 years with the same company. I learned quite a lot.

> "When I first arrived at EF, my intention was to stay until I could figure out what I wanted to do with the next phase of my life. Longevity in one place was the furthest notion from my mind. Within six months of arrival, I had moved to an apartment closer to work, as I began to realize that this was a company worth spending some time in. What made it worth uprooting my New York City lifestyle and moving to the suburbs, not to mention staying for another 22 years?
>
> "The company initially gave me an opportunity to explore many different types of work to see where I could add the most value. Where I have ended up couldn't be a better reflection of who I am as an individual and the sum of my prior professional and academic experiences. From the very beginning, I was viewed as a whole person, not just a set of skills on a resume. I was able to bring all the skills, knowledge, and interests acquired over my lifetime to the workplace. I have been surrounded by positive, nurturing people who really care about me as an individual.

"Nothing has been status quo. We are always in a process of self-reflection, considering how to improve upon our practices to make the company an even better place to work. There is a sense of gratitude and appreciation that permeates the walls. We all recognize how special the culture is, from Eileen's unconventional leadership and the collaborative workplace to the personal growth we experience through our work and our relationships with each other."

That ability to develop and deliver what really motivates her and her colleagues also reaches outside the company. She chairs the advisory board at Social Accountability International, keeper of the flame behind the SA8000 social-management systems standard while sitting on the board of the American Sustainable Business Council. That mix of business and standards roles reflects what she learned while studying for her MBA in sustainable business and graduate studies at Columbia's Teacher's College.

After many years of putting to good use her studies in Chinese from Georgetown University working with the Asia Society, the China Institute and the Institute for International Education, Amy took that first step with EF (as she calls the company) in 1993. Having been encouraged to work in a variety of areas to find her best fit doesn't now keep her narrowly defined or focused. That means she's busy at it.

"First and foremost, I lead a team of extraordinarily talented individuals. The day-to-day work of environmental sustainability, human rights, women & girls, philanthropy, and community partnerships happens with the team's oversight. I am not necessarily involved in their work unless they need me. Therefore, as a team leader, I offer support, advocacy, coaching, feedback and extra brain power.

"I am also a co-leader of our company's People & Culture area. This means that I partner with the leaders of our Human Resources, Leadership Learning & Development, and Internal Communications teams to confer on workplace issues facing our employee population.

"I'm also the advisory board chair of Social Account-ability International and board member of the American Sustainable Business Council and speak publicly about a dozen times per year and conduct media interviews as needed."

As for what this allowed her to do in practical terms in engagement with suppliers and communities, she filled me in on the current and upcoming objectives.

"We're about to go public with our Vision 2020 goals. These are a set of ambitious, some might say, 'bold' environmental and social sustainability goals for the year 2020. This initiative is called, 'No Excuses.' That phrase alone speaks to the boldness of the task ahead of us. The messaging of the campaign is clear. It means holding ourselves accountable with every decision we make by pinning our progress to a five-year timeline that is both sensible and scary.

"We are not the first apparel company to take this leap. But we seem to be the first 'designer' brand. This is not, for us, a marketing ploy, but rather a call to action. We *need* other brands to join us in this journey for there to be real, substantive healing of the planet. The goals we've set for 2020 are to achieve 100 percent organic cotton and linen, eliminate viscose, and offer 100 percent sustainable wool from humanely raised sheep on sustainably managed land. Just as important is ensuring fair wages and meaningful benefits for workers in our first-tier suppliers. Worker and community happiness is measurable and achievable."

Hilde-Gunn Vestad, Adidas

These are many of the same issues Hilde-Gunn Vestad deals with in her new role as the director of Group Legal and Compliance for German sportswear brand Adidas. Working out of Hong Kong, Hilde has been deep in it since arriving in Asia from her native Norway in 1998. This makes her a solid "China Hand" in this part of the world, where she originally began by building out H&M's approach and in-frastructure for CSR across Asia Pacific.

By 2003, Hilde had moved over to Adidas where she worked in a hands-on training and development capacity, collaborating with regional suppliers until late 2014. Since beginning her latest role, her immediate list of concerns certainly has living wages down as a hot topic, along with trafficking and slavery, which she thinks markets will continue to gain greater awareness about. She personally hopes for the continued growth of corporate responsibility efforts in the industry and believes this needs to strongly push down into the next tier, below the globally recognized brands as well, which she describes as "currently in the shadows."

> "Right now I work on various initiatives around migrant workers, forced labor, worker grievance mechanisms projects via SMS and voice hotlines, and empowerment projects for workers, such as reproductive health and financial literacy."

There are still some major challenges she sees as hot topics for the next few years as brands deal, she believes, with increased media attention and calls for responsible actions down to the worker level. Water pollution, hazardous chemicals and "where next after China?" are questions on her mind — as they are for many of us. Hilde also expressed some cynicism about the growth of solutions offered up by too many consulting firms, which distract from eliminating duplications of efforts. Pragmatically, she called out the opportunity to generate savings and make money by such efforts.

> "We take this work seriously; we are, after all, ranked third in the world! [She is referring to the Global 100 Most Sustainable Corporations Index.] We have a dedicated team of 65 people with diverse backgrounds, skills and passions who all go beyond the scope of monitoring. I think Asia will continue to be a strong player, though we do see shrinkage in China."

Go Local

The causes of that shrinkage, the loss of apparel industry orders placed to what used to be called "the factory of the world," are various, but for most of the mainstream industry it comes down to cost. It is what brought industry to China and what will push it out at a time when both the global economy and China's are bracing for what I would call a Great Retailing Leap Forward. Multinational brands who went to China to buy for export are now buying domestically for domestic markets. Those in it for the long haul have opened their own stores.

As much as other key countries in the region have built up capacity for garments, footwear and a host of consumer goods, this doesn't detract from the fact that China has built out the most complete and functioning infrastructure to allow for its past 30 years of manufacturing success. Still, lack of enforcement on many labor and environmental issues did provide the country with undue advantage, in the estimation of many. That advantage has narrowed significantly, in great part adding to production shifts across the world once again. As we have seen, this is nothing new for the trade, which has been transforming itself since its earliest mercantilist days.

How best to leverage the values imbedded in the industry for greater local and community benefits is a problem that has also been tackled since the Industrial Revolution by one group or another. And while production volumes represented by most 'buy local' efforts are in the 'drop in a bucket' evolutionary stage, the industry cannot afford to underestimate the trend's potential impact. The Internet age has enabled micro-marketing efforts to the extreme; bespoke, handmade, local apparel has begun to make a rebirth. The difficulty, besides the fact that local handmade goods are more costly, is in weaning ourselves off the mass production model we have evolved. There is also now much political and philosophical baggage resting on this new movement as well.

The good news is that there are literally thousands of small-scale efforts taking place across the world in reaction to modernism's attacks on all things traditional — crafts, jobs, economies, or what have you.

Sara Power, INLAND

Sarah Power's story behind the birth of Toronto-based INLAND speaks to those of many like-minded professionals within creative industries across the planet.

> "After graduating the Fashion Design program at George Brown [College in Toronto], I quickly realized that the

fashion industry in Canada was somewhat un-opportu-
nistic, and I wanted — needed — to earn a fair living. The
fashion world presented limited options. The small fashion labels I was interning with were never going to be able
to afford to hire me. They certainly revealed how incredibly hard it was to start your own collection. I decided
to shelve my aspirations and instead took a job in 2007
with The Clothing Show. My interest was in the small
'Boutique' section that was made up of local, independent labels. I completely fell in love with the community
of local design.

"The idea for INLAND came out of my time with
The Clothing Show. I always wanted to see designers
being represented and presented in more of a beautifully,
curated way. I also saw that Canadian designers needed
more overall exposure and opportunity to make money.
INLAND does all this.

"The defining moment that pushed me to take the
leap to actually start INLAND was in a small boutique
in Berlin. I had been humming and hawing over a bracelet. I loved it — but I was struggling to justify the price.
Then I noticed a girl talking with the shop owner, pulling a bunch of similar jewelry pieces out of a box. She
was the artist who'd made the piece I was holding, there
making her delivery to the shop. I introduced myself, and
that was it — I bought the bracelet instantly. I was so
energized by the experience of meeting with the designer,
and she was so thrilled to see her work on a customer that
loved it. It made me realize how important and meaningful that exchange was, and at that moment, I decided to
create INLAND, a place where that feeling and experience could happen. That was July 2013."

And compared to the mainstream industry in Canada?

"I think it's over-saturated. Retail in general is hurting
because we just have too much stuff sitting on shelves.
These massive warehouse shopping centers are churning

out so much product — cheap, but meaningless. I really see people craving and searching for more of a personal connection with the things they buy, and especially with the things they put on their body. What we wear speaks about who we are and, whether we like it or not, the concept of 'personal brand' is dominating. It's a wonderful time for independent fashion and design actually — they just need to be found out about. Hopefully INLAND can help."

Yumnaa Firfirey, Bodhisattva

That kind of support for local, independent designers and labels is something that Yumnaa Firfirey, founder and director of Cape Town's Bodhisattva label loves to hear about. Her grounding in business studies and graduate work in corporate social investment led the South African native to a career in community engagement and education at the international level. After eight years helping to lead sustainable and responsible tourism efforts with the Cape's Department of Economic Development, Yumnaa turned to consulting, out of which the Bodhisattva label was born.

> "I initially worked with government, but after eight years was quite frustrated that the wheels just turned too slowly. I then consulted to business [but] left this phase of my career feeling disappointed that business seemed to be much more concerned with the short-term profits. I realized that perhaps a more effective way of bringing about real economic and social development is to be a role model of a business that is successful and profitable, while having a positive impact. And even though I had no formal fashion qualifications, I had been designing my own clothes since the age of 11 and grew up with my grandparents and mother who were tailors, seamstresses and knitters.
>
> "I started all the planning and establishment of Bodhisattva at the end of June 2013, and we launched at the end of February 2014 at Design Indaba, a prestigious

South African design fair that takes place in Cape Town at the end of February every year. I've started other organizations — both commercially and in government — and run previous businesses, but I have never worked as hard as I have in the fashion industry. This is definitely not for the faint-hearted. The past 20 months has been very tough, possibly because up to the end of last year I have also consulted on economic development three days a week. It helps to have an additional income stream when you are starting a luxury fashion brand."

Like the start-up itself, Bodhisattva creations project a youthful strength and simplicity of design. Ethical relationships in the manufacturing of the lineup are process-mapped on the brand's website, identifying the local entrepreneurs and operators responsible each step of the way. This fits with Yumnaa's goals, taken from her economic development background, to ensure the impacts are positive, widespread and recognized.

A lot of people in the industry are looking to Africa once again, some on the scale of projects like those mentioned earlier in Kenya and Ethiopia, many at the individual designer level.

"This is an amazing country and continent that we live in, which is not only breathtakingly beautiful, but also has an incredible spirit of hope and resilience. There is so much goodwill out there, waiting to be transformed to its full potential. If we believe in the philosophy of *Ubuntu*, that I am because we are, then we are impoverished by the poverty, disease and crime and all the social ills 'out there.' The truth is that it is not 'out there.' It is in here. We are the society that we live in. If we are able to change it, then it is our responsibility to do so."

Kathryn Hilderbrand, Good Clothing Company

Connecting that need for change with efforts to support and bring local designers' work to a larger audience was behind Kathryn Hilderbrand's latest effort in launching Good Clothing Company in Cape Cod, Massachusetts. As the founder and design head of the GreenLinebyK brand, the step into manufacturing small runs for others grew out of necessity.

> "In 2010 I decided that I wanted to launch a collection of apparel that was a true representation of me and my principles. GreenLinebyK was launched and slowly grew in popularity. I spent most of the first three to four years developing a more cohesive collection, getting rid of things that just didn't work and expanding on things that did. By late last year, I realized I needed to take things to production. The volume of sewing had become too much for me and my very small staff. In searching for a US-based apparel manufacturing facility that not only adhered to my ethical and sustainable production principles, but also offered small runs, I realized something — there weren't any! It just didn't make sense to me. Surely there were many other designers like me who were in the same position. I did some research and discovered that the problem was much more prevalent than I had initially assumed. After a lot of thought, business planning and looking for the perfect spot, Good Clothing Company found its home and a well-received place in the fashion community."

And how has the reaction been from local area designers?

> "Relief! That's the word that consistently comes to mind. Designers are relieved and feel hopeful. The overwhelming response is that they finally have a chance to thrive. The response has been so much greater than I could have ever hoped for. Unfortunately, most of the textile industry in our area had closed up shop. So, many of our industry jobs have been outsourced for cheap labor in other countries. It's difficult to battle that whole beast. What Good Clothing Company is doing is filling a huge need in local industry. We are offering small runs. That's hard to find. Our goal is to change the way manufacturing is done on a local level. That will — and is — bringing jobs back in our case. This business model will hopefully inspire

others to follow suit and create their own micro manufacturing business in their hometown."

There's nothing intrinsically wrong with manufacturing in a developing country — if and when it's being done responsibly and respectfully. Going local has the same community impacts in Africa, Latin America or Asia as the movement does in the West. It's a challenge for larger factories because their product is not really the garments it makes for others, but their time and labor.

Rachel Faller, Tonlé

Rachel Faller was after a very different business model when her Fulbright-funded research into sustainable businesses took her back to Cambodia in 2009 to launch her first apparel endeavor.

> "In 2007, I visited Cambodia for the first time with a family friend who wanted to start a handicraft business in the country — and I fell in love with the people and the textiles. It was also the first time I started to learn about businesses that were trying to use fashion for good rather than all of the negative outputs I had usually associated with the fashion and garment manufacturing industry. So, I applied for a Fulbright grant to go back and do research for a year on such sustainable businesses. What I learned through my research shaped my plans to start my first fashion business. Trying to grow that business and shape it into something self-sustaining kept me in Cambodia for six years. But I wouldn't have stayed if it weren't for the amazing team of people I had the pleasure of working with."

Most people's understanding of Cambodia has been largely shaped by media, movies and the country's recent violet past. But having spent many years living and working there, Rachel's view might surprise some of them.

> "I think many Cambodians are ready to move past it and have their country seen as something other than a war-ravaged country. Many complex factors have shaped Cambodia to become what it is today and are still shaping

it. Like any culture or country, Cambodia is a complicated, multifaceted place where you will be constantly surprised and kept on your toes if you keep your mind open. Not everything is as it seems at a first glance. This is true of so many places, but especially in Cambodia, I think."

Tonlé is driven by a zero-waste philosophy; her design team in Phnom Penh scours secondhand fabric markets and sifts through industrial factories' fabric waste for their raw materials. The production team's own two to three percent waste is then collected, cut down and re-fabricated back into materials for use in additional garments. Pay is set well above industry minimum wages, and training is provided as part of the management team's effort to encourage upward mobility in the small organization. Keeping everyone in the process connected to and invested in their products was a key goal in Rachel's vision for a more equitable way to create value, work and a sustainable business. She remains somewhat skeptical about larger brand efforts.

> "While there has been a lot more talk about sustainable fashion, I don't know if this is really leading to large changes in numbers yet. Tonlé is tiny — we employ 50 people — no small feat, but still! Compare that to 500,000 people working in conventional factory jobs in Cambodia alone. I think that the role of Tonlé and other boutique sustainable fashion brands is to be advocates and tastemakers who are setting the example. Once that happens, I am definitely more optimistic about change, but in order for those larger brands to make even incremental changes, *customers have to take a strong position.* I think a lot of customers care in theory about things changing, but have not yet taken a hard line approach to what they purchase."

Tal Dehtiar, Oliberté

Canadian entrepreneur Tal Dehtiar takes an equally pragmatic view.

> "I am very careful about making bold statements I can't live up to. Is Oliberté singlehandedly creating true social change right now? No. But our hope is that we continue

to change lives one worker at a time, and in the process inspire other business to operate in a similar manner, eventually helping to create more widespread lasting and meaningful change."

Tal founded the Oliberté footwear brand and established its manufacturing center in Ethiopia in 2012; it is one of a number of social entrepreneurship efforts he has undertaken over the years, including rural support projects in Belize and Costa Rica. A year later, the facility became a certified Fair Trade factory, the first of its kind for footwear. I was, of course, curious as to why he had narrowed in on Ethiopia.

"Ethiopia has the skilled craftsmen and the high-quality, sustainably made materials I was looking for. We didn't need to show the Ethiopian craftspeople how to make shoes, rather, we hired the folks who were doing it best and gave them the most high-quality, readily available and environmentally responsible materials to work with. That's how we found Hafde Tannery in Addis Ababa, which is actually one of the most environmentally responsible tanneries in the world. It's the only tannery to have a chrome-3 recycling system, so it doesn't contaminate the (local) water source.

"It's been our experience that Ethiopia's economy is relatively stable and open to foreign investment. African countries are new territory for small foreign business, and, though it is expensive in terms of costs, mistakes and patience, we have been extremely patient, used our capital wisely and when the time required, brought on key investors and lenders to support our growth."

Mr. Dehtiar's philosophy regarding the use of the best possible makers and materials extended into the factory's commitments to going local at the management level as well.

"One of the best decisions we made was to hire local management instead of bringing in managers from Canada or the U.S. We wanted to hire an Ethiopian manager and take an NGO approach to staffing, which is to say, make use of local knowledge to navigate the local landscape. Entrusting our operations with Ethiopians gives them a stake in our joint success."

Tal and Oliberté entered Ethiopia just ahead of major global sourcing efforts there. Late in 2014, H&M and Swedish investment group Kinnevik announced plans to invest more than $US 1 million over the coming three years to help support local social entrepreneurial efforts. This came on the back of news earlier in the year that Turkish textile firm Ayka Textile was set to expand its local manufacturing capacity by 50 percent, in part to respond to local procurement by retailers such as H&M and the U.K.'s Tesco. According to Tal, they had best be prepared for some challenges.

"The biggest challenges we face as a company come with cash flow and logistics. While African economies are advancing at a rapid rate, the infrastructure of monetary instruments is not as sophisticated. Many people get frustrated because they cannot apply the same business policies for payments, which can be a hurdle. In our case, we have built trust and partnerships, so are comfortable with the potential risks.

"Regarding logistics, while the footwear industry is improving in Africa, the supply chain is not fully developed yet. As such, some materials must be imported, and once they arrive, the customs clearance can take time. With that said, we are very lucky in Ethiopia because the government is making huge steps to improve this; over five years now in the country, we have seen positive improvements. Like a lot of businesses, we have our challenges, but we've learned the most important way to operate successfully. Patience is #1 — without it you will be lost and gone before you know it. Cultural respect is also incredibly vital. It may sound a bit 'fluffy,' but in a place like Ethiopia if you can build relationships that extend beyond just business, it goes a long way. There are a number of people we could consider competitors, but because of our personal relationships we work together when someone is in a jam."

It's an attitude that seems pervasive among those with a commitment to manufacturing locally in both an ethical and sustainable way, across the world or just around the corner.

Innovators & Activists

Over the past few years, we have heard from a growing chorus of activists, media pundits and politicians about what it will take to manage real change in the industry. Like many of my collaborators and peers, I often vacillate between pessimism and hope. We sometimes do truly take two steps forward and three steps back. There are some who have called for the system to be torn asunder and others who believe wholeheartedly that only business itself can be relied on to see through institutional change. From my understanding of history and politics, rarely has change come cheaply or from the very top. More often it comes from rebellion within or by force from external sources. Of the many people who have made valuable contributions to these efforts, there are a number who particularly stand out for me, either because I have been fortunate enough to have collaborated with them or I've been impacted by their perspective and passion.

Kate Larsen, Ethical Supply Chain Advisor

There are few brains I have enjoyed picking regarding ethical trade issues as much as that of London-based Kate Larsen. A Kiwi by birth (a native of New Zealand, that is), Kate has also been one of few people in the industry to have successfully taken her background in supply chains, nonprofits and a deep knowledge of China (that comes only from having lived there and learned the language) and successfully molded a new role for herself helping others to engage.

When we first met in Asia, she was well into her seven-year stretch with iconic British fashion house Burberry. Despite her often hectic schedule, Kate always took the time to provide a newcomer to the region with advice and encouragement. Since launching her own advisory services CSRWinWin in 2012, it didn't seem that her pace had let up any.

> "Since Rana Plaza, I became quite busy as one of the many [people] supporting efforts for better conditions for Bangladeshi garment workers. I'm particularly involved

in worker empowerment issues, and whilst committees, unions and stable management-worker dialogue will be the best, in the short term I've been busy on roll-out of a helpline, advising on how to deal with issues raised. For this, I apply my earlier years of experience setting up — in partnership with brands like Nike, HP and NEXT — NGO-run worker helplines in China.

"Being based now in London after about ten years living and working on the ground in China, I'm now often called on to speak at industry events in the U.K. and Europe about worker empowerment, brand collaboration, and capacity building — three tools that support responsible sourcing efforts. I spend a lot of time helping people see that no one or two tools will ensure them better supplier factory conditions for workers. Just as you can't build a house with only a hammer and a chisel, so you also need more tools to help and cause suppliers and their factories to improve conditions."

I asked what specifically she was most focused on at the moment.

"I did a lot of brand collaboration with industry leaders on shared factories (Levis, Adidas, Nike, Puma, M&S, Nordstrom, Ralph Lauren, etc.), so I like to help others understand how that can be undertaken, the benefits, and how to scale, given that none of us can improve long lists of factories on our own. I'm taking it a further step though, and am involved in efforts with industry peers to send the right messages to governments regarding improved labor law governance, and to help investors understand more what works. At the end of the day, local government law enforcement or investor encouragement to brands can have even bigger impacts for workers and sustainable business. I'm also working on a tool to help consumers understand brand efforts better!"

Boutique firm advisory services tend to allow for a much more individualized approach to helping guide brands and retailers on systemic changes to their operations. This means that the work is often varied and challenging. Based on what she had been working on, I wanted to know what key trends and causes needed the most attention from Kate's point of view.

> "We need to support wider efforts to see more balance between worker and CEO, Board and Executive pay, to think about the medium- and long-term rather than merely short-term quarterly income targets, and to see a living wage paid to employees in the West and the supply chain too.
>
> "The industry's involvement in violations in worker rights also reflects international trade policy that has veered too much in favor of short-term unsustainable trade patterns, and this needs to be fixed to incentivize trading countries to implement their labor and environmental laws."

Values near and dear to the Kiwi heart, I imagined!

> "Coming from New Zealand, with a mother who ran for the Green Party, I'm an environmentalist by heart. I chose to write my Master's thesis on how we can better prevent wastewater pollution from the apparel and electronics sectors. I saw rivers run black in China, and we know that apparel is one of the largest water-using industries, so it feels right to work with an industry where we can cause, support and reward factories for cleaner production in more environmentally friendly and sustainable ways."

There are those however, who believe that industry simply can't be expected to take a real hand in fixing the damage they themselves have wrought.

Tansy Hoskins, Writer/Activist

Tansy Hoskins's first book, "Stitched Up: The Anti-Capitalist Book of Fashion," shocked more than a few fashion industry sensibilities when it hit the bookstands in the U.K. and North America in late 2014. Anyone familiar with her writing and commentary for Britain's influential *The Guardian* newspaper, the BBC or Al Jazeera certainly shouldn't have been. Share her politics or not, one cannot help but deeply respect and be moved by her passion. Fatema Ahmed's book review for *The Guardian* hit all the right nails on the head when she called out Hoskins's pointedly Marxist interpretations of the fashion industry. The dogma was accepted by some as a breath of fresh air, daring to say something clearly and honestly that had needed saying for a very long time, but at an entirely new level intellectually. There were also interpretations of the work as critical of the concept of sustainable fashion, which is what I was most interested to learn about from her directly.

> "Ethical and planet-friendly fashion is important as an innovator for creating new technologies or for reinvigorating old ones. It stands as proof that beauty and quality do not need to be based on toxicity or labor abuses. It is the only section of the fashion industry that serves as a blueprint for a better future and its role in inspiring people and helping them to imagine a new way of organizing clothing production is very important. What it isn't, however, is a way out of the mess we are in; for that, we need systemic change."

I've more and more come to support that particular view myself. But even changes to systems require a goal, process map or vision to break through to the next level. If that system creeps along organically, so to speak, it may go in the direction of least resistance versus where we might envision its ideal to be. Meanwhile, there's real work going on — on the ground. And Tansy's been on the road through Asia and Africa for a close-up look.

> "I was recently in Bangladesh, and the strength and determination of the unions there — particularly the National Garment Workers Federation — is seriously inspiring. It is these unions that are securing minimum wage increases and securing rights for garment workers. In addition, the development of the Bangladesh Accord on Building and Fire Safety is a game changer in that it is legally binding and worker-led, I would like to see initiatives like that

rolled out to more countries and covering areas such as the environment and a living wage.

"Holding the fashion industry to account for its environmental destruction is a serious challenge — it is the third worst water polluter in China and the tanneries in Bangladesh are horrific. It would need global legislation and prosecutions of the big brands who are environmental criminals to force them to pay compensation and clean up the mess they have made in the Global South.

"I am optimistic, though, as I think people now recognize the need for change like never before; we have seen huge demonstrations calling for climate justice and swathes of people are joining the fight for a fair fashion industry."

The people who usually speak out in this way have been considered too on the fringe to be given media attention, but when the message comes in a compelling and articulate argument, as Tansy's does in her book, it's much more difficult to dismiss. No doubt the foundation she gained at the London School of Economics and Political Science prepared her for campaign work at U.K.'s Stop the War Coalition and the Campaign for Nuclear Disarmament. But the connections to her personal convictions are older than her school years.

"My family certainly instilled in me a strong sense of right and wrong and the need for people to participate in organized campaigns to change the world. Other than that, I feel propelled by a strong sense of injustice and frustration about how the world is run and the terrible conditions that capitalism creates for people; by the urgency of the climate question and the knowledge that we are on the brink of catastrophe; and by the knowledge that another world is possible. We have everything we need to create a way of living that is based on ecology and equality."

Kelly Drennan, Founder/Educator

Having a vision of greater environmental sustainability in fashion was what inspired Canada's Kelly Drennan, founder and executive director of Fashion Takes Action (FTA). Since 2007, when I first connected with Kelly, FTA has been working from within a community of local Canadian designers on sustainable fashion issues and education. It was only natural for me to look her up once we had relocated back to Canada from Asia in late 2010. When she invited me to join FTA's board in 2014, I learned very quickly that this was someone who liked to keep busy.

> "Every day is different at Fashion Takes Action. Our main focus right now is on youth education, so most of our time is spent building our program, hiring and training teachers, and seeking sponsorship and other funding. This week, we are also in the process of coordinating a fashion show fundraiser and an information booth at the Green Living Show, and building a national campaign for Fashion Revolution Day. We're also working with the City of Toronto's Solid Waste Management Strategy to reduce the amount of textiles that are being put in landfill and planning for our next conference, WEAR2015."

Her background and experiences in communications and publicity first exposed her to industry issues.

> "I began as a publicist working with local fashion designers. As I became more familiar with what went on behind the scenes, I became motivated to make change happen. Sickened by the waste and excess, I wanted to be a part of a movement that would benefit the environment and the people who make our clothes. From that motivation, Fashion Takes Action was born, and since then the focus has grown to also include consumer awareness."

Since the recent demise of civil society and labor rights group Maquila Solidarity Network, FTA provides the only multi-stakeholder opportunity for apparel industry engagement in Canada. I asked Kelly to share what her expectations were of the market more than two years after Rana Plaza had put industry issues back on the radar of civil society in Canada.

> "I believe that more Canadian brands will engage in ethical sourcing and CSR practices, and will continue to look

to global leaders for best practices. I believe that collaboration will finally become a practice and not just something preached. I hope that with these positive changes comes an increase in transparency and stronger stakeholder engagement. I also believe that there will be an increase in domestic production over the next few years, with companies manufacturing both offshore and locally. Finally, to minimize waste, the selling of inventory at a discounted rate, or worse, being left with excessive amounts of inventory that ends up in landfill, I hope to see a shift in production that is based on consumer demand rather than in anticipation of such demand."

Stephanie Benedetto, Lawyer/Entrepreneur

Corporate lawyer Stephanie Benedetto is banking on that demand, but not, perhaps, for the reasons one might first think, considering her background in the legal profession. But she actually did a very brave thing and stepped over to the client's side of the table when she took her first steps into sustainable fashion.

> "After six years as a corporate attorney in New York, I found myself gravitating toward working with entrepreneurs and pro bono clients. It's through those experiences that my passion for sustainability and its role in fashion and technology really took hold. So in 2012, I co-founded Paper No. 9, a sustainable textile manufacturing facility based in Brooklyn. We developed a proprietary process that converts recycled paper into custom fabrics. Everything is crafted by hand using minimal waste and zero toxins — and without the use of stripping agents, bleach, or wastewater. Corporate attorney turned fashion tech entrepreneur in one fell swoop!
>
> "At Paper No. 9, I saw firsthand the problems in textile manufacturing and the fashion industry. Think of your favorite cotton t-shirt. It requires over 700 gallons of water and one third of a pound of chemicals to produce. *That's enough water for one person to drink for three years.*

And that's just one shirt! Over two billion shirts are sold worldwide each year. If we continue at the current pace, by 2025, two thirds of the entire world's population will face shortages of freshwater and be exposed to hazardous chemicals. That is what motivates me each and every day. Replacing conventional cotton with organic cotton in a single t-shirt cuts your chemical use down to zero and requires only ten gallons of water to produce. Sustainable fashion can literally save lives."

I had received a few online indications recently that she was up to new projects when I received the demo invite to Queen of Raw's web tool. Benedetto was looking beyond the current model she was helping to build and finding a solution she could share with others. She has moved quickly to apply past experiences to take advantage of new opportunities.

"Some of my work as a lawyer was in media, entertainment and technology. The technology industry was a natural fit to solve some of fashion's biggest challenges to the environment. On one hand, fabric mills were producing tons of excess fabrics in over 80 percent of their runs. On the other hand, there was a large community of students and emerging designers who were struggling to get access to these fabrics. My goal was to provide the bridge. Queen of Raw is a new e-commerce platform and mobile app that connects independent designers to suppliers of innovative and sustainable textiles. Its custom applications, including a mood board tool, empower designers to design smarter by encouraging them to bring sustainability into the sourcing process early on."

Using the tools that have evolved out of globalization's communication explosion to address its consumption habits seems fitting. And considering the ongoing issues with textile waste in municipal landfills, there is no medium-term end to a near-guaranteed source of supply.

While waste reduction opportunities attract some innovators' attention to new business models within apparel and textiles that are aligned with their personal philosophies, others are focused on tackling industry pollution issues through the power of education and images — "activism by film," if you will.

River Blue *Documentary*

This is the route Canadian documentary team made up of cinematographer Roger Williams, director David McIlvride, conservationist Mark Angelo, and co-producer Lisa Mazzotta took on their international journey to make *River Blue: The Story of Fashion Destroying the Rivers of the World*. The joint efforts of renowned naturalist Mark Angelo together with an award winning team who have produced some of the best work on Discovery Channel, National Geographic, NBC and Nickelodeon, promise an engaging film event. *River Blue* takes a harsh look at the impact that denim manufacturing is having on the world's rivers.

> "The goal of the production group," co-producer Lisa Mazzotta told me, "was to bring the message of river conservation to a larger audience, and during the research of the current state of rivers globally, the destructive effects of clothing manufacturing came to light. Our director, David, found an image from NASA that showed the rivers in China had turned indigo blue, the color of blue jeans, from the thousands of factories on the banks of the Pearl River that are dumping their dyes and toxic chemical waste. At that moment, we realized that by focusing on apparel and denim in particular, we can relay the message to all of us because we all wear clothes and we all know most of our clothes are made abroad."

My immediate thoughts went back to the innumerable trips up into China I had taken over my six years in Hong Kong. My second thought was to mentally count the number of jeans in my closet. Only two, thankfully (though, to my wife's displeasure, they might see the washing machine only once a month — but I'm doing my part for water conservation!). I was also curious what locals might have had to say during the team's investigations in India, Africa, China and Indonesia.

> "Local environmentalists and lawyers express the dire need for change. Local farmers and fisherman have had to resort to sifting through garbage, fishing for worms or other alternative means to make money since the rivers that they once lived off of are dead. There are no fish or other wildlife for many of them to survive on. The locals, and people who work in these factories and leather tanneries complain about the situation, but they don't feel like there is much they can do. They don't feel like they have any power to change things.
>
> "We hope that the movie will create a great concern and sense of urgency for the need for change within the apparel manufacturing industry. It's easy to think that what happens oversees doesn't affect us, but we are the ones buying the clothing made there, and people who use these rivers and live around these factories are getting cancers and other various diseases from the toxic waste. If that's not enough to propel change, it's important to note that the toxins from this chemical waste are flowing from these rivers into the oceans, and from the oceans, these chemicals can be found in the tissues of fish we eat here in North America. What goes around comes around."

The critical importance of river health and water conservation helped bring together activists and experts from around the world in support of the documentary's work. Greenpeace Asia's Tianjie Ma, Dr. Jamie Pittock with UNESCO, Chinese environmentalist Ma Jun, Sunita Narain of India's Centre for Science and Environment and others worked with Mark Angelo to bring his message home. Had they found any positive brand efforts they could report on?

> "There are a few brands that are working to make a change. We met with a young fashion designer in Los Angeles, Lukas Eichmann of Tortoise Jeans, who has developed

technology that uses laser and air to do the finishing on jeans, deleting the necessity for water.

"Greenpeace has put forth a Detox Campaign that challenges some of the world's most popular clothing brands to eliminate all releases of hazardous chemicals by the year 2020. Some major brands have signed onto this; however, there are many that haven't. It's also hard to see what the brands who have signed on are really doing to take action toward changing their manufacturing practices."

This theme of transparency popped up throughout all the research, interviews and discussions that took place around the writing of this book. The lack of transparency is built into auditing practices to shield buyers from risk while illegalities continue at the factory level largely unchecked. The invisible impacts of global warming and the all-too-visible, yet hotly denied, fallout from raw wastewater have all taken place for years out of sight from any but those deep inside the industry — and those fighting to break in with a flashlight. Transparency is without a doubt the next battleground within the global apparel industry.

The status quo system that has evolved over the past 20 years has, in large part, been built up out of sight and out of mind; it's a situation that's been facilitated by the growing distances between producers and consumers. Terms of trade were kept quiet; the public was generally excluded from trade deals and tax-free pacts between governments and business as the era of corporate economic diplomacy took hold. But true to the Law of Unintended Consequences, globalization had provided opportunities to many multinational brands and retailers who are selling in your hometown but domiciled in Switzerland, Barbados and Hong Kong so as to minimize their fair shares of social benefit to society. The Internet age has also enabled ever-greater numbers of people to exchange information, connect with their peers, search out truths for themselves, and sometimes just to find a great t-shirt! Multiple interpretations of transparency and methods to achieve it stream live to our smartphones, tables, laptops and TVs.

On the back of this trend toward expanded transparency came Rana Plaza, an event that should not have happened and which industry and government had assured us time and time again would not happen. Trust us, the apparel and textile industry bodies told us, to manage this on the honor system with voluntary codes of conduct, and we'll keep our noses clean. Voluntary plans, standards and schemes — over the span of two decades now — have only begun to crack open the door of global supply chains. Improvements have been incremental as best. Thousands have lost their lives, while millions more have been affected by employment shifts and environmental degradation. Time is up. It's time to take serious, legislative action to hold brands and retailers legally responsible for complying with the ethics they espouse at home regardless of where their production happens to be taking place.

The technological advances in communications that allowed marketing firms and ad agencies to sell us on a globalized standard of industrial fashion are now allowing many of us to build on our dreams of connecting again to the people who make our clothes. In my family's case, this means we know the team at Tonlé in Cambodia who selected the fabric and sewed it, then packaged it for my wife's Christmas present this year. It means my son can trade t-shirts online with the friends he has made and kept while living around the world in Asia, Mexico, Central America and the U.S. And it means I know where the next local clothes swap will be because @NRandCo here in Toronto flags it to her Tweet pals.

All the power that we need to effect real change in the world is now in our hands. Truly it is. We decide where we spend our money. We decide what we choose to buy and believe in. And, in the end, this has been a book about us, about what we know, about the brands we support and believe in, about what we can choose to do about their actions and how we choose to live.

To paraphrase part of the opinion article I wrote to fellow Canadians in the *Toronto Star* just weeks following Rana Plaza: as a society, as human beings, we must now decide firmly do our part, or, by our silence and acquiescence, mark clearly for our children, our community and our future what we have each personally deemed to be acceptable standards of dignity and justice.

> *No one saves us but ourselves. No one can and no one may.*
> *We ourselves must walk the path."*
>
> — The Buddha

Notes

CHAPTER 1

1. Ames, Glenn J. (2008), *The Globe Encompassed: The Age of European Discovery, 1500–1700*, Pearson, pp. 102–103.
2. Schnee, Heinrich (1908), *Unsere Kolonien*, Quelle & Meyer, pp. 37 and 54.
3. Van Boven, M. W. (2002), *Towards A New Age of Partnership (TANAP): An Ambitious World Heritage Project*, UNESCO Memory of the World– reg. form VOC Archives Appendix 2, p.14.
4. Ricklefs, M. C. (1991), *A History of Modern Indonesia since c. 1300*, 2nd edition, London: MacMillan, p. 110.
5. For the text of the charter granted by Queen Elizabeth I to the Honourable East India Company see http://en.wikisource.org/wiki/Charter_Granted_by_Queen_Elizabeth_to_the_East_India_Company
6. Jourdain, J. (1905), *The Journal of John Jourdain: 1608–1617, Describing His Experiences in Arabia, India, and the Malay Archipelago*, Cambridge: Hakluyt Society.
7. Sainsbury, W. Noel, ed. (1878), *Calendar of State Papers Colonial, East Indies, China and Japan 1622/1624*, Vol 4, London.
8. Shorto, R. (2004), *The Island at the Center of the World*, Doubleday.
9. Schmidt, B. (2001), *Innocence Abroad: The Dutch Imagination and the New World, 1570–1670*, Cambridge Press.
10. Bates Brown, Harry and Jacob Osborn Ware (1958), *Cotton*, New York: McGraw-Hill.
11. Volti, Rudi (1999), "Cotton," *The Facts on File Encyclopedia of Science, Technology, and Society*.
12. Tripathi, Rama Shankar (2003), *History of Ancient India*, New Delhi: Motilal Banarsidass Publishers Pvt. Ltd.
13. Backer, Patricia, "Technology in the Middle Ages," *History of Technology*. Accessed June 12, 2011.
14. Berg, Maxine (2013), "Useful knowledge, 'industrial enlightenment,' and the place of India," *Journal of Global History*, Vol. 8 issue 1, pp. 117–141.

15. Bell, Adrian R., Chris Brooks, and Paul Dryburgh (2007), *The English Wool Market, c. 1230–1327*, Cambridge Press.
16. Douglas, David Charles and Harry Rothwell (1995), *English Historical Documents, 1189–1327*, Psychology Press.
17. Cohn, Samuel K. (2002), "The Black Death: End of a paradigm" *American Historical Review*, Vol. 107 issue 3, pp. 703–737.
18. Dickerson, Oliver Morton (1951), *The Navigation Acts and the American Revolution*, University of Pennsylvania.
19. Epstein, Stephan R., "Craft guilds, apprenticeship, and technological change in preindustrial Europe," *Journal of Economic History*, Sept 1998.
20. Behrendt, Stephen D., David Richardson, and David Eltis (1999), *Records for 27,233 Voyages That Set Out to Obtain Slaves for the Americas*, W. E. B. Du Bois Institute for African and African-American Research, Harvard.
21. Morgan, Kenneth (2000), *Slavery, Atlantic Trade and the British Economy, 1660–1800*, Cambridge University Press.
22. Bayly, C. A. (1988), "Indian society and the making of the British Empire," in *The New Cambridge History of India*.
23. Chaudhuri, K. N. (1978), *The Trading World of Asia and the English East India Company 1600–1760*, Cambridge.
24. Espinasse, Francis (1874), *Lancashire Worthie*, London: Simpkin, Marshall & Co., p. 296.
25. Jones, Sam (Aug 27, 2013), "Follow the money: Investigators trace forgotten story of Britain's slave trade," *The Guardian*, online. http://www.theguardian.com/world/2013/aug/27/britain-slave-trade
26. Smith, Woodruff D. (2002), *Consumption and the Making of Respectability, 1600–1800*, New York: Routledge.
27. Lemire, Beverly (1991), *Fashion's Favourite: The Cotton Trade and the Consumer in Britain 1660–1800*, New York: Oxford University Press.
28. Fisher, Peter (2012), *The Calico Acts: Why Britain Turned Its Back On Cotton*, University of Puget Sound.
29. Cooper, Brian (1983), *Transformation of a Valley: The Derbyshire Derwent*, London: Heinemann.
30. Oyangen, Knut (2014), "The cotton economy of the Old South," in *American Agriculture History Primer*, Iowa State University.
31. Bruchey, Stuart, ed. (1967), *Cotton & the Growth of The American Economy, 1790–1860*, New York: Harcourt, Brace & World.
32. Hernon, Ian (2006), *Riot!: Civil Insurrection from Peterloo to the Present Day*, Pluto Press.
33. Walmsley, Robert (1969), *Peterloo: The Case Re-opened* Manchester, University Press.
34. Bush, Michael (2005), *The Casualties of Peterloo*, Carnegie Publishing.
35. Hutchins, B. L. and A. Harrison (1911), *A History of Factory Legislation*, P. S. King & Son.

36. Greg, R.H. (1837), *The Factory Question, Considered in Relation to Its Effects on the Health and Morals of Those Employed in Factories*, J. Ridgway and Sons.
37. Wells, Karen (2008), "Invisible hands: Child labour and the state in colonial Zimbabwe, by Beverly Grier (a review)," *The Journal of the History of Childhood and Youth*.
38. Hay, Douglas (2007), *Masters, Servants, and Magistrates in Britain and the Empire, 1562–1955* (Studies in Legal History), University of North Carolina Press.
39. Roosevelt, Franklin (1937), *Public Papers and Addresses*, Vol. VII, New York, Random House, p. 392.
40. U.S. child labor numbers. http://www.socialwelfarehistory.com/programs/child-labor/
41. Hindman, Hugh D. (2002), *Child Labor: An American History*, New York: Sharpe, M. E.
42. Mofford, Juliet H. ed. (1997), *Child Labor in America* History Compass.

CHAPTER 2

43. US apparel employment statistics. http://www.bls.gov/iag/tgs/iag315.htm
44. Canadian apparel jobs decline. http://www.statcan.gc.ca/daily-quotidien/050321/dq050321b-eng.htm
45. IFC Project details CSU Costa Rica. http://ifcext.ifc.org/ifcext/spiwebsite1.nsf/ProjectDisplay/DataConversion9233
46. Sara Lee plant closures, 1. http://articles.chicagotribune.com/1998–01–06/business/9801060323_1_yarn-and-textile-textile-plants-markets
47. Sara Lee plant closures, 2. http://articles.chicagotribune.com/1997–09–16/business/9709160325_1_sara-lee-john-bryan-textile-plants
48. Tursi, Frank (1994), *Winston Salem: A History*, John F. Blair.
49. "Hanes takeover re: Sheffield v. Consolidated Foods." http://law.justia.com/cases/north-carolina/supreme-court/1981/91–0.html
50. Consolidated Foods Corp history. http://www.encyclopedia.chicagohistory.org/pages/2623.html
51. Dietz, James (1986), *Economic History of Puerto Rico: Institutional Change and Capitalist Development*, Princeton.
52. Maldonado, A. W. (1997), *Teodoro Moscoso and Puerto Rico's Operation Bootstrap*, University Press of Florida.
53. Chomsky, Aviva (2008), *Linked Labor Histories: New England, Colombia, and the Making of a Global Working Class*, Duke University Press.
54. Lammert, de Jong and Dirk Kruijt, eds. (2005), *Extended Statehood in the Caribbean: Paradoxes of Quasi Colonialism, Local Autonomy, and Extended Statehood in the USA, French, Dutch, and British Caribbean*, Rosenberg Publishers.
55. Loeb, Lori Anne (1994), *Consuming Angels: Advertising and Victorian Women*, Oxford University Press.
56. Goffman, Erving (1979), *Gender Advertisements*, London: Macmillan.

57. Julian, Philippe and Diana Vreeland (1982), *La Belle Époque*, New York: The Metropolitan Museum of Art.
58. Farrell-Beck, J. and J. Starr Johnson (1992), *Remodeling and Renovating Clothes: 1870–1933*, Fairchild Books.
59. U.S. census statistical abstract 1951. http://www2.census.gov/prod2/statcomp/documents/1951–02.pdf
60. Linn, Susan (2004), *Consuming Kids: The Hostile Takeover of Childhood*, New Press.
61. Kanner, Allen (2003), *Psychology and Consumer Culture: The Struggle for a Good Life in a Materialistic World*, American Psychological Association.
62. "Driving teen egos and buying through 'branding,'" *Monitor on Psychology*, June, 2004, Vol. 35 no. 6, p. 60.
63. Underhill, Paco (2000), *Why We Buy: The Science of Shopping*, Simon & Schuster.
64. Lewis, David (2014), *The Brain Sell: When Science Meets Shopping*, Nicholas Brealey Publishing.
65. Khan, Humayun (2014), "How retailers manipulate sight, smell, and sound to trigger purchase behavior in consumers," *Shopify*. http://www.shopify.com/blog/14193377-how-retailers-manipulate-sight-smell-and-sound-to-trigger-purchase-behavior-in-consumers
66. Nobel Prize press release (2004), Axel and Buck's Nobel Prize in Physiology or Medicine. http://www.nobelprize.org/nobel_prizes/medicine/laureates/2004/press.html
67. Urwin, Rosamund (Sept 24, 2013), "Who's got your brain? The science of shopping uncovered," *London Evening Standard* online reference. http://www.standard.co.uk/lifestyle/london-life/whos-got-your-brain-the-science-of-shopping-uncovered-8835845.html
68. For a comprehensive overview of U.S. trade agreements see. https://www.ustr.gov/
69. Carroll, Katherine Blue (2003), *Business as Usual? Economic Reform in Jordan*, Lexington Books.
70. "Qualifying industrial zones in Jordan and Egypt," CRS Report for Congress. http://www.au.af.mil/au/awc/awcgate/crs/rs22002.pdf
71. Jordanian Ministry of Labour report on status of migrant workers in the qualified industrial zones (2006). http://www.dol.gov/ilab/submissions/pdf/20091027c.pdf
72. Pettygrove, Margaret (2006), "Obstacles to Women's political empowerment in Jordan: Family, Islam, and patriarchal gender roles," *Independent Study Project (ISP) Collection*, Paper 358. http://digitalcollections.sit.edu/isp_collection/358
73. Greenhouse, Steven and Michael Barbaro (May 3, 2006), *The New York Times*. http://www.nytimes.com/2006/05/03/business/worldbusiness/03clothing.html?pagewanted=all&_r=0

74. "International labor migration: A responsible role for business," (Oct 2008). http://www.bsr.org/reports/BSR_LaborMigrationRoleforBusiness.pdf

75. See article "Human trafficking and abusive conditions at the Mediterranean garments factory," (Sept 2008). http://www.globallabourrights.org/reports/human-trafficking-and-abusive-conditions-at-the-mediterranean-garments-factory-in-the-ad-dulayl-industrial-zone-in-jordan

76. See article: "Nygard, Dillard's, J.C. Penney, Wal-Mart linked to human trafficking and abuse of young women in Jordan sweatshop," (April 2010). http://www.globallabourrights.org/reports/dirty-clothes

77. Better Work Jordan (May 2010), "Garment industry 1st compliance synthesis report." http://betterwork.org/jordan/wp-content/uploads/Better-Work-Jordan-1st-Compliance-Synthesis-Report.pdf

78. Government of Canada, Standing Committee on International Trade (Oct 2010) re: Canada-Jordan FTA. http://www.parl.gc.ca/HousePublications/Publication.aspx?DocId=4694895&Language=E&Mode=1

79. Halaby, Jamal (Sept 2011), "Rape case turns focus to Jordan's factory problems," AP/Business Week. http://www.businessweek.com/ap/financial news/D9PJKTAO2.htm

80. Bustillo, Miguel (June 2011), "Sex abuse alleged at apparel maker," Wall Street Journal. http://www.wsj.com/articles/SB10001424052702304887904576395832981860412

81. Ross, Janell (July 2011), "Major American brands silent on alleged rights abuses at overseas factories," Huffington Post. http://www.huffingtonpost.com/2011/07/21/american-brands-abuses-factories-jordan-labor-conditions_n_903995.html

82. Institute for Global Labour and Human Rights (June 2011) report on allegations at Classic factory in Jordan. http://www.globallabourrights.org/reports/hanes-and-target-linked-to-sexual-abuse-classic-factory-in-jordan

83. Better Work Jordan (March 2011), "Garment industry, 2nd compliance synthesis report." http://betterwork.com/global/wp-content/uploads/Better-Work-Jordan-2nd-Compliance-Synthesis-Report.pdf

84. Statement of the project advisory committee of Better Work Jordan on the release of the 2nd ILO compliance synthesis report on working conditions in Jordan's garment sector (March 2011). http://betterwork.com/jordan/wp-content/uploads/Project-Advisory-Committee-Statement-2nd-Compliance-Synthesis-Report1.pdf

85. Better Work Jordan (Feb 2013), "Baseline report, worker perspectives from the factory and beyond." http://betterwork.org/jordan/wp-content/uploads/Jordan-Baseline-Report.pdf page 36.

86. Better Work Jordan (March 2013), "Addressing sexual harassment in Jordan's garment industry." http://betterwork.org/jordan/wp-content/uploads/ILO-1402-SHP-training-Case-Study-WEB.pdf

CHAPTER 3

87. Tuckman, Jo (Aug 2007), "Distressed denim trends cost Mexican farmers the earth," *The Guardian*. http://www.theguardian.com/environment/2007/aug/17/waste.pollution

88. Maquila Solidarity Network (2003), "Tehuacán: Blue jeans, blue waters & worker's rights." http://en.maquilasolidarity.org/sites/maquilasolidarity.org/files/MSN-Tehuacan-ENG-2003.pdf

89. ILO Conventions, Canada's ratification status. http://www.ilo.org/dyn/normlex/en/f?p=1000:11200:0::NO:11200:P11200_COUNTRY_ID:102582

90. Wohn, Alice (2001), "Towards GATT integration," *University of Pennsylvania*. https://www.law.upenn.edu/journals/jil/articles/volume22/issue2/Wohn22U.Pa.J.Int%27lEcon.L.375%282001%29.pdf

91. Saipan (1993). http://www.nytimes.com/1993/07/18/world/made-usa-hard-labor-pacific-island-special-report-saipan-sweatshops-are-no.html

92. Saipan (1992). http://articles.latimes.com/1992–02–12/news/mn-1585_1_labor-laws

93. NBC dateline (Dec 1992), "Where are Wal-Mart's 'Made in the USA' clothes really made?" http://webcache.googleusercontent.com/search?q=cache:xFrHOmamzwEJ:archives.nbclearn.com/portal/site/k-12/flatview%3Fcuecard%3D46414+&cd=3&hl=en&ct=clnk&gl=ca

94. Hayes, Thomas (Dec 1992), "Wal-Mart disputes report on labor," *The New York Times*. http://www.nytimes.com/1992/12/24/business/wal-mart-disputes-report-on-labor.html

95. Bobrowsky, David (1999), *Creating A Global Public Policy Network in the Apparel Industry: The Apparel Industry Partnership*, Bobrowsky.

96. US Department of Justice (April 2000), "Response to Apparel Industry Partnership." http://www.justice.gov/atr/public/busreview/4513.htm

97. Strom, Stephanie (June 1996), "A sweetheart becomes suspect: Looking behind those Kathie Lee labels," *The New York Times*. http://www.nytimes.com/1996/06/27/business/a-sweetheart-becomes-suspect-looking-behind-those-kathie-lee-labels.html

98. Borg, Gary (May 1996), "Child sweatshop worker tells of beatings," *Chicago Tribune*. http://articles.chicagotribune.com/1996–05–30/news/9605300075_1_kathie-lee-gifford-charles-kernaghan-child-labor

99. Full text of "Child labor: Hearings before the Subcommittee on International Operations and Human Rights of the Committee on International Relations," House of Representatives, 104th Congress, second session, June 11 and July 15, 1996. http://www.archive.org/stream/childlaborhearin00unit/childlaborhearin00unit_djvu.txt

100. Brandeis, Louis (Dec 1913), "What publicity can do," *Harper's Weekly*. http://www.law.louisville.edu/library/collections/brandeis/node/196

101. Ethical Trading Action Group (Sept 2003), "Transparency and disclosure: New regulatory tools to challenge sweatshop abuses." http://en.maquila

solidarity.org/sites/maquilasolidarity.org/files/ETAGTransparencyand
Disclosure.pdf

102. Haufler, Virginia (2013), "Public role, private sector: Industry self-regulation in a global economy," *Carnegie Endowment*.

103. USLEAP (Aug 2008), "Hanes signs contract: Workers win big victory in the Dominican Republic." http://www.usleap.org/hanes-signs-contract-workers-win-big-victory-dominican-republic

104. *Los Angeles Times* (Sept 1995), "Sweatshop workers." http://articles. latimes.com/1995-09-01/local/me-41102_1_sweatshop-workers-el-monte-apparel-industry

105. White, George (June 1996), "Gifford to help Reich in war on sweatshops," *Los Angeles Times.* http://articles.latimes.com/1996-06-01/business/fi-10685_1_gifford-s-signature-clothing

106. United States Department of Labor (April 1997), Apparel Industry Partnership Agreement. http://training.itcilo.it/actrav_cdrom1/english/global/guide/apparell.htm

107. Initial participating brands and labor/civil society groups were: Liz Claiborne, Phillips-Van Heusen, Warnaco, L.L. Bean, Patagonia, Nike, Nicole Miller, Tweeds, Karen Kane, Kathie Lee Gifford, UNITE, the AFL-CIO's Retail, Wholesale, and Department Store Union, the National Consumers League, Lawyers Committee for Human Rights and the Interfaith Center on Corporate Responsibility. A short while later they would be joined by Reebok, consulting group Business for Social Responsibility and two additional NGOs: the International Labor Rights Fund and the Robert F. Kennedy Memorial Center for Human Rights.

108. Benjamin, Medea (April 1997), "No Sweat for Companies to Agree," *Los Angeles Times.* http://articles.latimes.com/1997-04-17/local/me-49596_1_minimum-wage

109. Vietnam Labor Watch (March 1997), "Nike Labor Practices in Vietnam." http://www.saigon.com/nike/reports/report1.html

110. President Bill Clinton's White House statement re: Apparel Industry Partnership Agreement (April 1997). http://www.gpo.gov/fdsys/pkg/WCPD-1997-04-21/html/WCPD-1997-04-21-Pg518-2.htm

111. Greenhouse, Steve (Nov 1997), "A deep split on policing of sweatshops," *The New York Times.* http://www.nytimes.com/1997/11/21/us/a-deep-split-on-policing-of-sweatshops.html

112. Barrett, Joyce (March 29, 1996), "New anti-sweatshop bill will go to House in April," *Women's Wear Daily (WWD)*.

113. Staff writer (June 7, 1996), "AAMA in deal with database service for tracking contractors' compliance," *Women's Wear Daily (WWD)*.

114. US House of Representatives (1999), "The role of business in the competitive garment industry: Hearing before the Subcommittee on Oversight and Investigations of the Committee on Education and the Workforce,

House of Representatives," 105th Congress, second session. Hearing held in Washington, DC September 25, 1998. http://catalog.hathitrust.org/Record/007606975

115. Ramey, Joanna (28 Sept 1998), "AAMA tells Capitol Hill it will launch its own anti-sweatshop fight," *Women's Wear Daily (WWD)*.

116. Vickery, Tim (April 2001), "Who's watching the shop floor?" *Christian Science Monitor*. http://www.csmonitor.com/2001/0430/p11s1.html

117. O'Rourke, Dara (Sept 2000), "Monitoring the monitors: A critique of Pricewaterhouse Coopers (PwC) labor monitoring." http://nature.berkeley.edu/orourke/PDF/pwc.pdf

118. Developed by the German sociologist Robert Michels in his 1911 book, *Political Parties*, the iron law of oligarchy is a political theory that posits that all organizations, even those which appear democratic in nature, sooner or later come to be dominated by smaller groups of elites from within.

119. Hyland, James. (1995), *Democratic Theory: The Philosophical Foundations*, Manchester University Press n.d., p. 247.

120. Q1 2015 China salaries survey. http://www.gemini.com.hk/assets/doc/survey_china.pdf

121. Greenhouse, Steve and Clifford Stephanie (Sept 2013), "Fast and flawed inspections of factories abroad." http://www.nytimes.com/2013/09/02/business/global/superficial-visits-and-trickery-undermine-foreign-factory-inspections.html?pagewanted=5&_r=2

122. Intertek press release (July 2008), "Wal-Mart global procurement enhances quality control in China." http://www.intertek.com/news/2008/07-11-wal-mart/

123. http://www.cbc.ca/news/world/joe-fresh-continuing-garment-business-in-bangladesh-in-year-after-tragedy-1.2606120

124. Euromonitor International (March 2014), "Key highlights from Euromonitor's Apparel and Footwear Research 2014." http://go.euromonitor.com/rs/euromonitorinternational/images/key-highlights-apparel-footwear-2014.pdf

125. Bush, George W. (July 2002), text of speech. http://edition.cnn.com/2002/ALLPOLITICS/07/09/bush.transcript/index.html

CHAPTER 4

126. Staff (June 16, 2006), "Factory denies pumping waste water into river," *South China Morning Post*. http://www.scmp.com/article/552969/brief

127. He Huifeng (June 20, 2006), "HK-owned textiles factory in delta faces fines over pollution," *South China Morning Post*. http://www.scmp.com/article/553479/hk-owned-textile-factory-delta-faces-fines-over-pollution

128. Spencer, Jane (Aug 2007), "China pays steep price as textile exports boom," *Wall Street Journal*. http://www.wsj.com/articles/SB118580938555882301

129. For an in-depth understanding of the Better Cotton Initiative, see www.bettercotton.org

130. Natural Resources Defense Council, "Fiber selection: Understanding the impact of different fibers." http://www.nrdc.org/international/cleanbydesign/files/CBD-Fiber-Selection-FS.pdf

131. *The Guardian*, H&M Zone Partner Zone, "Organic cotton demand still on the rise." http://www.theguardian.com/sustainable-business/hm-partner-zone/sustainable-cotton-on-the-rise

132. Better Cotton Initiative 2013 Harvest Report. http://bettercotton.org/wp-content/uploads/2014/09/BCI-Harvest-Report-2013_compressed2.pdf

133. US Department of Labor, "List of goods produced by child or forced labor." http://www.dol.gov/ilab/reports/child-labor/list-of-goods/

134. Cotton Campaign, "Review of the 2013 cotton harvest in Uzbekistan." http://www.cottoncampaign.org/wp-content/uploads/2013/11/2013CottonHarvest_end_report.pdf

135. Uzbek-German Forum for Human Rights "Preliminary report on forced labor during Uzbekistan's 2014 cotton harvest." http://uzbekgermanforum.org/wp-content/uploads/2014/11/Forced-Labor-During-Uzbekistans-2014-Cotton-Harvest.pdf

136. BBC Newsnight (Oct 2007), "Child labour and the High Street." http://news.bbc.co.uk/2/hi/programmes/newsnight/7068096.stm

137. US/Canadian retail industry letter to Bangladesh Garment Manufacturers Association re: Uzbekistan cotton. http://www.retailcouncil.org/sites/default/files/advocacy/joint-association-letter-to-BGMEA-concerning-Uzbek-Cotton-MOU.pdf

138. Aulakh, Raveena (Oct 2013), "In Uzbekistan slave labour used to harvest cotton," *Toronto Star*. http://www.thestar.com/news/world/clothesonyourback/2013/10/25/in_uzbekistan_slave_labour_used_to_harvest_cotton.html

139. Responsible Sourcing Network, "Cotton Sourcing Survey of Corporate Practices." http://www.sourcingnetwork.org/storage/cotton-publications/cottonsourcingsnapshot-editedforprint.pdf

140. Cotton Campaign, companies active in Uzbekistan. http://www.cottoncampaign.org/frequently-asked-questions/

141. Cornell University Law School, "Corporations as legal personages." http://www.law.cornell.edu/wex/corporations

142. World Wildlife Fund, "Common impacts of the shipping industry." http://www.wwf.org.au/our_work/saving_the_natural_world/oceans_and_marine/marine_threats/commercial_shipping/impacts/

143. Sustainable Shipping Initiative, "Driving transformational change through the value chain." http://ssi2040.org/wp-content/uploads/2014/11/SSI_SustainableShipper_final-041114.pdf

144. Sustainable Shipping Initiative, "Our vision for a sustainable shipping industry." http://ssi2040.org/what-we-do/vision-2040/

145. H&M 2014 Full Year Financial Report. http://about.hm.com/content/dam/hm/about/documents/en/cision/2015/01/1460341_en.pdf

146. Shen, Bin (2014), *Sustainable Fashion Supply Chain: Lessons from H&M*, Shanghai: Donghua University.

147. Lewis, Barbara, David Ljunggren and Jeffrey Jones (May 2010), "Canada's oil sand battle with Europe." http://www.reuters.com/article/2012/05/10/us-oil-sands-idUSBRE8490OL20120510

148. O Ecotextiles (Oct 2014), "Climate change and the textile industry." https://oecotextiles.wordpress.com/tag/polyester/

149. Chevron El Segundo Refinery, "What is in a barrel of oil?" http://elsegundo.chevron.com/home/abouttherefinery/whatwedo/what_is_in_a_barrel_of_oil.aspx

150. O Ecotextiles (Feb 2013), "Antimony in fabrics." https://oecotextiles.wordpress.com/tag/polyester/

CHAPTER 5

151. Text of speech by His Highness The Aga Khan (Dec 2003). http://www.akdn.org/speech/596/Opening-of-Alltex-EPZ-Limited-at-Athi-River

152. Recommendations of the WTO Task Force on Aid for Trade [WT/AFT/1], July 27, 2006.

153. Razzaue, Abdur and Abu Eusuf (2007), "Trade, development and poverty linkage: A case study of ready made garment industry in Bangladesh." http://legacy.intracen.org/dbms/tirs/TIR_Publication_EK.Asp?DS=MONOGRAPHS&TY=F&CD=837&ID=39176

154. IDS Policy Briefing (March 2009), "Changing the Aid for Trade debate towards content." http://www.ids.ac.uk/files/dmfile/InFocus61.pdf

155. Transparency International Corruption Rankings (2014). http://www.transparency.org/cpi2014/results

CHAPTER 6

156. McFarland, Janet (Jan 2015), "Responsible investment vehicles see demand surge," *Globe and Mail*. http://www.theglobeandmail.com/report-on-business/economy/responsible-investment-vehicles-see-demand-surge/article22565321/

157. Pofeldt, Elaine (Oct 2003), "The Nurturer Eileen Fisher/Eileen Fisher Inc.," *Fortune Small Business*. http://money.cnn.com/magazines/fsb/fsb_archive/2003/10/01/353434/

Acknowledgments

ARLY IN THE PROCESS of bringing this book to market I joked
with editor Heather Nicholas about how the calendar to do so
— just about nine months — mirrored that of a pregnancy. Nearing
the end of that journey now, I'd have to say it's almost the inverse of a
birth in some ways ... nine relatively uncomfortable months with one
big effort of power and vitality at the end versus nine months of the
building power and vitality of the pen followed by a rather quiet end
in the editing of commas and apostrophes. Coincidentally, I remember
saying at the time, about the same number of weeks used to be needed
to turn a traditional department-store apparel collection around, from
designer's sketches to racks in the stores, with production shipping
from around the world.

What also seems true about the book-child analogy is that, not unlike the Nigerian proverb, it also takes a village to make a book. Well,
at least a large group of talented professionals. And much like my shirt
or my pants, odds are I will never meet many of those involved with
bringing this work to market. But I can certainly do my best to thank
and recognize a few of them here, along with a number of people who
have both encouraged and inspired me to think and look beyond the
end of my nose.

I am indebted to Heather Nicholas and the team at New Society
Publishers for the opportunity to bring this book to life and with it an
important reminder of the actions needed to take responsibility for the
state of our world. Thanks to Sara Reeves and EJ Hurst in marketing
and to Sue and Diane for a stunning cover concept beyond my highest expectations. As I write this, the editing team of Ingrid Witvoet

and Linda Glass are busy making final corrections to my incoherent phrases and misplaced semicolons. Everything that reads well, is properly constructed and sounds intelligent, I owe to them! Everything that might be an omission, is grammatically questionable or is found to be incorrect is certainly my own responsibility. Best of luck also to Heather in her new life in local politics, no doubt Gabriola Island, B.C. will be the better for it!

There have been many people throughout my life and career who have helped me grow as a person and as a professional. A few of them stand out as authentic mentors and leaders. Heartfelt thanks to Claudia Runkel, Mark Agius and Kirk Ehrlich for their support, guidance and professional encouragement.

A number of important voices over the years have helped shape my own thoughts on ethics, business, community and responsibility. From Dr. David Suzuki to former New Democratic Party leader Jack Layton to a little organization called "Greenpeace," Canada has had its fair share of champions for social and environmental justice to whom I have often looked for inspiration. The industry efforts, writing and activism of far too many people to mention have raised questions, challenged me and added to my own understanding. Here, Tansy Hoskins, Lucy Siegle, Kelly Drennan, Sass Brown and Carry Somers stand out as those I admire and thank for their contributions to a growing global movement. I must also make mention here of the long-term work and grassroots efforts of the Maquila Solidarity Network (MSN) which came to an end here in Canada earlier this year. Thanks to dozens of dedicated and passionate individuals of all nationalities; the MSN led a 20-year fight for the rights of workers across the Global South. The work of Bob Jeffcott, Lynda Yanz, Kevin Thomas, Ana Enriquez and so many others who struggled to bring us the voices of offshore apparel workers filled a significant gap in Canadian civil society which won't easily be filled.

Above all things, I have been deeply blessed with a friend, confidant, love, collaborator and life-partner for the past 19 years. She has accompanied me without a complaint around the world, living in five countries while coordinating the moves of ten different homes, all the while teaching, going back to school for a Master's degree, guiding our children through eight different schools and caring for the needs of a house full of boys. Angélica, you are our hero and words will never be enough to express our thanks and appreciation for you. *Ya sabes eres mi media naranja.*

— Michael Lavergne

Index

A

Adidas, 8, 36, 48, 116, 184, 196
African Growth and
  Opportunity Act (AGOA),
  59–61, 143, 147
Aga Khan Fund for Economic
  Development (AKFED),
  143–44
Agius, Mark, 54, 63
Aid for Trade (AfT), 89,
  144–45, 154
Alliance for Bangladesh Worker
  Safety, 153, 170–73, 177
American Apparel & Footwear
  Association (AAFA), 77, 86,
  95, 123
American Apparel
  Manufacturers Association
  (AAMA), 92–96
Angelo, Mark, 203–4
apparel and textile factories
  quality inspections in, 99, 105
  standard industry practices for,
  100
  work conditions in, 28, 73, 101
  See also manufacturing facilities

apparel and textile industry,
  15–16, 30, 77, 92–93, 141
  labor practices in, 67, 75, 79,
    85, 88, 90–91, 96
  offshore sourcing of, 2, 31, 53,
    70, 72, 76
  social and environmental
    impacts of, 5, 67, 118, 160,
    162
  supply chains for, 52, 89, 206
  transparency in, 137–38, 205
Apparel Industry Partnership
  (AIP), 86, 90–94, 96
Ara, Shatil, 175, 178, 181
Arkwright, Sir Richard, 25–27
auditing firms, 67, 76, 91, 97–99,
  101, 105, 110
auditing, of apparel industry
  as an industry, 77, 98, 106
  factory audits, 8, 65, 86, 96–97,
    99, 101, 107, 109, 127–28
  social compliance audits, 107,
    174, 179–80
  See also auditing firms; labor
    audits; monitoring, of
    apparel industry

About the Author

MICHAEL LAVERGNE is an ethical supply-chain professional who has spent the past 18 years leading sourcing initiatives across Asia, Latin America, the Middle East, Africa and North America markets. He gained experience in labor, human rights and environmental issues in Central America, Mexico and SE Asia and has supported responsible industry development in East Africa and the Middle East. Michael has written on ethical trade issues for *Canadian Business Magazine*, *Toronto Star*, and *National Post*, among others. He is a board member of Fashion Takes Action, and speaks regularly at industry events such as The Sustainable Fashion Forum and the World Ethical Apparel Roundtable.

If you have enjoyed *Fixing Fashion* you might also enjoy other

BOOKS TO BUILD A NEW SOCIETY

Our books provide positive solutions for people who want to
make a difference. We specialize in:

**Food & Gardening • Resilience • Sustainable Building
Climate Change • Energy • Health & Wellness • Sustainable Living
Environment & Economy • Progressive Leadership • Community
Educational & Parenting Resources**

New Society Publishers

ENVIRONMENTAL BENEFITS STATEMENT

New Society Publishers has chosen to produce this book on recycled paper made
with **100% post-consumer waste,** processed chlorine free, and old growth free.
For every 5,000 books printed, New Society saves the following resources:[1]

24	Trees
2,188	Pounds of Solid Waste
2,408	Gallons of Water
3,140	Kilowatt Hours of Electricity
3,978	Pounds of Greenhouse Gases
17	Pounds of HAPs, VOCs, and AOX Combined
6	Cubic Yards of Landfill Space

[1]Environmental benefits are calculated based on research done by the Environmental Defense Fund
and other members of the Paper Task Force who study the environmental impacts of the paper
industry.

For a full list of NSP's titles, please call 1-800-567-6772 *or check out our website* at:

www.newsociety.com

new society
PUBLISHERS